TAKING THE
MEASURE
OF WORK

To my wife,
Christy W. Fields,
who in this,
as in all things,
made life easier and more joyful

TAKING THE
MEASURE
OF WORK

A GUIDE TO
VALIDATED
SCALES FOR
ORGANIZATIONAL
RESEARCH
AND DIAGNOSIS

Hm
786
.F54
2002

Dail L. Fields
Regent University

*With support from the Regent University School of
Business and Center for Leadership Studies*

SAGE Publications
International Educational and Professional Publisher
Thousand Oaks ▪ London ▪ New Delhi

For information:

Sage Publications, Inc.
2455 Teller Road
Thousand Oaks, California 91320
E-mail: order@sagepub.com

Sage Publications Ltd.
6 Bonhill Street
London EC2A 4PU
United Kingdom

Sage Publications India Pvt. Ltd.
M-32 Market
Greater Kailash
New Delhi 110 048 India

Printed in the United States of America

Library of Congress Cataloging-in-Publication Data

Fields, Dail L.
Taking the measure of work : a guide to validated scales for organizational research and diagnosis / Dail L. Fields.
        p. cm.
Includes bibliographical references and index.
ISBN 0-7619-2425-6
    1. Organizational sociology—Research—Handbooks, manuals, etc. 2. Quality of work life—Evaluation—Handbooks, manuals, etc. 3. Questionnaires. I. Title.
HM786 .F54 2002
302.3'5—dc21   2002001441

02   03   04   05   10 9 8 7 6 5 4 3 2 1

Acquiring Editor:	Marquita Flemming
Editorial Assistant:	Mary Ann Vail
Production Editor:	Claudia A. Hoffman
Copy Editor:	Kate Peterson
Typesetter:	Tina Hill
Indexer:	Molly Hall
Cover Designer:	Michelle Lee

Contents

2. *Organizational Commitment*   *43*

6. *Organizational Justice*   *163*

7. *Work-Family Conflict*   *197*

10. *Workplace Values* *263*

Preface

This book grew out of frustrations I had experienced over years of working as a consultant and manager trying to locate validated and reliable ways to measure aspects of how employees view their work and their organizations. Frequently, managers disagreed about what was ailing an organization and the only way to get to the "real story" was to get information from workers. But choosing what to ask proved to be a time-consuming and painful task. Consultants and managers were faced with a choice of digging through journals of organizational studies to find proven measures, or more likely, throwing up their hands and "cooking up" some questions to meet the immediate need. Later, in the academic research world, I found that researchers faced exactly the same problem when trying to design a questionnaire. After more than 60 years of documented organizational studies, it just should not be so difficult to locate validated measures for employee surveys, diagnostic inquiries, or research studies of organizational members. And that is the purpose of this book—to make life easier for those who want to measure how employees think and feel about work and organizations. I designed this book as a handy tool for researchers, consultants, managers, and organizational development specialists to efficiently obtain reliable and valid information about how employees view their jobs and organizations.

Acknowledgments

There are a few individuals that I thank for their help in preparing this book. The first is Christy W. Fields for her persistent and tireless help in solving software mysteries and obtaining copyright permissions from publishers here and afar. Second is Kathleen Patterson, a doctoral fellow in the Center for Leadership Studies, who collected and analyzed source materials and participated in the writing of two chapters of the book. Third is Roman Gaiduk, for his persistent and accurate work in searching electronic databases and obtaining source materials. Finally, I thank both John Mulford, Dean of the Regent University School of Business, and Kathaleen Reid-Martinez, Dean of the Regent University Center for Leadership Studies, for their encouragement and support of this project.

Introduction

Background

This book has been written for researchers and consultants interested in measuring the judgments that organizational members make about the nature of jobs and the related work environment. It is a guide to measures that operationalize, describe, or assess employee perceptions about and affective responses to the experience of their work within an organization. The measures included in the book are those that can be completed as part of a questionnaire or survey, or administered as part of an interview. The book includes only measures for which the responses are closed-ended, where the respondent must choose one of a several predefined response options. Measures that use open-ended questions or observational or behavioral rating scales are not included.

The measures in this book cover the areas of

- Job satisfaction
- Organizational commitment
- Job characteristics
- Job stress
- Job roles
- Organizational justice
- Work-family conflict
- Person-organization fit

- Work behaviors
- Work values

The book identifies and describes measures that have demonstrated reliability and validity and that have been used in research studies published during 1990-1999. Each measure is described in terms of basic information important to potential users. The book is designed to serve its readers in three primary ways:

1. *Reduce the time and effort required to select and assemble validated measures for organizational research and consulting.* The book includes numerous alternative measures for ten major aspects of work perceptions and related judgments. Whether preparing questionnaires or interviews for an employee survey, organizational assessment, dissertation, or research program, this book guides users to a summary-level understanding of each topic area, the measurement issues in the area, and a selection of measures from which to choose. This should help eliminate an often time-consuming and occasionally haphazard search for validated measures within published studies. Organizational consultants, in particular, should find this book useful, because using validated measures can

help them focus discussions with clients on the substance of their findings and away from the quality of their measurements.

2. Increase the frequency and variety of uses of the measures described. Over time, repeated use of measures for key concepts inherent to employee perceptions of their work leads to increased scrutiny, refinement, and improvement in the measures. Repeated use of such measures may also increase our understanding of not only the relationship among these concepts but also their antecedents and consequences. That is, our ability to generalize about the relationships among organizational variables is limited when studies use different measures of the key concepts. Studies that use the same measures of the focal variables can be compared without having to worry about how similarities or differences of substance are augmented or attenuated by unmeasured effects of differences in the measures used.

3. Improve the quality and quantity of validated measures available to organizational researchers and consultants. For example, many of the measures described in this book have been subjected to limited tests of reliability and validity. That is, internal consistency is frequently the only test provided, while test-retest reliability is rarely investigated. On the other hand, the few measures that have been used in numerous different studies have been subjected to a wide variety of test of both reliability and validity. In addition, as suggested by Brief (1998), our future measurement efforts may be well served by challenges to the dimensions of existing measures of employee perceptions of and related attitudes about work.

Identification of Measures

Validated measures were identified by reviewing studies that were published during

1990-1999 in 15 respected organization research journals:

- *Academy of Management Journal*
- *Journal of Applied Psychology*
- *Administrative Science Quarterly*
- *Educational and Psychological Measurement*
- *Human Relations*
- *Work and Occupations*
- *Journal of Applied Social Psychology*
- *Journal of Management*
- *Journal of Management Studies*
- *Journal of Occupational and Organizational Psychology*
- *Journal of Organizational Behavior*
- *Journal of Vocational Behavior*
- *Organizational Behavior and Human Decision Processes*
- *Personnel Psychology*
- *Group & Organization Management*

The relevant studies were first identified through key word searches using several electronic databases, such as ABI-Inform, Expanded Academic, and Dow-Jones Interactive. As measures were identified and reviewed, a database was developed cataloguing the studies as well as cumulative information about the uses, reliability, and validity of each measure. The database also included sources published in years prior to 1990 that in many cases contained information about the development of the original measures and the items that comprise each measure. A total of 605 studies were catalogued, along with 200 sources published prior to 1990. This effort resulted in the identification of 270 measures. Of these measures, 136 are described in this book.

Selection Criteria

Meyer and Allen (1997) outline a set of recommendations for the psychometric evaluation of measures used in organizational behavior research. First, items within a scale should measure the same construct and thus the measure should have acceptable internal reliability. Internal reliability is typically assessed with coefficient alpha (Cortina, 1993). Although a coefficient alpha value of .70 is generally suggested as a minimum acceptable level, Cortina (1993) has noted the importance of taking the number of measure items into account when evaluating what constitutes adequate levels of coefficient alpha. That is, measures with more items will yield higher coefficient alpha values than measures with fewer items, other things being equal. Thus, scales with fewer items are preferable to scales with many items given comparable alpha values and construct validity estimates.

Second, scale scores should be relatively stable across time, assuming no major changes in conditions that influence the construct. This is assessed with measures of test-retest reliability such as the correlation of the scale scores between two points in time. Third, items that measure one construct should not correlate highly with items intended to measure unrelated constructs. This is assessed with factor analysis of both groups of items together, or through examination of alternative confirmatory factor models (Netemeyer, Boles, & McMurrian, 1996).

The construct validity of a measure—evidence that it measures what it purports to measure—can be assessed by examining its correlations with other constructs and comparing these correlations with what is expected theoretically. In addition, confirmatory factor analysis is appropriate for investigating construct validity of multi-item scales because it allows for direct examination of the degree to which specific items jointly are associated with hypothesized factors (i.e., convergent validity) and display negligible cross-loadings on other factors (i.e., discriminant validity). For example, in a four-dimensional measure, if the dimensions do not have discriminant validity, the fit of a single-factor model will be no worse than will the fit of a four-factor model (Kraimer, Seibert, & Liden, 1999).

Taking these issues into account, measures were selected for inclusion in this book based on meeting the following minimum criteria:

- The measure is based on sound theoretical foundation and clear conceptual definitions.
- Studies using the measure provide evidence of internal reliability, such as coefficient alpha, and empirical evidence of convergent validity, such as correlations with appropriate variables.
- The measure uses at least three items (statements or questions) to operationalize employee perceptions and attitudes. Three items are considered a minimum for capturing the types of latent variables that are the foci of the measures in this book (Bearden & Netemeyer, 1999; Spector, 1992).
- The measure was used in two or more studies in the period 1990-1999, or if only used in a single study, it provides a unique perspective on measurement of the focal concept.
- The items used in the measure were available from a published source with offices that could be contacted to obtain permission to reprint items for this book and that provide a point of contact for future users of the measure. I did not include measures when the items used could only be obtained from an individual author, since individuals move, and the copyright status of such items may require clarification.

Presentation of the Measures

Each chapter begins with a summary of the definitions of the constructs measured and a discussion of relevant issues noted during review of studies conducted during the 1990s. The introduction to each chapter also highlights measurement issues that researchers attempting to study the constructs have identified and investigated. This introductory material is not meant to be comprehensive, but is provided to make the reader a more informed consumer of the measures that follow. The measures are presented in the book using the following format:

Description This section identifies the original developers of the measure and describes the focal concept that the measure assesses. This section also describes unique features as well as its dimensions.

Reliability This section contains information about the reliability the measure has demonstrated in uses in the 1990s. At minimum, the reliability information describes internal consistency of the measure as measured by coefficient alpha. Some measures also have information about test-retest reliability. If available, this section also describes the measure's factor structure. This evidence might include results of exploratory factor analysis or confirmatory factor analysis in a separate sample. The various measures that describe the goodness of fit of confirmatory factor analyses are not reported, but readers interested in these data are referred to the studies cited.

Validity This section provides evidence indicating the measure is operationalizing the construct that it intends to represent. In most cases, this evidence is in the form of statistically significant correlations of the measure with other variables that are consistent with theoretically based expectations. That is, this evidence shows that the measure correlated positively or negatively with other variables in ways that it should if it is indeed measuring what it promises to measure. The only correlations reported are those that were statistically significant ($p < .05$) in the studies reviewed. The size of the correlations is not reported because the correlations were observed in samples of varying size and homo-

geneity. For example, a correlation of $r = .50$ may appear to be of great practical value unless we find that it occurs in a sample of employees who are similar in many other characteristics that may be related to the focal measure. Alternately, a correlation of $r = .20$ may not seem to represent much until it is discovered that it was calculated from a very diverse sample of the general population.

In some cases, this section also provides evidence showing that a measure is empirically distinct from other variables that measure similar constructs or that it has different dimensions than originally thought. Much of this evidence is derived from confirmatory analyses or structural models. Again, the various measures of the goodness of fit are not reported, but interested readers are referred to the studies cited.

Source This provides the reference from which I obtained the questions, statements, instructions, and response scales used by the measure.

Items This section contains the questions or statements that employees respond to and the response scale the measure uses. Many of the measures use a Likert-type response scale with various response ranges. Measures commonly use response scales with from four to seven alternative choices for the respondent. Response patterns with five or seven options contain a neutral point. Response scales using an even number of options avoid the middle-point response. The usefulness and interpretability of a neutral point varies from measure to measure. A typical example of this rating method is "Please indicate how much you agree or disagree with each of the following statements using the numbers 1 through 7 where 1 = *strongly disagree*, 2 = *disagree*, 3 = *slightly (or somewhat) disagree*, 4 = *neutral*, 5 = *slightly (or somewhat) agree*, 6 = *agree*, and 7 = *strongly agree*." All of the response options have been included when they were available from the sources consulted. In many cases, the studies reviewed provided only the number of possible responses and the anchoring statements for the endpoints. When available, instructions for respondents that had been developed and used with each measure are also included.

Cautions

It is important to remember that the information provided about each measure is derived from interpretation of published studies. The studies reviewed for this book vary a great deal in the detail they provide about the measures used and their psychometric properties. The information provided herein is as accurate as the sources used. The fact that a measure is described in this book should not be construed as a comment on its quality or suitability for use in all situations.

The information provided in this book should reduce the time and effort it takes to identify measures for which there is some degree of reliability and validity information. However, the user must examine the face validity of a measure, consider its appropriateness for the objectives of the research or consulting endeavor to be undertaken, evaluate its suitability for the work environment to be investigated, and make choices based on the theoretical underpinnings of the study or diagnostic project.

Considerations in Using the Measures

First, it is crucial for the users of this book to remember that with a few exceptions, these measures ask employees to describe aspects of their job or work environment by choosing preselected responses to a series of questions or statements. In essence, these measures attempt to capture meaningful aspects of individual perceptions as well as an employee's evaluation of these perceptions. Indeed, the use of multiple items to attempt to capture

employee perceptions and related evaluations is tacit recognition of the difficulty of the task at hand. That is, if a large percentage of workers would all agree on the concept of organizational commitment, much as they would agree about the color red, then a single question or statement could measure commitment in nearly all situations. However, the reality is that organizational commitment is the result of an employee evaluating numerous aspects of the work situation. As Brief (1998) notes, attitudes such as commitment to an organization may have affective and cognitive aspects. Thus, comprehensive measures of commitment must attempt to capture multiple aspects of how employees feel about the organization and how they think about the organization.

Because the measurement foci are employee perceptions and attitudes, the use of validated measures is particularly crucial. As Roznowski and Hulin (1992) note, general intelligence provides us with key information about an individual outside of an organizational context. Within an organizational context, the key information about an individual is provided by his or her job satisfaction, organizational commitment, perceptions of the nature of a job, and fit with the organization. Most researchers or consultants would not consider a measure of general intelligence to be credible if it consisted of a dozen "homegrown" questions. For the same reason, these researchers and consultants should not consider measures of job satisfaction, commitment, or organizational fit to be credible if they are the result of the homegrown approach.

Although the measures described in this book have all been validated, it is important to evaluate validated measures before adopting them. For example, in evaluating a measure for possible use, it is important to consider the types of samples that have been used to develop and validate the measure (Bearden & Netemeyer, 1999). Do the previous samples have similar characteristics to employees in the proposed study group? If not, is there reason to be concerned that the differences will affect the way that respondents interpret the questions or statements that make up the measure?

In addition, numerous measures included in this book have multiple dimensions. However, with a few exceptions, the dimensionality of the measures has been investigated in a small number of samples. Clearly, it is important for users to be prepared to test whether the dimensions expected in fact appear in a new study sample. Typically, this step will involve the use of factor analysis of the responses from a study sample. The same concern applies to convergent and discriminant validity. That is, users of these measures should be prepared, at minimum, to examine the patterns of correlations within a study sample to determine if the expected relationships are present.

It is also important for users of the measures in this book to bear in mind that most of these measures ask for self-reports about jobs and related work environments. It is important to remember that self-reports do not describe objective job conditions, such as might be measured by trained observers. Self-report measures also may be capturing other influences besides the particular focus of measurement. For example, it is likely that an employee's descriptions of the autonomy and variety present in his or her job may be influenced by the nature of the employee's relationship with his or her supervisor (Spector, 1994). Self-reports about jobs and work environments provide very meaningful and valuable insights. However, they have limitations that are worth keeping in mind (Spector, 1994).

Similarly, users must bear in mind that responses to items used in these measures may be subject to bias. In particular, users should be concerned and possibly be prepared to test for the existence of two types of response bias. One is acquiescence, which describes the tendency of respondents to respond in a positive or negative direction to measure items (also described as "yea-saying" and

"nay-saying" tendencies). The other is social desirability bias, which describes the tendency of respondents to want to make a positive impression (Bearden & Netemeyer, 1999). Spector (1987) found that both forms of response bias were present to very slight degrees and seemed to have no substantial affects on the relationships among organizational measures. Nonetheless, users of the measures in this book should be prepared to consider checking for the presence and effects of these forms of response bias (see Podsakoff & Organ, 1986, and Spector, 1987, for examples of tests and detection). In addition, the use of multiple measures within a single questionnaire in order to examine the relationship among constructs is a common design in organizational research. Users of such designs must be concerned with the extent to which the relationships among variables are inflated because the measures are all collected within a single instrument. Again, Spector (1987) found that the presence of such common method variance did not substantively affect the results of the studies he reviewed. However, several alternative statistical methods are available for assessing the degree of impact of method variance, and users of this book should be aware of these and plan to incorporate their use as needed (Sweeney & McFarlin, 1997).

Some research suggests it is possible that the directional wording of questions or statements in a measure may result in a set of responses that correlated more highly with one another than with other questions or statements that are worded in an opposite direction (Spector, Van Katwyk, Brannick, & Chen, 1997). For example, positively worded items may appeal more to respondents with positive affectivity. As a result, people with positive affectivity may be more likely to agree or strongly agree with positively worded items, but react less severely to negatively worded items. Of course, the opposite may be true for respondents who have negative affectivity. In addition, regardless of a respondent's affective tendency, a person reading a positively worded item may agree with the item, but may not disagree with a negatively worded item and vice versa. The result of these response possibilities is that dimensions may be introduced into a measure as an artifact of the directional wording of the items. Spector et al. (1997) examined a set of items describing job satisfaction, some of which were negatively worded and some positively worded. They found that the item response patterns differed between the two types of items after reverse scoring. Within the same study, factor analysis of negatively and positively worded items describing the same construct produced two factors each corresponding to direction of the wording. Similar artifacts have been found in validation studies of other measures (Idaszak & Drasgow, 1987; Mathieu, 1991). Thus, direction of the wording of items represents a phenomenon worthy of investigation when using a measure with items that use both positive and negative wording.

Finally, users of these measures should be aware that the use of English-language instruments in other cultures may be fraught with problems. For example, Wong, Hui, and Law (1998) used four versions of a measure, each version varying according to the language and the response scale used. There were two reasons for adopting the four versions. First, by comparing the responses of the two language versions, the researchers were able to determine whether respondents were interpreting the Chinese and English questions in a similar way. Second, they could examine the response bias of the Chinese research participants induced by different scales. That is, past studies have found that people in Eastern populations are reluctant to make known their opinion on politically sensitive matters. This lack of extreme response style in survey research will lower the true variances and covariances of the underlying measures. This can lead to misleading results when statistical procedures involving the structures of variances and covariances are employed. Thus, it is important to examine whether or not this effect is present when using English-language measures in other cultures. Riordan and Vandenberg (1994) provide guidance and procedures for empirically evaluating measure for use across cultures.

1

Job Satisfaction

The Construct

For decades, organizational researchers have been intrigued by employee satisfaction with work. Some studies have examined antecedents of job satisfaction, specific dimensions of job satisfaction, and the relationship between job satisfaction and outcomes such as job performance or turnover. Meta-analyses have shown that the relationship between performance and job satisfaction is positive, but small (George & Jones, 1997). However, analysis at the organizational level has shown that organizations with higher average levels of job satisfaction outperform other organizations (Ostroff, 1992). Some have suggested that we still lack a workable understanding of the way different factors such as work values, job satisfaction, and performance interact with one another (George & Jones, 1997).

Job satisfaction is generally defined as an employee's affective reactions to a job based on comparing actual outcomes with desired outcomes (Cranny, Smith, & Stone, 1992). It is generally recognized as a multifaceted construct that includes employee feelings about a variety of both intrinsic and extrinsic job elements (Howard & Frink, 1996). Porter and Steers (1973) argued that the extent of

employee job satisfaction reflected the cumulative level of met worker expectations. That is, employees expect their job to provide a mix of features (e.g., pay, promotion, autonomy) for which the employee has certain preferential values. The range and importance of these preferences vary across individuals, but when the accumulation of unmet expectation becomes sufficiently large there is less job satisfaction, and greater probability of withdrawal behavior (Pearson, 1991). Indeed, some interest in job satisfaction is focused primarily on its impact on employee commitment, absenteeism, intentions to quit, and actual turnover (Agho, Mueller, & Price, 1993). However, across studies, the proportion of variance in turnover explained by levels of satisfaction may be smaller than originally thought (Hom & Griffeth, 1991; Lee, Mitchell, Holtom, McDaniel, & Hill, 1999). On the other hand, a 2-year longitudinal study showed that employees who changed jobs and moved into a new occupation had higher levels of work satisfaction in the new job than employees who changed jobs and stayed in the same occupation and employees who did not change jobs at all (Wright & Bonett, 1992). In particular, satisfaction with the facets of meaningful work and promotion opportunities were significant predictors of intentions to leave an organization. Mathieu's (1991) tests of the causal ordering of job satisfaction and organizational commitment found that the effects of a variety of antecedents on organizational commitment were mediated by their impact on job satisfaction (Tsui, Egan, & O'Reilly, 1992).

Aspects of the work situation have been shown to be determinants of job satisfaction (Arvey, Carter, & Buerkley, 1991). For example, a broad situational factor, job level, is positively correlated with satisfaction with all aspects of the job probably because higher-level jobs tend to have better working conditions, pay, promotion prospects, supervision, autonomy, and responsibility (Robie, Ryan, Schmieder, Parra, & Smith, 1998). Zeitz (1990) found that perceptions that employees have about numerous aspects of their work environment (management climate, job content, reward fairness, employee influence on work group, and promotion opportunities) explained job satisfaction. This study also found distinct patterns of work satisfaction at different age levels for non-college graduates (U shape), non-elite professionals (downward sloping), and elite professionals (upward sloping). Personal characteristics such as age, gender, education level, and pay grade did not contribute incrementally to explaining the variance in work satisfaction beyond that explained by variables describing the job situation. In Agho, Price, and Mueller (1992), evaluation of alternative confirmatory factor models found that job satisfaction and the personality tendencies of negative and positive affectivity were empirically distinct.

Judge and Hulin (1993) tested the differential effects of employee affective disposition on job satisfaction. The study found that affective disposition was antecedent to general well-being, and well-being was reciprocally related with job satisfaction. Judge and Watanabe (1993) found in a longitudinal study that the effects of life satisfaction on job satisfaction were considerably larger than the effects of job satisfaction on life satisfaction. It is possible that people with higher levels of satisfaction with life pay more attention to the positive aspects of jobs and less attention to the negative aspects. However, it appears that under conditions of organizational change, job satisfaction has larger effects on life satisfaction, suggesting that job satisfaction is an essential component of an employee's life (Judge & Watanabe, 1993).

A qualitative study (Bussing, Bissels, Fuchs, & Perrar, 1999) suggested that job satisfaction is developed through assessment of the match among expectations, needs, motives, and the work situation. Based on this assessment, a person builds up satisfaction (steady feeling of relaxation as a result of met expectations and needs) or dissatisfaction (feeling of tension as a result of unsatisfied needs and expectations) with her or his work. In the case of dissatisfaction, employees may maintain or reduce their level of aspiration. Maintaining aspirations in the face of work dissatisfaction can result in pseudo work satisfaction, fixated dissatisfaction, and constructive dissatisfaction. Fixated and constructive work dissatisfaction may result in mobilization of an employee's problem-solving behavior (Bussing et al., 1999). Problem-solving behaviors seem to depend largely on variables such as control or social support at work. Alternately, a more cynical view is that decreases in aspirations may lead to "resigned" job satisfaction. That is, some proportion of satisfied workers found in attitudinal studies may be explained by some workers who have passively resigned or given up on their work situation (Bussing et al., 1999).

The Measures

Measures of job satisfaction may assess global satisfaction with a job or satisfaction with several key aspects of the job such as pay, supervision, promotion, co-worker, and the job itself. Sometimes facet measures are averaged together for an overall measure of satisfaction (Wright & Bonett, 1992). Some studies have used measures of both global and specific job facet satisfaction because specific facet satisfaction measures may better reflect changes in relevant situational factors, whereas a global measure may more likely reflect individual differences than responses to specific items (Witt & Nye, 1992). For example, Watson and Slack (1993) used the Job Descriptive Index (JDI) to measure satisfaction with several facets, such as the work itself, pay, promotion, supervision, and co-workers. This study also used the Minnesota Satisfaction Questionnaire (MSQ) to measure global or overall job satisfaction. The levels of facet satisfaction had varying degrees of relationship with global satisfaction. Satisfaction with supervision had the largest positive correlation, whereas satisfaction with pay had the lowest. In Taber and Alliger (1995), significant relationships were found between task-level experiences assessed through job analysis, facet satisfaction (the work itself), and global job satisfaction. The percentage of time an employee spends in enjoyable tasks was correlated positively with higher levels of facet and global satisfaction. It is possible that workers form a perception pattern about their jobs that is influenced by the task experiences (Taber & Alliger, 1995). Howard and Frink (1996) found that individuals in an organization undergoing change who perceived growth opportunities were more satisfied with their job overall. Although co-workers were more important than supervisors for keeping workers internally motivated, supervisors were more critical than co-workers for keeping employees satisfied with their jobs.

Rice, Gentile, and McFarlin (1991) found that facet importance moderated the relationship between facet amount and job satisfaction for each of 12 job facets: pay, hours worked, commuting time, promotion opportunity, interaction with co-workers, customer/client contact, opportunity to learn new skills, decision making, physical effort required, mental effort required, supervisor contact, and a worker's control over his or her schedule. I have included several alternative validated measures for global job satisfaction as well as several alternatives that measure satisfaction with specific job facets.

Some researchers have suggested that job satisfaction measures may differ in the extent to which they tap affective satisfaction or cognitive satisfaction (Moorman, 1993). Affective satisfaction is based on an overall positive emotional appraisal of the job and focuses on whether the job evokes a good mood and positive feelings. Cognitive satisfaction is based on logical and rational evaluation of the job, such as conditions, opportunities, or outcomes (Moorman, 1993). Organ and Near (1985) noted that most satisfaction measures asked respondents to compare facets of their job to some referent (a cognitive process) and did not really ask for judgments about feelings and emotions. Brief and Roberson (1992) tested the relative effect of cognition and affect in frequently used job satisfaction measures and found that the MSQ and JDI were predominantly cognitive, but with some affective influence present. For example, the Brayfield-Rothe measure of job satisfaction (Brayfield & Rothe, 1951) includes questions on the degree to which a respondent is bored, interested, happy, enthusiastic, disappointed, or enjoying work. These questions center not on specific appraisals about job conditions, but on the emotional reactions to the work. Therefore, job satisfaction measures appear to differ in the degree they reflect cognition and affect with the mix depending on the nature of the items used in the measure.

A final measurement consideration is the extent to which job satisfaction measures reflect "true variance" in satisfaction as opposed to error or method variance. Buckley, Carraher, and Cote (1992) found that for the JDI composite measure of job satisfaction, trait (actual job satisfaction) variance accounted for approximately 43% of the total variance, with common method and random error variance comprising the balance. For the JDI measures of facet satisfaction, trait variance accounted for approximately 41% for the measure of supervision, 34% for the measure of satisfaction with work itself, 38% of the variance in satisfaction with co-workers, 56% of satisfaction with pay, and 61% of the satisfaction with promotions. The same study estimated that trait variance accounted for approximately 46% of the total variance in other measures of job satisfaction including the MSQ.

Overall Job Satisfaction

Description   This measure, developed by Cammann, Fichman, Jenkins, and Klesh (1983) as part of the Michigan Organizational Assessment Questionnaire (OAQ), uses three items to describe an employee's subjective response to working in his or her job and organization. This is a global indication of worker satisfaction with a job.

Reliability   Coefficient alpha values ranged from .67 to .95 (Hochwarter, Perrewé, Igalens, & Roussel, 1999; McFarlin & Rice, 1992; McLain, 1995; Pearson, 1991; Sanchez & Brock, 1996; Siegall & McDonald, 1995).

Validity   Job satisfaction correlated positively with leader's positive affectivity, leader's job involvement, distribution of risk exposure in the workplace, the economic value placed on health and safety, organizational commitment, job involvement, job focus, and work complexity (George, 1995; McLain, 1995; Siegall & McDonald, 1995). Job satisfaction correlated negatively with employees' off-job focus, perceived danger, perceived risk, task distractions, and intent to leave (Siegall & McDonald, 1995). In Sanchez, Kraus, White, and Williams (1999), confirmatory factor analysis showed that organizational munificence, high-involvement human resources (HR) practices, benchmarking, and job satisfaction were empirically distinct constructs.

Source   Cammann, C., Fichman, M., Jenkins, D., & Klesh, J. (1983). Assessing the attitudes and perceptions of organizational members. In S. Seashore, E. Lawler, P. Mirvis, & C. Cammann (Eds.), *Assessing organizational change: A guide to methods, measures and practices.* New York: John Wiley. Items were taken from Table 4-2, p. 84. Copyright © 1983. Reprinted by permission of John Wiley and Sons, Inc.

Items   Responses are obtained using a 7-point Likert-type scale where 1 = *strongly disagree*, 2 = *disagree*, 3 = *slightly disagree*, 4 = *neither agree nor disagree*, 5 = *slightly agree*, 6 = *agree*, and 7 = *strongly agree*.

Items:

1. All in all, I am satisfied with my job
2. In general, I don't like my job (R)
3. In general, I like working here

Items denoted with (R) are reverse scored.

Job Satisfaction Relative to Expectations

Description   This measure, developed by Bacharach, Bamberger, and Conley (1991), assesses the degree of agreement between the perceived quality of broad aspects of a job and employee expectations. The measure is particularly useful to assess the extent to which job stresses, role conflicts, or role ambiguities prevent job expectations from being met.

Reliability   Coefficient alpha was .88 (Bacharach et al., 1991).

Validity   Job satisfaction relative to expectations correlated negatively with role conflict, role overload, and work-home conflict (Bacharach et al., 1991).

Source   Bacharach, S., Bamberger, P., & Conley, S. (1991). Work-home conflict among nurses and engineers: Mediating the impact of role stress on burnout and satisfaction with work. *Journal of Organizational Behavior, 12*, 39-53. Items were taken from text, p. 45. Copyright © 1991. Reproduced by permission of John Wiley & Sons Limited.

Items   Responses are obtained using a 4-point Likert-type scale where 1 = *very dissatisfied* and 4 = *very satisfied*.

1. Your present job when you compare it to others in the organization
2. The progress you are making toward the goals you set for yourself in your present position
3. The chance your job gives you to do what you are best at
4. Your present job when you consider the expectations you had when you took the job
5. Your present job in light of your career expectations

Minnesota Satisfaction Questionnaire

Description

The Minnesota Satisfaction Questionnaire (MSQ) "long form" consists of 100 questions that make up 20 subscales measuring satisfaction with ability utilization, achievement, activity, advancement, authority, company policies and practices, compensation, co-workers, creativity, independence, moral values, recognition, responsibility, security, social service, social status, supervision-human relations, supervision-technical, variety, and working conditions (Weiss, Dawis, England, & Lofquist, 1967). Twenty of these items make up a frequently used measure of general job satisfaction. These 20 items are referred to as the short form of the MSQ. The items can be separated into a 12-item subscale for intrinsic satisfaction (such as satisfaction with the chance to use abilities and feelings of accomplishment from the job) and an 8-item subscale measuring extrinsic satisfaction (such as satisfaction with pay, chances for advancement, and supervision). The MSQ has been translated into French and Hebrew (Igalens & Roussel, 1999; Sagie, 1998).

Reliability

Coefficient alpha values for the 20-item MSQ ranged from .85 to .91 (Hart, 1999; Huber, Seybolt, & Venemon, 1992; Klenke-Hamel & Mathieu, 1990; Mathieu, 1991; Mathieu & Farr, 1991; Riggs & Knight, 1994; Roberson, 1990; Scarpello & Vandenberg, 1992; Smith & Brannick, 1990; Wong, Hui, & Law, 1998). Coefficient alpha values for the intrinsic satisfaction subscale ranged from .82 to .86 (Breeden, 1993; Davy, Kinicki, & Scheck, 1997; Wong et al., 1998). For the extrinsic satisfaction subscale, coefficient alpha values ranged from .70 to .82 (Breeden, 1993; Davy et al., 1997; Wong et al., 1998). A Hebrew-language version of the MSQ had a coefficient alpha of .70 (Sagie, 1998). Overall job satisfaction measured with the 20-item MSQ had test-retest reliability across three time periods of $r = .58$ (Wong et al., 1998).

Validity

Overall job satisfaction was negatively correlated with role conflict and role ambiguity, and propensity to leave (Klenke-Hamel & Mathieu, 1990; Smith & Brannick, 1990). Overall job satisfaction correlated positively with life satisfaction, non-work satisfaction, job involvement, and performance expectancy (Hart, 1999; Smith & Brannick, 1990). In both cross-sectional and longitudinal analysis, job and non-work satisfaction were predictors of life satisfaction (Scarpello & Vandenberg, 1992). In Sagie (1998), the Hebrew-language version correlated positively with organizational commitment and negatively with intention to quit.

In confirmatory analysis, Mathieu and Farr (1991) found that organizational commitment, job involvement, and job satisfaction were empirically distinct. Scarpello and Vandenberg (1992) found that job satisfaction and occupational commitment were independent constructs. Moorman (1993) factor analyzed the MSQ and found two factors: one assessing satisfaction with intrinsic aspects of the job and the other assessing satisfaction with the extrinsic aspects. In Mathieu (1991), an exploratory factor analysis of the

MSQ yielded four factors. These four subscales included satisfaction with working conditions (six items), leadership (two items), responsibility (six items), and extrinsic rewards (six items). In Igalens and Roussel (1999), confirmatory factor analysis of a French-language version of the MSQ showed that a four-factor model fit the data best. The four factors were intrinsic satisfaction, extrinsic satisfaction, recognition, and authority/social utility.

Source

Weiss, D., Dawis, R., England, G., & Lofquist. L. (1967). *Manual for the Minnesota Satisfaction Questionnaire (Minnesota Studies on Vocational Rehabilitation, Vol. 22)*. Minneapolis: University of Minnesota, Industrial Relations Center. Items were taken from pp. 110-111. Copyright © 1967. Reprinted with permission.

Items

Responses are obtained on a 5-point Likert-type scale where 1 = *very dissatisfied with this aspect of my job*, 2 = *dissatisfied with this aspect of my job*, 3 = *can't decide if I am satisfied or not with this aspect of my job*, 4 = *satisfied with this aspect of my job*, and 5 = *very satisfied with this aspect of my job*.

Instructions and items:

On the following pages, you will find statements about your present job. Read each statement carefully; decide how satisfied you are about the aspect of your current job described by the statement. Then check the box that corresponds to your level of satisfaction with that aspect of your job.

1. The chance to work alone on the job
2. The chance to do different things from time to time
3. The chance to be "somebody" in the community
4. The way my boss handles his men
5. The competence of my supervisor in making decisions
6. Being able to do things that don't go against my conscience
7. The way my job provides for steady employment
8. The chance to do things for other people
9. The chance to tell people what to do
10. The chance to do something that makes use of my abilities
11. The way the company policies are put into practice
12. The pay and the amount of work that I do
13. The chance for advancement on this job
14. The freedom to use my own judgment
15. The chance to try my own methods of doing the job
16. The working conditions
17. The way my co-workers get along with each other
18. The praise I get for doing a good job
19. The feeling of accomplishment I get from the job
20. Being able to keep busy all the time

Job in General Scale

Description This measure, developed by Ironson, Smith, Brannick, Gibson, and Paul (1989), uses 18 items to describe global job satisfaction. The measure can be used alone or in conjunction with the Job Descriptive Index (JDI), which assesses satisfaction with five job facets. Because individuals may use different frames of reference when responding to questions about facet and overall job satisfaction, this measure was developed to assess global satisfaction independent from satisfaction with facets.

Reliability Coefficient alpha values ranged from .82 to .94 (Konovsky & Cropanzano, 1991; Long, 1993; Major, Kozlowski, Chao, & Gardner, 1995; Rowley, Rosse, & Harvey, 1992; Wanberg, 1995).

Validity Global job satisfaction correlated positively with affective organizational commitment, trust in management, satisfaction with the job itself, tenure with a supervisor, pay satisfaction, satisfaction with supervision, satisfaction with promotion prospects, and judgments about procedural and outcome fairness (Cropanzano, James, & Konovsky, 1993; Konovsky & Cropanzano, 1991; Long, 1993; Major et al., 1995; Rowley et al., 1992). Global job satisfaction correlated negatively with turnover intentions (Cropanzano et al., 1993; Major et al., 1995).

Source Ironson, G., Smith, P., Brannick, M., Gibson, M., & Paul, K. (1989). Construction of a Job in General Scale: A comparison of global, composite and specific measures. *Journal of Applied Psychology, 74,* 193-200. Items were taken from Table 1, p. 195. Copyright © 1989 by the American Psychological Association. Reprinted with permission.

Items Responses are obtained as "yes" if the employee agrees that the item describes his or her job in general, "no" if the item does not and "?" if the employee is undecided.

1.	Pleasant	10.	Superior
2.	Bad (R)	11.	Better than most
3.	Ideal	12.	Disagreeable (R)
4.	Waste of time (R)	13.	Makes me content
5.	Good	14.	Inadequate (R)
6.	Undesirable (R)	15.	Excellent
7.	Worthwhile	16.	Rotten (R)
8.	Worse than most (R)	17.	Enjoyable
9.	Acceptable	18.	Poor (R)

Items denoted with (R) are reverse scored.

Overall Job Satisfaction

Description   This measure was developed by Taylor and Bowers (1974) as part of a survey of organizations questionnaire. The measure assesses job satisfaction by combining employee responses to single items that describe the degree of employee satisfaction with the work, co-workers, supervision, promotional opportunities, pay, progress, and the organization to assess overall job satisfaction.

Reliability   Coefficient alpha values ranged from .67 to .71 (Larwood, Wright, Desrochers, & Dahir, 1998; Singh, 1994).

Validity   In Singh (1994), overall job satisfaction correlated negatively with employee equity comparisons outside the organization. Overall job satisfaction also correlated negatively with turnover intention and job market fluidity (Larwood et al., 1998).

Source   Cook, J. D., Hepworth, S. J., Wall, T. D., & Warr, P. B. (1981). *The experience of work: A compendium of 249 measures and their use.* London: Academic Press. Items were taken from p. 26. Copyright © 1981 by Academic Press. Reproduced with permission.

Items   Responses are obtained on a 5-point Likert-type scale where 1 = *completely satisfied* and 5 = *completely unsatisfied*.

Items:

1. All in all, how satisfied are you with the persons in your work group?
2. All in all, how satisfied are you with your supervisor?
3. All in all, how satisfied are you with your job?
4. All in all, how satisfied are you with this organization, compared to most?
5. Considering your skills and the effort you put into your work, how satisfied are you with your pay?
6. How satisfied do you feel with the progress you have made in this organization up to now?
7. How satisfied do you feel with your chance for getting ahead in this organization in the future?

Overall Job Satisfaction

Description

This measure was developed by Judge, Boudreau, and Bretz (1994). It uses three items to assess overall job satisfaction. These include the Gallop poll question about job satisfaction (respondents are asked if they are satisfied with their job with a yes/no reply option), the G. M. Faces scale (asks for employees to choose 1 of 11 faces that best described how they feel about their job overall), and a question that asks the percentage of time respondents are satisfied with their jobs on average. The responses to the three questions are standardized and then added to form the composite measure of overall job satisfaction.

Reliability

Coefficient alpha values ranged from .78 to .85 (Judge et al., 1994; Judge, Thoresen, Pucik, & Welbourne, 1999).

Validity

Judge et al. (1994) evaluated alternative measurement models and found that job satisfaction, life satisfaction, job stress, and work-family conflict were empirically distinct. In Judge et al. (1999), job satisfaction was positively correlated with perceived job performance, coping with change, and organizational commitment. Satisfaction was negatively correlated with having reached a career plateau.

Sources

Judge, T. A., Boudreau, J. W., & Bretz, R. D., Jr. (1994). Job and life attitudes of male executives. *Journal of Applied Psychology, 79*(5), 767-782. Items were taken from text, p. 771. Copyright © 1994 by the American Psychological Association. Reprinted with permission.

Kunin, T. (1955). The construction of a new type of attitude measure. *Personnel Psychology, 8*(1), 65-77. Faces graphic taken from Figure 2, p. 68, and Figure 3, p. 69. Reproduced with permission.

Items

1. Are you satisfied with your current job? (Responses are obtained as yes = 2 or no = 1.)
2. Circle the face that best describes how you feel about your job in general. (Responses range from 11 = *happiest non-graphic face* to 1 = *unhappiest non-graphic face*.)

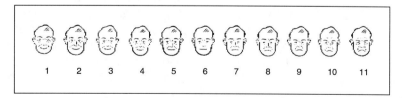

3. What percentage of the time are you satisfied with your job on average (percentage response)?

Global Job Satisfaction

Description   This measure was originally developed by Quinn and Shepard (1974) and subsequently modified by Pond and Geyer (1991) and Rice et al. (1991). It uses six items to measure an employee's general affective reaction to his or her job without reference to any specific facets. Other studies have used three of the items (Fields & Blum, 1997), four (Eisenberger, Cummings, Armeli, & Lynch, 1997; Taber & Alliger, 1995), and five of the items (Birnbaum & Somers, 1993; McFarlin & Rice, 1992; Mossholder, Bennett, & Martin, 1998; Williams, Gavin, & Williams, 1996). Rice et al. (1991) substituted a revised sixth item.

Reliability   Coefficient alpha for the six-item measure was .89 (Pond & Geyer, 1991). Coefficient alpha for the five-item measure ranged from .81 to .89 (Birnbaum & Somers, 1993; McFarlin & Rice, 1992; Mossholder, Bennett, & Martin, 1998; Williams et al., 1996). Coefficient alpha values for the four-item measure ranged from .75 to .85 (Eisenberger et al., 1997; Martin & Roman, 1996; Taber & Alliger, 1995). In Fields and Blum (1997), coefficient alpha for the three-item version was .78.

Validity   Global job satisfaction correlated positively with satisfaction with the facets of the job itself, supervision, promotion, pay, interactions with a boss, customer contact, job freedom, learning opportunities, amount of decision making, and satisfaction with co-workers (Fields & Blum, 1997; McFarlin & Rice, 1992; Pond & Geyer, 1991). It also correlated positively with affective commitment to an occupation and the organization, job involvement, the importance of interaction with a boss, and the importance of customer contact (Birnbaum & Somers, 1993; McFarlin & Rice, 1992; Mossholder, Bennett, & Martin, 1998; Pond & Geyer, 1991). Global job satisfaction correlated negatively with continuance commitment to an occupation and an organization, the extent of perceived job alternatives, role conflict, role ambiguity, turnover, and the importance of pay and promotion (Birnbaum & Somers, 1993; McFarlin & Rice, 1992; Mossholder, Bennett, & Martin, 1998; Pond & Geyer, 1991).

Eisenberger et al. (1997) performed a confirmatory factor analysis of the measure and found that perceived organizational support and overall job satisfaction were empirically distinct. In Rice et al. (1991), multivariate analysis indicated that overall job satisfaction was empirically distinct from satisfaction with each of 12 job facets. In Williams et al. (1996), exploratory and confirmatory factor analysis showed the measure had one dimension and was empirically distinct from organizational commitment, role ambiguity, role overload, role conflict, job complexity, and negative affectivity.

Sources   Pond, S. B., & Geyer, P. D. (1991). Differences in the relation between job satisfaction and perceived work alternatives among older and younger blue-collar workers. *Journal of Vocational Behavior, 39,* 251-262. Items were taken from text, p. 254. Copyright © 1991 by Academic Press. Reprinted with permission.

Revised sixth item from Rice, R. W., Gentile, D. A., & McFarlin, D. B. (1991). Facet importance and job satisfaction. *Journal of Applied Psychology, 76*(1), 31-39. Item was taken from text, p. 33. Copyright © 1991 by the American Psychological Association. Reprinted with permission.

Items   Items and response scales:

The original wording of the items is in parentheses.

1. (Knowing what you know now), If you had to decide all over again whether to take the job you now have, what would you decide?

   Responses range from 1 = *definitely not take the job* to 5 = *definitely take the job.*

2. If a (good) friend asked if he/she should apply for a job like yours with your employer, what would you recommend?

   Responses range from 1 = *not recommend at all* to 5 = *recommend strongly.*

3. How does this job compare with your ideal job (job you would most like to have)?

   Responses range from 1 = *very far from ideal* to 5 = *very close to ideal.*

4. (In general) how does your job measure up to the sort of job you wanted when you took it?

   Responses range from 1 = *not at all like I wanted* to 5 = *just like what I wanted.*

5. All (in all) things considered, how satisfied are you with your current job?

   Responses range from 1 = *not at all satisfied* to 5 = *completely satisfied.*

6. In general, how much do you like your job?

   Responses range from 1 = *not at all* to 5 = *a great deal.*

   Revised sixth item from Rice et al. (1991):

   How do you feel about your job overall?

   Possible responses are 1 = *terrible*, 2 = *unhappy*, 3 = *mostly dissatisfied*, 4 = *mixed (about equally dissatisfied and satisfied)*, 5 = *mostly satisfied*, 6 = *pleased*, and 7 = *delighted.*

Job Satisfaction Survey

Description   This measure, developed by Spector (1985), uses 36 items to describe nine job facets (four items per facet). The job facets include pay, promotion, supervision, benefits, contingent rewards, operating procedures, co-workers, nature of work, and communication. It was originally developed to assess job satisfaction in human service, nonprofit, and public organizations.

Reliability   In Blau (1999), coefficient alpha was .89.

Validity   In a longitudinal study, job satisfaction correlated positively with expected job utility and professional commitment in the previous year, and the extent of downsizing, shift assignment, and professional commitment in the current year (Blau, 1999). Spector (1997) found that the nine facets were all positively intercorrelated.

Source   Spector, P. (1997). *Job satisfaction.* Thousand Oaks, CA: Sage. Copyright © 1997 by Sage Publications, Inc. Items were taken from the appendix, pp. 75-76. Reprinted by permission of Sage Publications, Inc.

Items   Responses are obtained on a 6-point Likert-type scale where 1 = *disagree very much*, 2 = *disagree moderately*, 3 = *disagree slightly*, 4 = *agree slightly*, 5 = *agree moderately*, and 6 = *agree very much*.

Pay satisfaction items:

1. I feel I am being paid a fair amount for the work I do
2. Raises are too few and far between (R)
3. I am unappreciated by the organization when I think about what they pay me (R)
4. I feel satisfied with my chances for salary increases

Promotion satisfaction items:

1. There is really too little chance for promotion on my job (R)
2. Those who do well on the job stand a fair chance of being promoted
3. People get ahead as fast here as they do in other places
4. I am satisfied with my chances for promotion

Supervision satisfaction items:

1. My supervisor is quite competent in doing his/her job
2. My supervisor is unfair to me (R)
3. My supervisor shows too little interest in the feelings of subordinates (R)
4. I like my supervisor

Benefits satisfaction items:

1. I am not satisfied with the benefits I receive (R)
2. The benefits we receive are as good as most other organizations offer
3. The benefit package we have is equitable (R)
4. There are benefits we do not have which we should have (R)

Rewards satisfaction items:

1. When I do a good job, I receive the recognition for it that I should receive
2. I do not feel that the work I do is appreciated (R)
3. There are few rewards for those who work here (R)
4. I don't feel my efforts are rewarded the way they should be (R)

Operating procedure satisfaction items:

1. Many of our rules and procedures make doing a good job difficult (R)
2. My efforts to do a good job are seldom blocked by red tape
3. I have too much to do at work (R)
4. I have too much paperwork (R)

Co-workers satisfaction items:

1. I like the people I work with
2. I find I have to work harder at my job than I should because of the incompetence of people I work with (R)
3. I enjoy my co-workers
4. There is too much bickering and fighting at work (R)

Work itself satisfaction items:

1. I sometimes feel my job is meaningless (R)
2. I like doing the things I do at work
3. I feel a sense of pride in doing my job
4. My job is enjoyable

Communication satisfaction items:

1. Communications seem good within this organization
2. The goals of this organization are not clear to me (R)
3. I often feel that I do not know what is going on with the organization (R)
4. Work assignments are often not fully explained (R)

Items denoted with (R) are reverse scored.

Job Satisfaction Index

Description   This measure was developed by Schriesheim and Tsui (1980). It uses six items to form an index that describes overall job satisfaction. The scale includes single questions to assess the degree of satisfaction with the work itself, supervision, co-workers, pay, promotion opportunities, and the job in general.

Reliability   Coefficient alpha ranged from .73 to .78 (Cohen, 1997; Tsui et al., 1992).

Validity   Overall job satisfaction correlated positively with age, tenure, psychological commitment to the organization, personal coping ability, organizational support for non-work activities, and intention to stay. It correlated negatively with frequency of absences, job level, conflict between work and non-work roles, and years in an occupation (Cohen, 1997; Tsui et al., 1992).

Source   Tsui, A. S., Egan, T. D., & O'Reilly, C. A., III. (1992). Being different: Relational demography and organizational attachment. *Administrative Science Quarterly, 37*(4), 549-580. Items were taken from the appendix, p. 588. Copyright © 1992 by *Administrative Science Quarterly*. Reprinted with permission.

Items   Responses are obtained on a 5-point Likert-type scale where 1 = *strongly disagree* and 5 = *strongly agree*.

1. How satisfied are you with the nature of the work you perform?
2. How satisfied are you with the person who supervises you—your organizational superior?
3. How satisfied are you with your relations with others in the organization with whom you work—your co-workers or peers?
4. How satisfied are you with the pay you receive for your job?
5. How satisfied are you with the opportunities which exist in this organization for advancement or promotion?
6. Considering everything, how satisfied are you with your current job situation?

Job Perception Scale

Description   The Job Perception Scale was developed by Hatfield, Robinson, and Huseman (1985). It uses semantic differential responses to 21 items that describe aspects of a job. These include the work itself, pay, promotions, supervision, and co-workers. The Job Perception Scale was selected for use in Smith, Smits, and Hoy (1998) because it was likely to be easily understood by workers with a wide range of educational backgrounds. The items of the Job Perception Scale can also be collapsed to form one summed measure of job satisfaction (Smith et al., 1998).

Reliability   Coefficient alpha values ranged from .87 to .93 for the 21-item composite measure (Miles, Patrick, & King, 1996; Smith et al., 1998).

Validity   Overall job satisfaction correlated positively with age, supervisory positive relationship communications, positive communications about the job, and perceptions of the quality of management. It correlated negatively with negative relationship communications (Miles et al., 1996; Smith et al., 1998).

Source   Hatfield, J., Robinson, R. B., & Huseman, R. C. (1985). An empirical evaluation of a test for assessing job satisfaction. *Psychological Reports, 56,* 39-45. Items were taken from Table 2, p. 42. © Psychological Reports, 1985. Reprinted with permission of the authors and publisher.

Items   Respondents are asked to choose a level from 1 to 5 that describes their present job using each pair of words as end-point anchors.

Work items:

1. Exciting/Dull
2. Pleasant/Unpleasant
3. Clear/Hazy
4. Challenging/Unchallenging
5. Satisfying/Unsatisfying

Pay items:

6. Rewarding/Unrewarding
7. Large/Small
8. Right/Wrong
9. Positive/Negative

Promotion items:

10. Just/Unjust
11. Reliable/Unreliable
12. Positive/Negative
13. Reasonable/Unreasonable

Supervisor items:

14. Near/Distant
15. Sincere/Insincere
16. Friendly/Unfriendly
17. Qualified/Unqualified

Co-workers items:

18. Careful/Careless
19. Loyal/Disloyal
20. Pleasant/Unpleasant
21. Boring/Interesting

Overall Job Satisfaction

Description   This measure, developed by Brayfield and Rothe (1951), uses 18 items to describe overall job satisfaction. The items form a one-dimensional measure of overall job satisfaction. A six-item version has also been used to measure overall job satisfaction (Agho et al., 1993; Aryee, Fields, & Luk, 1999).

Reliability   Coefficient alpha values for the entire measure ranged from .88 to .91 (Moorman, 1991; Pillai, Schriesheim, & Williams, 1999; Shore, Newton & Thornton, 1990). Coefficient alpha values for the six-item version ranged from .83 to .90 (Agho et al., 1993; Agho et al., 1992; Aryee et al., 1999; Judge, Locke, Durham, & Kluger, 1998).

Validity   Overall job satisfaction correlated positively with a composite measure of job facets, autonomy, distributive justice, supervisory support, task significance, sensitivity to equity, employee perceptions of performance, and job involvement (Agho et al., 1993; Aryee et al., 1999; Judge et al., 1998; O'Neill & Mone, 1998). Overall job satisfaction correlated negatively with family-work conflict, work routinization, role ambiguity, and role conflict (Agho et al., 1993; Aryee et al., 1999). Brooke, Russell, and Price (1988) examined the measure using confirmatory factor analysis and found that this measure of job satisfaction was empirically distinct from measures of organizational commitment and job involvement. In Judge et al. (1998), an employee's significant other also reported about their perceptions of the employee's job satisfaction. The correlation of self and significant other perceptions was .68.

Sources   Original items: Cook, J. D., Hepworth, S. J., Wall, T. D., & Warr, P. B. (1981). *The experience of work: A compendium of 249 measures and their use.* London: Academic Press. Items were taken from pp. 18-19. Copyright © 1981 by Academic Press. Reproduced with permission.

Six-item version: Agho, A. O., Price, J. L., & Mueller, C. W. (1992). Discriminant validity of measures of job satisfaction, positive affectivity and negative affectivity. *Journal of Occupational and Organizational Psychology, 65,* 185-196. Items were taken from the appendix, p. 195. Copyright © 1992. Reproduced with permission.

Items   Original measure:

Responses are obtained using a 5-point Likert-type scale where 5 = *strongly agree*, 4 = *agree*, 3 = *undecided*, 2 = *disagree*, and 1 = *strongly disagree.*

1. My job is like a hobby to me
2. My job is usually interesting enough to keep me from getting bored

3. It seems that my friends are more interested in their jobs (R)
4. I consider my job rather unpleasant (R)
5. I enjoy my work more than my leisure time
6. I am often bored with my job (R) (Used in six-item version)
7. I feel fairly well satisfied with my present job (Used in six-item version)
8. Most of the time I have to force myself to go to work (R)
9. I am satisfied with my job for the time being (Used in six-item version)
10. I feel that my job is no more interesting than others I could get (R)
11. I definitely dislike my work (R)
12. I feel that I am happier in my work than most other people
13. Most days I am enthusiastic about my work (Used in six-item version)
14. Each day of work seems like it will never end (R)
15. I like my job better than the average worker does (Used in six-item version)
16. My job is pretty uninteresting (R)
17. I find real enjoyment in my work (Used in six-item version)
18. I am disappointed that I ever took this job (R)

Items denoted with (R) are reverse scored.

Six-item measure:

Responses are obtained using a 5-point Likert-type scale where 5 = *strongly agree*, 4 = *agree*, 3 = *undecided*, 2 = *disagree*, and 1 = *strongly disagree*.

Items:

1. I am often bored with my job (R)
2. I feel fairly well satisfied with my present job
3. I am satisfied with my job for the time being
4. Most days I am enthusiastic about my work
5. I like my job better than the average worker does
6. I find real enjoyment in my work

Items denoted with (R) are reverse scored.

Job Diagnostic Survey

Description

The Job Diagnostic Survey (JDS), developed by Hackman and Oldham (1974), measures overall and facet specific job satisfaction. Overall job satisfaction is measured in terms of three dimensions including general satisfaction (five items), internal work motivation (six items), and growth satisfaction (four items). These dimensions are often combined into a single measure of job satisfaction. The JDS also measures satisfaction with the job facets of security, compensation, co-workers, and supervision. Satisfaction with these facets and growth satisfaction have also been combined to form a composite measure (Duffy, Ganster, & Shaw, 1998).

Reliability

Coefficient alpha for the measure encompassing general satisfaction, internal work motivation, and growth satisfaction ranged from .55 to .92 (Adkins, 1995; Mannheim, Baruch, & Tal, 1997; Munz, Huelsman, Konold, & McKinney, 1996; Netemeyer, Johnston, & Burton, 1990; Pearson, 1992; Rothausen, Gonzalez, Clarke, & O'Dell, 1998). General satisfaction had a coefficient alpha of .77, internal work motivation had an alpha of .67, and growth satisfaction had an alpha of .85 (Munz et al., 1996). In Duffy et al. (1998), coefficient alpha for a composite of facet and growth satisfaction was .91. Coefficient alphas for the facet satisfaction subscales were .89 for satisfaction with supervision, .84 for satisfaction with growth, .73 for satisfaction with job security, .88 for satisfaction with pay, and .63 for satisfaction with co-workers (Mathieu, Hofmann, & Farr, 1993).

Validity

Overall job satisfaction correlated positively with organizational commitment, organizational citizenship behaviors, and interrole facilitation. It correlated negatively with tenure (Duffy et al., 1998; Thompson & Werner, 1997). In confirmatory factor analysis, Mathieu and Farr (1991) found that organizational commitment, job involvement, and overall job satisfaction were empirically distinct.

Source

Hackman, J. R., & Oldham, G. R. (1974). *The Job Diagnostic Survey: An instrument for the diagnosis of jobs and the evaluation of job redesign projects* (Tech. Rep. No. 4). New Haven, CT: Yale University, Department of Administrative Sciences. Prepared in connection with research sponsored by the Office of Naval Research (Contract No. N00014-67A-0097-0026, NR170-744) and the U.S. Department of Labor (Manpower Administration, Grant No. 21-09-74-14).

Items

General satisfaction instructions and items:
Each of the statements below is something that a person might say about his or her job. You are to indicate your own personal feelings about your job by marking how much you agree with each of the statements. How much do you agree with the statement?

(1 = *disagree strongly*, 2 = *disagree*, 3 = *disagree slightly*, 4 = *neutral*, 5 = *agree slightly*, 6 = *agree*, 7 = *agree strongly*)

1. Generally speaking, I am very satisfied with this job
2. I am generally satisfied with the kind of work I do in this job
3. I frequently think of quitting this job (R)

Now please think of the other people in your organization who hold the same job you do. If no one has exactly the same job as you, think of the job which is most similar to yours. Please think about how accurately each of the statements describes the feelings of those people about the job. It is quite all right if your answers here are different from when you described your own reactions to the job. Often different people feel quite differently about the same job. How much do you agree with the statement?

(1 = *disagree strongly*, 2 = *disagree*, 3 = *disagree slightly*, 4 = *neutral*, 5 = *agree slightly*, 6 = *agree*, 7 = *agree strongly*)

4. Most people on this job are very satisfied with the job
5. People on this job often think of quitting (R)

Internal work motivation items:

Now please indicate how you personally feel about your job. Each of the statements below is something that a person might say about his or her job. You are to indicate your own personal feelings about your job by marking how much you agree with each of the statements. How much do you agree with the statement?

(1 = *disagree strongly*, 2 = *disagree*, 3 = *disagree slightly*, 4 = *neutral*, 5 = *agree slightly*, 6 = *agree*, 7 = *agree strongly*)

1. My opinion of myself goes up when I do this job well
2. I feel a great sense of personal satisfaction when I do this job well
3. I feel bad and unhappy when I discover that I have performed poorly on this job
4. My own feelings generally are not affected much one way or the other by how well I do on this job (R)

Now please think of the other people in your organization who hold the same job you do. If no one has exactly the same job as you, think of the job which is most similar to yours. Please think about how accurately each of the statements describes the feelings of those people about the job. It is quite all right if your answers here are different from when you described your own reactions to the job. Often different people feel quite differently about the same job. How much do you agree with the statement?

(1 = *disagree strongly*, 2 = *disagree*, 3 = *disagree slightly*, 4 = *neutral*, 5 = *agree slightly*, 6 = *agree*, 7 = *agree strongly*)

5. Most people on this job feel a great sense of personal satisfaction when they do the job well
6. Most people on this job feel bad or unhappy when they find that they have performed the work poorly

Growth satisfaction items:

Now please indicate how satisfied you are with each aspect of your job listed below. How satisfied are you with this aspect of your job?

(1 = *extremely dissatisfied*, 2 = *dissatisfied*, 3 = *slightly dissatisfied*, 4 = *neutral*, 5 = *slightly satisfied*, 6 = *satisfied*, 7 = *extremely satisfied*)

1. The amount of personal growth and development I get in doing my job
2. The feeling of worthwhile accomplishment I get from doing my job
3. The amount of independent thought and action I can exercise in my job
4. The amount of challenge in my job

Facet satisfaction items:

Now please indicate how satisfied you are with each aspect of your job listed below. How satisfied are you with this aspect of your job?

(1 = *extremely dissatisfied*, 2 = *dissatisfied*, 3 = *slightly dissatisfied*, 4 = *neutral*, 5 = *slightly satisfied*, 6 = *satisfied*, 7 = *extremely satisfied*)

Satisfaction with security:

1. The amount of job security I have
2. How secure things look for me in the future in this organization

Satisfaction with compensation (pay):

1. The amount of pay and fringe benefits I receive
2. The degree to which I am fairly paid for what I contribute to this organization

"Social" satisfaction:

1. The people I talk to and work with on my job
2. The chance to get to know other people while on the job
3. The chance to help other people while at work

"Supervisory" satisfaction:

1. The degree of respect and fair treatment I receive from my boss
2. The amount of support and guidance I receive from my supervisor
3. The overall quality of the supervision I receive in my work

Job Descriptive Index

Description   The Job Descriptive Index (JDI) was originally developed by Smith, Kendall, and Hulin (1969). It uses 72 items to assess five facets of job satisfaction. The five facets are the work itself, pay, promotions, supervision, and co-workers. The ratings of satisfaction with the facets can be combined into a composite measure of job satisfaction. The JDI was updated by Roznowski (1989) to recognize changes in work atmospheres, job content, and work technologies. The items for the updated version of the JDI are presented below. The revised JDI showed somewhat higher alpha reliabilities than the scales composed of the original items (Roznowski, 1989). Gregson (1990) used a 30-item shortened version of the JDI based on choosing the 6 items that loaded the highest on each dimension (work, pay, promotions, supervision, and co-workers) in a factor analysis of the job satisfaction items.

Reliability   Coefficient alpha values for satisfaction with the work itself ranged from .75 to .94; for satisfaction with pay, alpha ranged from .78 to .91; for satisfaction with supervision, alpha values ranged from .87 to .92; for satisfaction with promotions, alpha ranged from .82 to .87; for satisfaction with co-workers, alpha ranged from .87 to .92 (Buckley et al., 1992; Callen, 1993; Cropanzano et al., 1993; Gregson, 1990; Judge, 1993a; Judge & Hulin, 1993; Kushnir & Melamed, 1991; Lefkowitz, 1994; Mossholder, Bedeian, Niebuhr, & Wesolowski, 1994; Smart, 1998; Taber & Alliger, 1995; Wanberg, 1995).

Validity   Satisfaction with the work itself, satisfaction with supervision, satisfaction with promotion, and satisfaction with co-workers were all positively correlated (Smart, 1998). Satisfaction with the work itself correlated positively with quantity and quality of communication between supervisor and subordinate and correlated negatively with lack of perceived control over job, employee anxiety, and employee irritability (Callen, 1993; Kushnir & Melamed, 1991). In Cropanzano et al. (1993), the composite job satisfaction measure was correlated positively with affective commitment to the organization and negatively correlated with turnover intentions.

In Roznowski (1989), factor analysis showed that the JDI items loaded on five distinct factors and that the items of each subscale loaded on a single factor. Judge (1993a) found a second-order factor interpreted as overall job satisfaction. In Gregson (1990), factor analysis of a modified 30-item version of the JDI showed that communication satisfaction and job satisfaction were empirically distinct. Buckley et al. (1992) found that for the JDI composite measure of job satisfaction, trait (actual job satisfaction) variance accounted for approximately 43% of the total variance, with common method and random error variance comprising the balance. For the JDI measures of facet satisfaction, trait variance accounted for 41% for the measure of supervision, 34% for the measure of satisfaction with work itself, 38% of the variance in satisfaction with co-workers, 56% of satisfaction with pay, and 61% of the satisfaction with promotions. The same study estimated that trait variance accounted for approximately 46% of the total variance in other measures of job satisfaction such as the Minnesota Satisfaction Questionnaire. The JDI is a copyrighted measure. Users should contact Professor Patricia Smith, Department of Psychology, Bowling Green State University, Bowling Green, OH 43403.

Source   Roznowski, M. (1989). An examination of the measurement properties of the Job Descriptive Index with experimental items. *Journal of Applied Psychology, 74*, 805-814. Items were taken from Tables 1, 2, 3, 4, and 5, pp. 807-810. Copyright © 1989 by the American Psychological Association. Reprinted with permission.

Items   Updated items for the Job Descriptive Index:

Respondents are asked to put Y beside each item if it describes the feature in question, N if the item does not describe that feature, or ? if they cannot decide.

Work on present job:

1.	Fascinating	10.	Challenging
2.	Routine	11.	Frustrating
3.	Satisfying	12.	Simple
4.	Boring	13.	Gives sense of accomplishment
5.	Creative	14.	A source of pleasure
6.	Respected	15.	Dull
7.	Pleasant	16.	Interesting
8.	Useful	17.	Awful
9.	Tiresome	18.	Important

Present pay:

1. Income adequate for normal expenses
2. Barely live on income
3. Bad
4. Insecure
5. Less than I deserve
6. Underpaid
7. Well paid
8. Unfair
9. Enough for what I need

Opportunities for promotion:

1. Good opportunity for promotion
2. Opportunity somewhat limited
3. Promotion on ability
4. Dead-end job
5. Good chance for promotion
6. Infrequent promotions
7. Regular promotions
8. Fairly good chance for promotion
9. Easy to get ahead

Supervision on present job:

1. Hard to please
2. Impolite
3. Praises good work
4. Tactful
5. Up-to-date
6. Quick-tempered
7. Tells me where I stand
8. Annoying
9. Stubborn
10. Knows job well
11. Bad
12. Intelligent
13. Around when needed
14. Lazy
15. Interferes with my work
16. Gives confusing directions
17. Knows how to supervise
18. Cannot be trusted

People on your present job:

1. Stimulating
2. Boring
3. Slow
4. Ambitious
5. Stupid
6. Responsible
7. Intelligent
8. Easy to make enemies
9. Talk too much
10. Smart
11. Lazy
12. Unpleasant
13. Active
14. Narrow interests
15. Loyal
16. Work well together
17. Bother me
18. Waste of time

Satisfaction With Job Facets

Description   This measure, developed by Andrews and Withey (1976), uses five items to measure overall job satisfaction. The questions each assess satisfaction with specific job facets. The response scale is unique, obtaining responses ranging from *delighted* to *terrible*.

Reliability   Coefficient alpha values for the measure range from .79 to .81 (McFarlin & Rice, 1992; Rentsch & Steel, 1992; Steel & Rentsch, 1995, 1997).

Validity   The Andrews and Withey measure correlated positively with organizational commitment, self-rated performance, supervisory rated performance, pay level, promotion opportunities, positive conversations with boss, customer/client contact, freedom to work the employee's own way, learning opportunities, amount of decision making, and mental effort required. It correlated negatively with intention to quit (McFarlin & Rice, 1992; Steel & Rentsch, 1995, 1997). Rentsch and Steel (1992) found that the Andrews and Withey measure correlated highly with overall satisfaction scores from both the Job Descriptive Index (JDI) and the Minnesota Satisfaction Questionnaire. It also correlated positively with satisfaction with the five JDI facets of pay, supervision, promotions, co-workers, and the work itself.

Source   Rentsch, J. R., & Steel, R. P. (1992). Construct and concurrent validation of the Andrews and Withey Job Satisfaction Questionnaire. *Educational and Psychological Measurement, 52,* 357-367. Copyright © 1992 by Sage Publications, Inc. Items were taken from text, p. 359. Reprinted by permission of Sage Publications, Inc.

Items   Responses are obtained on a 7-point Likert-type scale where 7 = *delighted*, 6 = *pleased*, 5 = *mostly satisfied*, 4 = *mixed (about equally satisfied and dissatisfied)*, 3 = *mostly dissatisfied*, 2 = *unhappy*, and 1 = *terrible*.

1. How do you feel about your job?
2. How do your feel about the people you work with—your co-workers?
3. How do you feel about the work you do on your job—the work itself?
4. What is it like where your work—the physical surroundings, the hours, the amount of work you are asked to do?
5. How do you feel about what you have available for doing your job— I mean the equipment, information, good supervision, and so on?

Global Job Satisfaction

Description   This measure, developed by Warr, Cook, and Wall (1979), uses 15 items to describe overall job satisfaction. The measure has two subscales assessing satisfaction with extrinsic (eight items) and intrinsic (seven items) aspects of a job.

Reliability   Coefficient alpha values for the composite measure of overall job satisfaction ranged from .80 to .91 (Abraham & Hansson, 1996; Norman, Collins, Conner, Martin, & Rance, 1995). For satisfaction with intrinsic aspects of a job, alpha ranged from .84 to .88. For satisfaction with extrinsic job aspects, alpha was .76 (Cordery, Vevastos, Mueller, & Parker, 1993; Wright & Cordery, 1999).

Validity   In Winefield, Winefield, Tiggemann, and Goldney (1991), global job satisfaction was used to separate subjects into satisfied employees and dissatisfied employees. The two groups differed significantly in a variety of variables describing psychological well-being. In Abraham and Hansson (1996), job satisfaction correlated negatively with both job-related tension and control problems. Job satisfaction correlated positively with job-related well-being, satisfaction with rate of pay, perceived job competence, and perceived job control (Norman et al., 1995; Wright & Cordery, 1999).

Source   Cook, J. D., Hepworth, S. J., Wall, T. D., & Warr, P. B. (1981). *The experience of work: A compendium of 249 measures and their use.* London: Academic Press. Items were taken from pp. 33-34. Copyright © 1981 by Academic Press. Reproduced with permission.

Items   Responses are obtained on a 7-point Likert-type scale where 1 = *I'm extremely dissatisfied,* 2 = *I'm very dissatisfied,* 3 = *I'm moderately dissatisfied,* 4 = *I'm not sure,* 5 = *I'm moderately satisfied,* 6 = *I'm very satisfied,* and 7 = *I'm extremely satisfied.*

Items: (E) denotes extrinsic satisfaction subscale; (I) denotes intrinsic satisfaction subscale.

1. The physical work conditions (I)
2. The freedom to choose your own method of working (I)
3. Your fellow workers (I)
4. The recognition you get for good work (E)
5. Your immediate boss (E)
6. The amount of responsibility you are given (I)
7. Your rate of pay (E)
8. Your opportunity to use your abilities (I)
9. Industrial relations between management and workers in your firm (E)

10. Your chance of promotion (E)
11. The way your firm is managed (E)
12. The attention paid to suggestions you make (I)
13. Your hours of work (E)
14. The amount of variety in your job (I)
15. Your job security (E)

Career Satisfaction

Description   This measure was developed by Greenhaus, Parasuraman, and Wormley (1990). It measures satisfaction with career success, an internally generated and defined career outcome. Besides general satisfaction with career progress, the measure assesses the extent to which an employee has made satisfactory progress toward goals for income level, advancement, and development of skills.

Reliability   Coefficient alpha ranged from .83 to .89 (Aryee, Chay, & Tan, 1994; Greenhaus et al., 1990; Seibert, Crant, & Kraimer, 1999).

Validity   Career satisfaction correlated positively with having a job in general management, salary level, number of promotions received, perceptions of upward mobility, sponsorship within an organization, acceptance, job discretion, supervisory support, career strategies, perceived personal-organization value congruence, presence of an internal labor market, and job performance. It correlated negatively with having reached a career plateau (Aryee et al., 1994; Greenhaus et al., 1990; Seibert et al., 1999). Confirmatory factor analysis showed that general perceptions of career satisfaction are empirically distinct from financial success and hierarchical success in an organization (Aryee et al., 1994).

Source   Greenhaus, J. H., Parasuraman, A., & Wormley, W. M. (1990). Effects of race on organizational experiences, job performance evaluations, and career outcomes. *Academy of Management Journal 33*(1), 64-86. © 1990 by Academy of Management. Items were taken from the appendix, p. 66. Items are reproduced with permission of Academy of Management in the format textbook via Copyright Clearance Center.

Items   Responses are obtained on a 5-point Likert-type scale where 5 = *strongly disagree*, 4 = *disagree to some extent*, 3 = *uncertain*, 2 = *agree to some extent*, and 1 = *strongly agree*.

1. I am satisfied with the success I have achieved in my career
2. I am satisfied with the progress I have made toward meeting my overall career goals
3. I am satisfied with the progress I have made toward meeting my goals for income
4. I am satisfied with the progress I have made toward meeting my goals for advancement
5. I am satisfied with the progress I have made toward meeting my goals for the development of new skills

Employee Satisfaction With Influence and Ownership

Description   This measure, developed by Rosen, Klein, and Young (1986), contains two subscales that measure influence due to ownership associated with holding stock through an employee stock ownership program (ESOP) and satisfaction with the ESOP. The influence subscale has been used to measure workers' perceived actual amount of influence and desired amount of influence by changing item wording to *should* (Buchko, 1992).

Reliability   In Buchko (1992), the ESOP satisfaction subscale had a coefficient alpha of .86 and the influence subscale had a coefficient alpha of .87.

Validity   In Buchko (1992), perceived influence and ESOP satisfaction correlated positively with organizational commitment, job involvement, and overall job satisfaction. Both measures correlated negatively with turnover intentions and unionization. ESOP satisfaction also correlated positively with ESOP participation.

Source   Rosen, C., Klein, K., & Young, K. (1986). *Employee ownership in America: The equity solution.* Lexington, MA: D. C. Heath. Items were taken from Appendix 6-A, pp. 139-140. Copyright © 1986 by Corey Rosen. Reproduced with permission.

Items   Influence subscale instructions and items:

How much say or influence do non-managerial workers in your company actually have over the following areas? (Possible responses are 1 = *workers have no say*, 2 = *workers receive information*, 3 = *workers are asked for their opinion*, 4 = *workers decide with management*, and 5 = *workers decide alone.*)

1. Social events
2. Working conditions
3. The way workers perform their own jobs
4. Pay and other compensation
5. Hiring, firing, and other personnel decisions
6. Selection of supervisors and management
7. Company policy (investment in new equipment, planning for the company future)

ESOP satisfaction subscale items:

(Responses are obtained on a 7-point Likert-type scale where 1 = *completely disagree* and 7 = *completely agree*)

1. Because of employee ownership, my work is more satisfying
2. I really don't care about the employee ownership plan in this company (R)
3. I'm proud to own stock in this company
4. Employee ownership at this company makes my day-to-day work more enjoyable
5. Owning stock in this company makes me want to stay with this company longer than I would if I did not own stock
6. It is very important to me that this company has an employee stock ownership plan
7. Owning stock in this company makes me more interested in the company's financial success
8. Employee ownership at this company gives me a greater share in the company profit

Items denoted with (R) are reverse scored.

Satisfaction With Work Schedule Flexibility

Description   This measure, developed by Rothausen (1994), uses a five-item scale to measure employee satisfaction with work schedule flexibility. It measures the extent to which an employee feels he or she has flexibility in scheduling work, in doing part-time or flextime work, and in balancing work and family responsibilities.

Reliability   In Aryee, Luk, and Stone (1998), coefficient alpha was .79.

Validity   Satisfaction with schedule flexibility correlated positively with organizational commitment and supervisor work-family support. Satisfaction with flexibility correlated negatively with turnover intentions (Aryee et al., 1998).

Source   Rothausen, T. J. (1994). Job satisfaction and the parent worker: The role of flexibility and rewards. *Journal of Vocational Behavior, 44*, 317-336. Items were taken from text, p. 326. Copyright © 1994 by Academic Press. Reproduced with permission.

Items   Responses are obtained on a 5-point Likert-type scale where 1 = *very dissatisfied* and 5 = *very satisfied*.

1. The extent to which management accommodates family responsibility needs without any negative consequences
2. The opportunity to perform your job well and yet be able to perform home-related duties adequately
3. The ease of getting time off for family as needed
4. The opportunity to do part-time or flextime work without being penalized
5. The amount of flexibility in work scheduling

Pay Satisfaction Questionnaire

Description   The Pay Satisfaction Questionnaire (PSQ) was developed by Heneman and Schwab (1985). It uses four subscales to measure satisfaction with pay level, amount of last raise, benefits, and pay structure/administration. The subscales can also be combined into a composite measure for overall pay satisfaction. Heneman and Schwab initially hypothesized five dimensions of pay satisfaction: pay level, pay raises, benefits, structure, and administration. Based on factor analysis results, the pay level, raises, and benefits dimensions were supported, but the structure and administration dimensions were combined into a single fourth dimension (Judge, 1993b).

Reliability   Coefficient alpha for the composite measure of pay satisfaction ranged from .77 to .88. Coefficient alpha values for the four subscales ranged from .73 to .96 (Blau, 1994; Carraher & Buckley, 1996; DeConinck, Stilwell, & Brock, 1996; Huber et al., 1992; Jones, Scarpello, & Bergmann, 1999; Judge, 1993b; Lee & Farh, 1999; Welbourne, 1998; Welbourne & Cable, 1995).

Validity   Expectations about the level of equitable pay were negatively correlated with satisfaction with pay level, pay structure/administration, and amount of last raise. The four subscales of the pay satisfaction questionnaire were also positively correlated with overall job satisfaction (Huber et al., 1992). Carraher and Buckley (1996) used confirmatory factor analysis to show the number of dimensions best used to measure pay satisfaction differed by cognitive complexity of employees. Four dimensions (pay level, benefits, raises, and pay structure-administration) fit the data better for more cognitively complex employees. In Shaw, Duffy, Jenkins, and Gupta (1999), confirmatory factor analysis showed that a four-factor model had the best fit with the data. Confirmatory factor analyses by Judge (1993b) and DeConinck et al. (1996) both found that the items from the PSQ loaded on the hypothesized dimensions, and the overall fit supported the four dimensional model. The factor loadings were similar across job classifications and the dimensions of the PSQ were empirically separable. Judge (1993b) found that the PSQ dimensions displayed differing patterns of correlations with hypothesized predictors. For example, salary level correlated positively with satisfaction with pay level; pay relative to others doing similar work in other companies correlated positively with all the PSQ dimensions; pay raise history correlated positively with satisfaction with raises; understanding of the pay system correlated positively with satisfaction with pay level, satisfaction with raises and satisfaction with pay structure and administration, but not with satisfaction with benefits. Pay satisfaction measured with the PSQ correlated positively with pay satisfaction measured by the Minnesota Satisfaction Questionnaire and pay satisfaction measured by the Job Descriptive Index. All three measures of pay satisfaction correlated negatively with perceived inequity in pay and positively with an employee's amount of pay. Correlations among pay level, pay raises, and structure/

administration were substantially larger than the correlations of these dimensions with satisfaction with benefits (Judge, 1993b; Welbourne & Cable, 1995). DeConinck and colleagues (1996) found that the four PSQ dimensions were empirically distinct from distributive justice.

Source   Heneman, H. G., & Schwab, D. P. (1985). Pay satisfaction: Its multidimensional nature and measurement. *International Journal of Psychology, 20,* 129-141. © 1985, Elsevier. Reprinted with permission.

Items   Responses are obtained on a 5-point Likert-type scale where 1 = *very dissatisfied* and 5 = *very satisfied.*

1.   My take-home pay
2.   My benefit package
3.   My most recent raise
4.   Influence my supervisor has on my pay
5.   My current salary
6.   Amount the company pays towards my benefits
7.   The raises I have typically received in the past
8.   The company's pay structure
9.   Information the company gives about pay issues of concern to me
10. My overall level of pay
11. The value of my benefits
12. Pay of other jobs in the company
13. Consistency of the company's pay policy
14. Size of my current salary
15. The number of benefits I receive
16. How my raises are determined
17. Differences in pay among jobs in the company
18. How the company administers pay

Index of Organizational Reactions

Description   The Index of Organizational Reactions (IOR), developed by Dunham and Smith (1979), assesses employee satisfaction with his or her job and organization. The IOR assesses satisfaction with supervision, financial rewards, kind of work, physical conditions, amount of work, company identification, co-workers, and career future.

Reliability   Coefficient alpha values ranged from .82 to .83 (Lee & Johnson, 1991; McLain, 1995; Taylor, Tracy, Renard, Harrison, & Carroll, 1995).

Validity   In Lee and Johnson (1991), workplace satisfaction measured with the IOR correlated positively with organizational commitment for both permanent and temporary employees and distribution of risk exposure in the workplace. The IOR correlated negatively with education level and pay levels for exempt staff, perceived danger, perceived risk, task distractions, and risk experience (Lee & Johnson, 1991; McLain, 1995; Taylor et al., 1995).

Source   Cook, J. D., Hepworth, S. J., Wall, T. D., & Warr, P. B. (1981). *The experience of work: A compendium of 249 measures and their use.* London: Academic Press. Items were taken from pp. 42-45. Copyright © 1981 by Academic Press. Reproduced with permission.

Items   Items and possible responses:

Supervision items:

1. Do you ever have the feeling you would better off working under different supervision?

   Possible responses are 1 = *I almost always feel this way,* 2 = *I frequently feel this way,* 3 = *I occasionally feel this way,* 4 = *I seldom feel this way,* 5 = *I never feel this way.*

2. How do you feel about the supervision you receive?

   Possible responses are 5 = *I am extremely satisfied,* 4 = *I am well satisfied,* 3 = *I am only moderately satisfied,* 2 = *I am somewhat dissatisfied,* 1 = *I am very dissatisfied.*

3. How does the way you are treated by those who supervise you influence you overall attitude toward your job?

   Possible responses are 1 = *It has a very unfavorable influence,* 2 = *It has a slightly unfavorable influence,* 3 = *It has no real effect,* 4 = *It has a favorable influence,* 5 = *It has a very favorable influence.*

4. How much do the efforts of those who supervise you add to the success of your organization?

    Possible responses are 5 = *a very great deal*, 4 = *quite a bit*, 3 = *only a little*, 2 = *very little*, 1 = *almost nothing*.

5. The people who supervise me have:

    Possible responses are 5 = *many more good traits than bad ones*, 4 = *more good traits than bad ones*, 3 = *about the same number of good traits as bad ones*, 2 = *more bad traits than good ones*, 1 = *many more bad traits than good ones*.

6. The supervision I receive is the kind that:

    Possible responses are 1 = *greatly discourages me from giving extra effort*, 2 = *tends to discourage me from giving extra effort*, 3 = *has little influence on me*, 4 = *encourages me to give extra effort*, 5 = *greatly encourages me to give extra effort*.

Company identification items:

7. There is something about working for this organization that:

    Possible responses are 5 = *greatly encourages me to do my best*, 4 = *definitely encourages me to do my best*, 3 = *only slightly encourages me to do my best*, 2 = *tends to discourage me from doing my best*, 1 = *definitely discourages me from doing my best*.

8. From my experience, I feel this organization probably treats its employees:

    Possible responses are 1 = *poorly*, 2 = *somewhat poorly*, 3 = *fairly well*, 4 = *quite well*, 5 = *extremely well*.

9. How does working for this organization influence your overall attitude toward your job?

    Possible responses are 1 = *it has a very unfavorable influence*, 2 = *it has an unfavorable influence*, 3 = *it has no influence one way or the other*, 4 = *it has a favorable influence*, 5 = *it has a very favorable influence*.

10. How do you describe this organization as a company to work for?

    Possible responses are 5 = *couldn't be much better*, 4 = *very good*, 3 = *fairly good*, 2 = *just another place to work*, 1 = *poor*.

11. I think this organization, as a company, considers employee welfare:

    Possible responses are 1 = *much less important than sales and profits*, 2 = *less important than sales and profits*, 3 = *about as important as sales and profits*, 4 = *more important than sales and profits*, 5 = *much more important than sales and profits*.

Kind of work items:

12. Work like mine:

    Possible responses are 1 = *discourages me from doing my best*, 2 = *tends to discourage me from doing my best*, 3 = *makes little difference*, 4 = *slightly encourages me to do my best*, 5 = *greatly encourages me to do my best.*

13. How often when you finish a day's work do you feel you've accomplished something really worthwhile?

    Possible responses are 5 = *all of the time*, 4 = *most of the time*, 3 = *about half of the time*, 2 = *less than half of the time*, 1 = *rarely.*

14. How does the kind of work you do influence your overall attitude toward your job?

    Possible responses are 1 = *it has a very unfavorable influence*, 2 = *it has a slightly unfavorable influence*, 3 = *it has no influence one way or the other*, 4 = *it has a fairly favorable influence*, 5 = *it has a very favorable influence.*

15. How many of the things you do on your job do you enjoy?

    Possible responses are 5 = *nearly all*, 4 = *more than half*, 3 = *about half*, 2 = *less than half*, 1 = *almost none.*

16. How much of the work you do stirs up real enthusiasm on your part?

    Possible responses are 5 = *nearly all of it*, 4 = *more than half of it*, 3 = *about half of it*, 2 = *less than half of it*, 1 = *almost none of it.*

17. How do you feel about the kind of work you do?

    Possible responses are 1 = *don't like it, would prefer some other kind of work*; 2 = *it's OK, there's other work I like better*; 3 = *I like it, but there is other work I like as much*; 4 = *I like it very much*; 5 = *it's exactly the kind of work I like best.*

Amount of work items:

18. I feel my workload is:

    Possible responses are 5 = *never too heavy*, 4 = *seldom too heavy*, 3 = *sometimes too heavy*, 2 = *often too heavy*, 1 = *almost always too heavy.*

19. How does the amount of work you're expected to do influence the way you do your job?

    Possible responses are 1 = *it never allows me to do a good job*, 2 = *it seldom allows me to do a good job*, 3 = *it has no effect on how I do my job*, 4 = *it usually allows me to do a good job*, 5 = *it always allows me to do a good job.*

20. How does the amount of work you're expected to do influence your overall attitude toward your job?

    Possible responses are 5 = *it has a very favorable influence*, 4 = *it has a favorable influence*, 3 = *it has no influence one way or the other*, 2 = *it has an unfavorable influence*, 1 = *it has a very unfavorable influence*.

21. How do you feel about the amount of work you're expected to do?

    Possible responses are 1 = *very dissatisfied*, 2 = *somewhat dissatisfied*, 3 = *neither satisfied nor dissatisfied*, 4 = *somewhat satisfied*, 5 = *very satisfied*.

Co-workers items:

22. How do you generally feel about the employees you work with?

    Possible responses are 5 = *they are the best group I could ask for*, 4 = *I like them a great deal*, 3 = *I like them fairly well*, 2 = *I have no feeling one way or the other*, 1 = *I don't particularly care for them*.

23. How is your overall attitude toward your job influenced by the people you work with?

    Possible responses are 5 = *it is very favorably influenced*, 4 = *it is favorably influenced*, 3 = *it is not influenced one way or the other*, 2 = *it is unfavorably influenced*, 1 = *it is very unfavorably influenced*.

24. The example my fellow employees set:

    Possible responses are 1 = *greatly discourages me from working hard*, 2 = *somewhat discourages me from working hard*, 3 = *has little effect on me*, 4 = *somewhat encourages me to work hard*, 5 = *greatly encourages me to work hard*.

25. How much does the way co-workers handle their jobs add to the success of your organization?

    Possible responses are 1 = *it adds almost nothing*, 2 = *it adds very little*, 3 = *it adds only a little*, 4 = *it adds quite a bit*, 5 = *it adds a very great deal*.

26. In this organization, there is:

    Possible responses are 1 = *a very great deal of friction*, 2 = *quite a bit of friction*, 3 = *some friction*, 4 = *little friction*, 5 = *almost no friction*.

Physical work conditions items:

27. How much pride can you take in the appearance of your work place?

Possible responses are 5 = *a very great deal*, 4 = *quite a bit*, 3 = *some*, 2 = *little*, 1 = *very little.*

28. How do you feel about your physical working conditions?

Possible responses are 5 = *extremely satisfied*, 4 = *well satisfied*, 3 = *only moderately satisfied*, 2 = *somewhat dissatisfied*, 1 = *very dissatisfied.*

29. How do your physical working conditions influence your overall attitude toward your job?

Possible responses are 1 = *they have a very unfavorable influence*, 2 = *they have a slightly unfavorable influence*, 3 = *they have no influence one way or the other*, 4 = *they have a favorable influence*, 5 = *they have a very favorable influence.*

30. The physical working conditions make working here:

Possible responses are 1 = *very unpleasant*, 2 = *unpleasant*, 3 = *neither pleasant nor unpleasant*, 4 = *pleasant*, 5 = *very pleasant.*

31. For the work I do, my physical working conditions are:

Possible responses are 1 = *very poor*, 2 = *relatively poor*, 3 = *neither good nor poor*, 4 = *reasonably good*, 5 = *very good.*

32. How do your physical working conditions affect the way you do your job?

Possible responses are 5 = *they help me a great deal*, 4 = *they help me a little*, 3 = *they make little difference*, 2 = *they tend to make it difficult*, 1 = *they make it very difficult.*

Financial rewards items:

33. For the job I do, I feel the amount of money I make is:

Possible responses are 5 = *extremely good*, 4 = *good*, 3 = *neither good nor poor*, 2 = *fairly poor*, 1 = *very poor.*

34. To what extent are your needs satisfied by the pay and benefits you receive?

Possible responses are 1 = *almost none of my needs are satisfied*, 2 = *very few of my needs are satisfied*, 3 = *a few of my needs are satisfied*, 4 = *many of my needs are satisfied*, 5 = *almost all of my needs are satisfied*

35. Considering what it costs to live in this area, my pay is:

Possible responses are 1 = *very inadequate*, 2 = *inadequate*, 3 = *barely adequate*, 4 = *adequate*, 5 = *more than adequate.*

36. Does the way pay is handled around here make it worthwhile for a person to work especially hard?

Possible responses are 5 = *it definitely encourages hard work*, 4 = *it tends to encourage hard work*, 3 = *it makes little difference*, 2 = *it tends to discourage hard work*, 1 = *it definitely discourages hard work.*

37. How does the amount of money you now make influence your overall attitude toward your job?

Possible responses are 5 = *it has a very favorable influence*, 4 = *it has a fairly favorable influence*, 3 = *it has no influence one way or the other*, 2 = *it has a slightly unfavorable influence*, 1 = *it has a very unfavorable influence.*

Career future items:

38. How do you feel about your future with this organization?

Possible responses are 1 = *I am very worried about it*, 2 = *I am somewhat worried about it*, 3 = *I have mixed feelings about it*, 4 = *I feel good about it*, 5 = *I feel very good about it.*

39. How do your feelings about your future with the company influence your overall attitude toward your job?

Possible responses are 5 = *they have a very favorable influence*, 4 = *they have a favorable influence*, 3 = *they have no influence one way or the other*, 2 = *they have a slightly unfavorable influence*, 1 = *they have a very unfavorable influence.*

40. The way my future with the company looks to me now:

Possible responses are 5 = *hard work seems very worthwhile*, 4 = *hard work seems fairly worthwhile*, 3 = *hard work seems worthwhile*, 2 = *hard work hardly seems worthwhile*, 1 = *hard work seems almost worthless.*

41. Do you feel you are getting ahead in the company?

Possible responses are 5 = *I'm making a great deal of progress*, 4 = *I'm making some progress*, 3 = *I'm not sure*, 2 = *I'm making very little progress*, 1 = *I'm making no progress.*

42. How secure are you in your present job?

Possible responses are 1 = *I feel very uneasy about it*, 2 = *I feel fairly uneasy about it*, 3 = *I feel somewhat uneasy about it*, 4 = *I feel fairly sure of it*, 5 = *I feel very sure of it.*

Satisfaction With My Supervisor

Description   This measure, developed by Scarpello and Vandenberg (1987), describes an employee's satisfaction with his or her immediate supervisor. The measure was developed over a 3-year period using samples of more than 2,000 employees from seven manufacturing firms and tested with more than 1,000 employees in the insurance industry.

Reliability   Coefficient alpha values ranged from .95 to .96 (Jones et al., 1999; Scarpello & Vandenberg, 1987).

Validity   Although factor analysis of the 18 items making up the scale found that the items loaded on two factors, the factors were highly correlated (mean *r* across eight samples = .60). The items loading on the second factor also loaded on the first factor, suggesting the existence of a single underlying construct, rather than independent dimensions (Jones et al., 1999; Scarpello & Vandenberg, 1987).

Source   Scarpello, V., & Vandenberg, R. (1987). The Satisfaction With My Supervisor scale: Its utility for research and practical application. *Journal of Management, 3*, 451-470. Items were taken from Figure 1, p. 455. Reprinted with permission.

Items   Responses are obtained using a 5-point Likert-type scale where 1 = *very dissatisfied* and 5 = *very satisfied.*

1. The way my supervisor listens when I have something important to say
2. The way my supervisor sets clear work goals
3. The way my supervisor treats me when I make a mistake
4. My supervisor's fairness in appraising my job performance
5. The way my supervisor is consistent in his/her behavior toward subordinates
6. The way my supervisor helps me to get the job done
7. The way my supervisor gives me credit for my ideas
8. The way my supervisor gives me clear instruction
9. The way my supervisor informs me about work changes ahead of time
10. The way my supervisor follows through to get problems solved
11. The way my supervisor understands the problems I might run into doing the job
12. The way my supervisor shows concern for my career progress
13. My supervisor's backing me up with other management
14. The frequency with which I get a pat on the back for doing a good job

15. The technical competence of my supervisor
16. The amount of time I get to learn a task before I'm moved to another task
17. The time I have to do the job right
18. The way my job responsibilities are clearly defined

2

Organizational Commitment

The Construct

Employee commitment to an organization has been defined in a variety of ways including an attitude or an orientation that links the identity of the person to the organization, a process by which the goals of the organization and those of the individual become congruent, an involvement with a particular organization, the perceived rewards associated with continued participation in an organization, the costs associated with leaving, and normative pressures to act in a way that meets organizational goals (Meyer & Allen, 1997). Mowday, Porter, and Steers (1982), who did much of the original research about organizational commitment, characterized it as a strong belief in and acceptance of the organization's goals and values, a willingness to exert considerable effort on behalf of the organization, and a strong desire to maintain membership in an organization. The various definitions reflect three broad themes: commitment reflecting an affective orientation toward the organization, recognition of costs associated with leaving the organization, and moral obligation to remain with an organization (Meyer & Allen, 1997).

An employee's liking for an organization is termed *affective commitment* and includes identification with and involvement in the or-

ganization. Employees with a strong affective commitment continue employment with the organization because they want to do so (Cohen, 1993). *Continuance commitment* refers to an awareness of the costs associated with leaving the organization. Employees whose primary link to the organization is based on continuance commitment remain with their employer because they need to do so. Finally, *normative commitment* reflects a feeling of obligation to continue employment. Employees with a high level of normative commitment feel that they ought to remain with the organization (Meyer & Allen, 1997).

Others have argued that commitment reflects the psychological bond that ties the employee to the organization but that the nature of the bond can take three forms, labeled *compliance, identification,* and *internalization* (O'Reilly & Chatman, 1986). Compliance occurs when attitudes and behaviors are adopted not because of shared beliefs but simply to gain specific rewards. In this case, public and private attitudes may differ. Identification occurs when an individual accepts influence to establish and maintain a relationship; that is, an individual may respect a group's values without adopting them. On the other hand, internalization occurs when influence is accepted because the induced attitudes and beliefs are congruent with one's own values (Caldwell, Chatman, & O'Reilly, 1990; Meyer & Allen, 1997; O'Reilly & Chatman, 1986; O'Reilly, Chatman, & Caldwell, 1991).

Clearly, not all of these views are in agreement. For example, some researchers have questioned whether compliance should be viewed as a component of commitment because it is distinct from other common definitions and can be viewed as the antithesis of commitment. That is, compliance has been found to correlate positively with employee turnover (O'Reilly & Chatman, 1986), whereas commitment generally reduces turnover (Mowday et al., 1982). The studies I reviewed from the 1990s suggest there is a growing consensus that commitment is a multidimensional construct that certainly includes an affective dimension and may include components that reflect normative pressures as well as practical considerations such as the costs of leaving an organization and locating another job with similar pay and benefits.

The Measures

This chapter describes 11 measures of organizational commitment. There are three primary issues to be addressed in measuring organizational commitment: the basis for the commitment (how does it form?), the manifestation of the commitment (what is the evidence of commitment—attitude or behavior?), and the focus of the commitment (what or who is the employee committed to?).

Each of the multiple dimensions of organizational commitment such as affective, normative, and so on describes a basis of commitment. For example, affective commitment is a product of the employee's psychological attachment, liking, and identification with aspects of an organization; normative commitment may arise from an employee's internalization of values and mission of the organization; and continuance

commitment may arise through pressures for compliance or conformity that is driven by rewards and punishments. The measures that follow include some that describe only the affective basis for commitment and others that include separate scales for affective-, normative-, and compliance-based commitment.

A second consideration is whether to describe commitment in terms of attitudes or behaviors. In general, researchers have tended to recognize the importance of both components, labeling affective commitment as representing the attitudinal focus and continuance commitment as representing the behavioral focus. To some extent, the distinction depends on the process by which commitment forms. It is possible, for example, that commitment comes about when an individual is "bound to his acts." That is, an individual may identify himself with a particular behavior. The strength of the commitment of the individual to the behavior depends on how visible, revocable, and volitional the behavior is (Mowday et al., 1982). Once a commitment is made, employees may find mechanisms for adjusting. Hence, if an employee has worked for a major corporation for 20 years, he or she is likely to develop attitudes that justify remaining with the organization in the face of alternative positions. All of the measures that follow in this chapter ask employees to respond to statements or questions that reflect the employees' beliefs and attitudes about their relationship with the organization, not their behaviors.

The third measurement issue is the focus of an employee's commitment. Much of the theoretical and empirical work on commitment has focused on the organization. This emphasis has raised some concern, because organizations are not monolithic entities. Various constituencies to which an employee might be committed within an organizational setting include top management, supervisors, work groups, occupations, and departments. Although studies have generally shown significant positive relationships between commitment to these constituencies and global organizational commitment, it is useful to have validated measures available for alternative foci more specific than the organization as a whole. I have identified and included validated measures for commitment to an occupation or profession, supervisor-related commitment, and commitment to a parent company or local operation.

An additional concern is the possibility that organizational commitment is redundant with other work-related constructs such as job involvement, career commitment, and job satisfaction. Fortunately, several of the studies published in the 1990s investigated the empirical distinction between various measures of organizational commitment and other work variables using tools such as confirmatory factor analysis. The specific results are noted in the discussion of validity for each measure. In general, these analyses found that measures of organizational commitment are empirically distinct from variables such as job satisfaction, job involvement, career commitment, intention to leave, and the Protestant work ethic.

Organizational Commitment Questionnaire

Description   The Organizational Commitment Questionnaire (OCQ) was originally developed by Mowday, Steers, and Porter (1979). It uses 15 items to describe *global* organizational commitment. This widely used measure has been modified to examine professional commitment by replacing the word *organization* with *profession*. It has also been used to assess job commitment by changing the wording from *organization* to *job* (Gunz & Gunz, 1994; Millward & Hopkins, 1998). Sagie (1998) developed and used a Hebrew-language version of the measure.

Reliability   Coefficient alpha values ranged from .81 to .93 (Becker, 1992; Brett, Cron, & Slocum, 1995; Cohen & Hudecek, 1993; Gunz & Gunz, 1994; Hackett, Bycio, & Hausdorf, 1994; Hochwarter, Perrewé, Ferris, & Gercio, 1999; Johnston & Snizek, 1991; Kacmar, Carlson, & Brymer, 1999; Lee & Johnson, 1991; Marsden, Kalleberg, & Cook, 1993; Mathieu, 1991; Mathieu & Farr, 1991; Millward & Hopkins, 1998; Riggs & Knight, 1994; Sommer, Bae, & Luthans, 1996; Zeffane, 1994). The Hebrew-language version of the OCQ had alpha = .62 (Sagie, 1998).

Validity   Organizational commitment correlated positively with involvement in an organization for both calculative and moral reasons, job satisfaction, leader-member exchange (LMX), perception of organizational justice, job satisfaction, job involvement, and the perceived utility of organizational and task feedback (Brett et al., 1995; Johnston & Snizek, 1991; Kacmar et al., 1999; Lee & Johnson, 1991; Mathieu, 1991). Organizational commitment correlated negatively with the extent of hierarchy, more specialized jobs, employee education level, intention to turnover, role strain, perceptions of organizational politics, job tension, and voluntary turnover (Brett et al., 1995; Hochwarter, Perrewé, Ferris, & Gercio, 1999; Johnston & Snizek, 1991; Kacmar et al., 1999; Lee & Johnson, 1991; Mathieu, 1991). The Hebrew-language version correlated positively with job satisfaction and negatively with intention to quit (Sagie, 1998).

In Riggs and Knight (1994), structural equation analysis showed discriminate validity between organizational commitment, job satisfaction, and personal efficacy. In a study by Zeffane (1994), a factor analysis found two principal factors within the 15 items of the OCQ. The first factor was made up of six items measuring corporate loyalty/citizenship. The second was made up of nine items and measured attachment to the organization. Mathieu (1991) found that a factor analysis yielded two factors—one containing nine positively worded items and the other containing six negatively worded items. The meaning of the second factor was unclear and possibly was an artifact of the item wording. Cohen and Hudecek (1993) found in a meta-analysis that the full 15-item scale includes six items that measure an employee's desire to remain with the organization and may overlap with turnover intentions. These six items had a stronger relationship with employee turnover than did the nine-item subscale that did not include these items. However, Kacmar et al. (1999) used confirmatory factor analysis to compare a one-factor model (one dimension for the 15 items) with a two-factor model (value commitment and commitment to stay). The one-factor model fit the data better. This confirmatory analysis also found that the OCQ is empirically distinct from an alternative organizational commitment measure developed by Balfour and Wechsler (1996). Dunham, Grube, and Castaneda (1994) found in a multisample confirmatory factor analysis that the 15 items of the OCQ loaded with the eight affective commitment items of the Meyer and Allen affective commitment scale on a single factor, suggesting that the OCQ primarily measures affective commitment.

Source   Mowday, R. T., Steers, R. M., & Porter, L. W. (1979). The measurement of organizational commitment. *Journal of Vocational Behavior, 14*, 224-247. Items were taken from Table 1, p. 228. Copyright © 1979 by Academic Press. Reproduced with permission.

Items   Responses are obtained using a 7-point Likert-type scale where 1 = *strongly disagree*, 2 = *moderately disagree*, 3 = *slightly disagree*, 4 = *neither disagree nor agree*, 5 = *slightly agree*, 6 = *moderately agree*, and 7 = *strongly agree*.

The OCQ instructions and items:

Listed below is a series of statements that represent possible feelings that individuals might have about the company or organization for which they work. With respect to your own feelings about the particular organization for which you are now working [company name], please indicate the degree of your agreement or disagreement with each statement by checking one of the seven alternatives below each statement.

1. I am willing to put in a great deal of effort beyond that normally expected in order to help this organization be successful
2. I talk up this organization to my friends as a great organization to work for
3. I feel very little loyalty to this organization (R)
4. I would accept almost any types of job assignment in order to keep working for this organization
5. I find that my values and the organization's values are very similar
6. I am proud to tell others that I am part of this organization
7. I could just as well be working for a different organization as long as the type of work was similar (R)
8. This organization really inspires the very best in me in the way of job performance
9. It would take very little change in my present circumstance to cause me to leave this organization (R)
10. I am extremely glad that I chose this organization to work for over others I was considering at the time I joined

11. There's not too much to be gained by sticking with this organization indefinitely (R)
12. Often, I find it difficult to agree with this organization's policies on important matters relating to its employees (R)
13. I really care about the fate of this organization
14. For me, this is the best of all possible organizations for which to work
15. Deciding to work for this organization was a definite mistake on my part (R)

Items denoted with (R) are reverse scored.

Shortened Organizational Commitment Questionnaire

Description   This measure is a nine-item shortened version of the 15-item Organization Commitment Questionnaire (OCQ) (Mowday et al., 1982). It measures attitudinal or affective commitment. The shortened OCQ has been shown to have a large positive correlation with the 15-item OCQ (Huselid & Day, 1991). This measure has also been used to describe commitment to a profession by inserting the profession name in place of *organization* in each item (Vandenberg & Scarpello, 1994).

Reliability   Coefficient alpha values ranged from .74 to .92 (Aryee, Luk, & Stone, 1998; Cohen, 1995, 1996; Dulebohn & Martocchio, 1998; Huselid & Day, 1991; Jones, Scarpello, & Bergmann, 1999; Kirchmeyer, 1992; Mathieu & Farr, 1991; Mossholder, Bennett, Kemery, & Wesolowski, 1998; Netemeyer, Burton, & Johnston, 1995; Somers & Casal, 1994; Thompson & Werner, 1997; Wahn, 1998; Wayne, Shore, & Liden, 1997). Vandenberg and Lance (1992) found the test-retest reliability to be .74.

Validity   Organizational commitment correlated positively with power and success of an employee's work unit, perceived opportunity for advancement, employee income level, work involvement, and employee satisfaction with work schedule flexibility. It correlated negatively with arbitrary personnel practices, turnover intentions, and employee turnover (Aryee et al., 1998; Huselid & Day, 1991; Kirchmeyer, 1992; Wahn, 1998).

Cohen (1996) found through confirmatory factor analysis that the nine-item version of the OCQ was empirically distinct from job involvement, career commitment, work involvement, and the Protestant work ethic. In Mathieu and Farr (1991), confirmatory factor analysis in two samples showed that commitment, job satisfaction, and job involvement were empirically distinct measures.

Source   Mowday, R. T., Steers, R. M., & Porter, L. W. (1979). The measurement of organizational commitment. *Journal of Vocational Behavior, 14*, 224-247. Items were taken from Table 1, p. 228. Copyright © 1979 by Academic Press. Reproduced with permission.

Items   Responses are obtained on a 7-point Likert-type scale where 1 = *strongly disagree*, 2 = *moderately disagree*, 3 = *slightly disagree*, 4 = *neither disagree nor agree*, 5 = *slightly agree*, 6 = *moderately agree*, and 7 = *strongly agree*.

Instructions and items:

Listed below is a series of statements that represent possible feelings that individuals might have about the company or organization for which they work. With respect to your own feelings about the particular organization for which you are now working [company name], please indicate the degree of your agreement or disagreement with each statement by checking one of the seven alternatives below each statement.

1. I am willing to put in a great deal of effort beyond that normally expected in order to help this organization be successful
2. I talk up this organization to my friends as a great organization to work for
3. I would accept almost any types of job assignment in order to keep working for this organization
4. I find that my values and the organization's values are very similar
5. I am proud to tell others that I am part of this organization
6. This organization really inspires the very best in me in the way of job performance
7. I am extremely glad that I chose this organization to work for over others I was considering at the time I joined
8. I really care about the fate of this organization
9. For me, this is the best of all possible organizations for which to work.

Affective, Normative, and Continuance Commitment

Description   These measures, developed by Meyer and Allen (1997), describe three types of organizational commitment. Affective commitment measures an employee's emotional attachment to, identification with, and involvement in the organization. Normative commitment reflects pressures on an employee to remain with an organization resulting from organizational socialization. Continuance commitment refers to commitment associated with the costs that employees perceive are related to leaving the organization. These measures have also been applied to describe commitment to an occupation or profession by substituting the profession name in place of *organization* in the items (Coleman, Irving, & Cooper, 1999; Meyer, Allen, & Smith, 1993). Meyer and Allen (1997) shortened the original eight-item measures to six items for each type of commitment. The items for both the original and revised measures are provided below.

Reliability   Coefficient alpha values ranged from .77 to .88 for affective commitment (ACS), from .65 to .86 for normative commitment (NCS), and from .69 to .84 for continuance commitment (CCS) (Allen & Meyer, 1990a; Cohen, 1996, 1999; Cohen & Kirchmeyer, 1995; Hackett et al., 1994; Meyer & Allen, 1997; Meyer, Irving, & Allen, 1998; Somers, 1995; Somers & Birnbaum, 1998).

Validity   In multisample confirmatory factor analysis, Hackett et al. (1994) and Dunham et al. (1994) found support for the three-component model, with affective, normative, and continuance commitment each comprising a separate dimension. Cohen (1999) used confirmatory analysis to show discriminate validity among affective organizational commitment, career commitment, and continuance organizational commitment. Confirmatory factor analysis has also shown that the three Allen and Meyer scales were empirically distinct from job involvement, career commitment, work involvement, and Protestant work ethic (Cohen, 1996). This analysis also showed that a model in which continuance commitment was divided into two subscales fit the data better than models that used continuance commitment as one eight-item scale. One four-item component described continuance commitment due to the availability of limited alternatives. The other four-item subscale measured continuance commitment due to high sacrifices required to leave an organization. Meyer and colleagues (1991) suggest using the two continuance commitment subscales unless these components do not have differential relationships with outcome variables, in which case there may be just cause for combining them into one eight-item scale for continuance commitment.

Somers (1995) found that affective and normative commitment both correlated positively with turnover, whereas continuance commitment correlated negatively with employee turnover. In addition, the low alternatives subscale of continuance commitment correlated negatively with career commitment. The personal sacrifices subscale of continuance commit-ment correlated positively with career commitment. Allen and Meyer (1990b) found that affective commitment correlated positively with six dif-ferent types of organizational socialization programs and negatively with having an innovative role orientation within the first 6 months of entering an organization.

Source   Meyer, J. P., & Allen, N. J. (1997). *Commitment in the workplace.* Thousand Oaks, CA: Sage. Copyright © 1997 by Sage Publications, Inc. Items were taken from Table A-1, pp. 118-119. Reprinted by permission of Sage Publi-cations, Inc.

Items   Employee responses are obtained on a 7-point Likert-type scale where 1 = *strongly disagree* and 7 = *strongly agree.*

Original and revised affective commitment items:

Items denoted with (R) are reversed scored. Items denoted with (RS) are those included in the revised affective commitment measure.

1. I would be very happy to spend the rest of my career with this organization (RS)
2. I enjoy discussing my organization with people outside of it
3. I really feel as if this organization's problems are my own (RS)
4. I think that I could easily become as attached to another organization as I am to this one
5. I do not feel like "part of the family" at my organization (R) (RS)
6. I do not feel "emotionally attached" to this organization (R) (RS)
7. This organization has a great deal of personal meaning for me (RS)
8. I do not feel a strong sense of belonging to my organization. (R) (RS)

Original normative commitment items:

Items denoted with (R) are reversed scored.

1. I think that people these days move from company to company too often
2. I do not believe that a person must always be loyal to his or her organization (R)
3. Jumping from organization to organization does not seem at all unethical to me (R)
4. One of the major reasons I continue to work for this organization is that I believe that loyalty is important and therefore feel a sense of moral obligation to remain
5. If I got another offer for a better job elsewhere I would not feel it was right to leave my organization
6. I was taught to believe in the value of remaining loyal to one organization

7. Things were better in the days when people stayed with one organization for most of their careers
8. I do not think that wanting to be a "company man" or "company woman" is sensible anymore (R)

Revised normative commitment items:

Items denoted with (R) are reversed scored.

1. I do not feel any obligation to remain with my current employer (R)
2. Even if it were to my advantage, I do not feel it would be right to leave my organization now
3. I would feel guilty if I left my organization now
4. This organization deserves my loyalty
5. I would not leave my organization right now because I have a sense of obligation to the people in it
6. I owe a great deal to this organization

Original and revised continuance commitment items:

Items denoted with (R) are reversed scored. Items denoted with (RS) are those included in the revised affective commitment measure.

(High sacrifice subscale)

1. I am not afraid of what might happen if I quit my job without having another one lined up (R)
2. It would be very hard for me to leave my organization right now, even if I wanted to (RS)
3. Too much in my life would be disrupted if I decided I wanted to leave my organization now (RS)
4. It wouldn't be too costly for me to leave my organization right now (R)

(Lack of alternative subscale)

5. Right now staying with my organization is a matter of necessity as much as desire (RS)
6. I feel that I have too few options to consider leaving this organization (RS)
7. One of the few serious consequences of leaving this organization would be the scarcity of available alternatives (RS)
8. One of the major reasons I continue to work for this organization is that leaving would require considerable personal sacrifice—another organization may not match the overall benefits that I have here (RS)

Psychological Attachment Instrument

Description   This measure was developed by O'Reilly and Chatman (1986). It uses 12 items to describe three dimensions of organizational commitment: (1) internalization, defined as an employee adopting the organization's mission as the employee's own; (2) identification, defined as the employee's belief that the organization's values are very similar to the employee's; and (3) compliance, defined as continuing to remain an organization member because the costs of changing are too high.

Reliability   Coefficient alpha values ranged from .86 to .91 (Harris, Hirschfeld, Field, & Mossholder, 1993; Martin & Bennett, 1996; Pillai, Schriesheim, & Williams, 1999; Sutton & Harrison, 1993).

Validity   Sutton and Harrison (1993) examined the items with factor analysis and showed that the 12 items formed two subscales. The first contained eight items and combines identification and internalization as sources of commitment. The second contains four items and corresponds to the compliance source of commitment. The identification/internalization and compliance components of commitment were not correlated. Martin and Bennett (1996) also found that the eight items corresponding to the identification and internalization sources of commitment formed a single factor.

Organizational commitment correlated positively with perceived job importance, procedural and distribution fairness of performance appraisals, pay, benefits and work conditions, and satisfaction with performance appraisals, pay, benefits, and work conditions (Martin & Bennett, 1996). Internalization correlated positively with identification and negatively with compliance. Internalization and identification both correlated positively with job level, task autonomy, job involvement, development through management exposure, and job satisfaction. Internalization also correlated positively with tenure. Internalization and identification both correlated negatively with turnover intentions. Compliance correlated positively with turnover intentions. Compliance correlated negatively with job level, job involvement, and development through management exposure (Harris et al., 1993).

Source   Caldwell, D. F., Chatman, J. A., & O'Reilly, C.A., III. (1990). Building organizational commitment: A multi-firm study. *Journal of Occupational and Organizational Psychology, 63,* 245-261. Items were taken from Table 2, p. 252. Copyright © 1990. Reproduced with permission.

Items   Responses are obtained on a 7-point Likert-type scale where 1 = *strongly agree* and 7 = *strongly disagree.*

Identification and internalization subscale:

1. What this organization stands for is important to me
2. I talk up this organization to my friends as a great organization to work for
3. If the values of the organization were different, I would not be as attached to this organization
4. Since joining this organization, my personal values and those of the organization have become more similar
5. The reason I prefer this organization to others is because of what it stands for, that is, its values
6. My attachment to this organization is primarily based on the similarity of my values and those represented by the organization
7. I am proud to tell others that I am a part of this organization
8. I feel a sense of "ownership" for this organization rather than just being an employee

Compliance subscale:

1. How hard I work for this organization is directly linked to how much I am rewarded
2. In order for me to get rewarded around here, it is necessary to express the right attitude
3. My private views about this organization are different from those I express publicly
4. Unless I am rewarded for it in some way, I see no reason to expend extra effort on behalf of this organization

Organizational Commitment

Description   This measure, developed by Cook and Wall (1980), describes an employee's overall organizational commitment. The measure uses nine items. The items can be grouped to form subscales for organizational identification, organizational involvement, and organizational loyalty. Each subscale contains three items.

Reliability   Coefficient alpha values ranged from .71 to .87 (Furnham, Brewin, & O'Kelly, 1994; Oliver, 1990; Sanchez & Brock, 1996).

Validity   The identification, involvement, and loyalty subscales correlated positively with work rewards and committed behaviors, which included such actions as reading in-house publications, attending general meetings, voting frequently in internal elections, activism, and job effort. The three subscales all correlated negatively with the range of other employment alternatives (Oliver, 1990). Furnham et al. (1994) found that a personality style that tends to attribute positive events at work to internal causes correlated positively with the combined measure of organizational commitment.

Source   Cook, J., & Wall, T. D. (1980). New work attitude measures of trust, organizational commitment and personal need for non-fulfillment. *Journal of Organizational and Occupational Psychology, 53*, 39-52. Items were taken from Appendix A, section 10, p. 51. Copyright © 1980. Reproduced with permission.

Items   Responses are obtained using a 7-point Likert-type scale where 1 = *strongly disagree* and 7 = *strongly agree*.

Instructions and items:

In this section we look at what it means to you being a member of your organization. Some people feel themselves to be just an employee, there to do a lot of work, while others feel more personally involved in the organization they work for. The following items express what people might feel about themselves as members of their organization. Will you please indicate on this scale how much you agree or disagree with each statement in turn?

1. I am quite proud to be able to tell people who it is that I work for
2. I sometimes feel like leaving this employment for good (R)
3. I'm not willing to put myself out just to help the organization (R)
4. Even if the firm were not doing too well financially, I would be reluctant to change to another employer
5. I feel myself to be part of the organization
6. In my work I like to feel I am making some effort, not just for myself, but for the organization as well

7. The offer of a bit more money with another employer would not seriously make me think of changing my job
8. I would not recommend a close friend to join our staff (R)
9. To know that my own work had made a contribution to the good of the organization would please me

Items denoted with (R) are reverse scored.

Organizational Commitment

Description   This measure, which was developed for and used in the 1991 General Social Survey, describes overall organizational commitment. It assesses commitment with only six items, meeting the needs of large-sample survey research where parsimony is essential. The items were derived from Lincoln and Kalleberg's (1990) American-Japanese work commitment study (cited in Marsden et al., 1993).

Reliability   In Marsden et al. (1993), coefficient alpha was .78.

Validity   Organizational commitment correlated positively with higher position of authority, job autonomy, and higher-quality workplace relationships. Commitment correlated negatively with the use of non-merit reward criteria, workplace size, and frequency of job-home conflict (Marsden et al., 1993).

Source   Marsden, P. V., Kalleberg, A. L., & Cook, C. R. (1993). Gender differences in organizational commitment: Influences of work positions and family roles. *Work and Occupations, 20*(3), 368-390. Copyright © 1993 by Sage Publications, Inc. Items were taken from Table 1, p. 376. Reprinted by permission of Sage Publications, Inc.

Items   Responses are obtained on a 4-point Likert-type scale where 1 = *strongly disagree*, 2 = *disagree*, 3 = *agree*, and 4 = *strongly agree*.

1. I am willing to work harder than I have to in order to help this organization succeed
2. I feel very little loyalty to this organization (R)
3. I would take almost any job to keep working for this organization
4. I find that my values and the organization's are very similar
5. I am proud to be working for this organization
6. I would turn down another job for more pay in order to stay with this organization

Items denoted with (R) are reverse scored.

Organizational Commitment Scale

Description   The Organizational Commitment Scale (OCS), developed by Balfour and
Wechsler (1996), uses nine items to measure three dimensions of overall
organizational commitment: commitment based on affiliation or pride in the
organization, commitment based on identification with the organization,
and commitment based on satisfactory exchange with the organization
resulting in appreciation of the individual by the organization. It has been
used to measure organizational commitment of public sector employees
(Balfour & Wechsler, 1996).

Reliability   Coefficient alpha values were .81 for affiliation commitment, .72 for identification commitment, and .83 for exchange commitment (Balfour &
Wechsler, 1996; Kacmar et al., 1999).

Validity   Kacmar et al. (1999) found through confirmatory factor analysis that
the three-dimensional model of the OCS fit the data better than a one-
dimensional version. The OCS and the 15-item Organizational Commitment Questionnaire were also found to be empirically distinct. The
subscales for the identification, affiliation, and exchange dimensions were
related somewhat differently to antecedents and consequences of organizational commitment in a multivariate path model. For example, affiliation
was negatively related to age, but identification and exchange commitment
were not. Commitment based on identification and exchange was negatively
related to job involvement, whereas commitment based on affiliation was
positively related to job involvement (Kacmar et al., 1999).

Source   Balfour, D., & Wechsler, B. (1996). Organizational commitment: Ante-
cedents and outcomes in public organizations. *Public Productivity and
Management Review, 29,* 256-277. Copyright © 1996 by Sage Publications,
Inc. Items were taken from Appendix B, p. 273. Reprinted by permission of
Sage Publications, Inc.

Scale items   Responses are obtained on a 7-point Likert-type scale where 1 = *strongly
disagree* and 7 = *strongly agree*.

Identification commitment items:

1. I am quite proud to be able to tell people who it is that I work for
2. What this organization stands for is important to me
3. I work for an organization that is incompetent and unable to
    accomplish its mission (R)

Affiliation commitment items:

4. I feel a strong sense of belonging to this organization
5. I feel like "part of the family" at this organization
6. The people I work for do not care about what happens to me (R)

Exchange commitment items:

7. This organization appreciates my accomplishments on the job
8. This organization does all that it can to recognize employees for good performance
9. My efforts on the job are largely ignored or overlooked by this organization (R)

Items denoted with (R) are reverse scored.

Organizational Commitment

Description   This measure, developed by Jaros, Jermier, Koehler, and Sincich (1993), describes affective organizational commitment with 14 bipolar adjective items. Using a 7-point scale with two extreme emotional responses as end-anchors, respondents are asked to report the degree of feelings they usually experience when thinking of their employing organization. Other measures of affective commitment use a Likert-type format, possibly tapping cognitive beliefs about emotional attachments more than the feelings themselves (Jaros et al., 1993). Although there is usually a strong relationship between beliefs and feelings toward a referent, the bipolar adjective approach may enable measurement of a more purely affective domain of experience (Jaros et al., 1993).

Reliability   Coefficient alpha was .94 (Jaros et al., 1993).

Validity   In three validation studies, this measure of affective commitment correlated positively with Meyer and Allen's (1997) measure of affective commitment and an independent moral commitment measure. Affective commitment measured with bipolar adjectives correlated negatively with role conflict and role ambiguity, thinking of quitting, search intentions, and intent to quit (Jaros et al., 1993).

Source   Jaros, S. J., Jermier, J. M., Koehler, J. W., & Sincich, T. (1993). Effects of continuance, affective, and moral commitment on the withdrawal process: An evaluation of eight structural equation models. *Academy of Management Journal, 36*(5), 951-996. © 1993 by Academy of Management. Items were taken from the appendix, p. 994. Reproduced with permission of Academy of Management in the format textbook via Copyright Clearance Center.

Items   Instructions and items:

Most people have specific feelings about their employing organization. When you think of your employing organization, what feelings do you experience? Please choose the number which best represents your feelings and enter it to the right of each question.

The 14 bipolar adjective items are presented in the following format:

Cold   1   2   3   4   5   6   7   Warm

The other anchor pairs are:

Hate-love
Affection-contempt (R)
Detachment-belonging
Loyalty-disloyalty (R)
Boredom-excitement
Sadness-happiness

Disgust-fondness
Comfort-discomfort (R)
Lifelessness-spiritedness
Anger-peace
Ecstasy-agony (R)
Pleasure-pain (R)
Despair-hope

Items denoted with (R) are reverse scored.

Career Commitment

Description   This measure, developed by Blau (1989), has been widely used to examine individuals' commitment toward their occupations, profession, and careers. Reilly and Orsak (1991) modified the items to fit the nursing profession. The measure could be similarly adapted to fit other specific professions.

Reliability   Coefficient alpha values ranged from .76 to .88 (Cohen, 1995, 1996, 1999; Reilly & Orsak, 1991; Somers & Birnbaum, 1998).

Validity   Career commitment correlated negatively with work stress, emotional exhaustion, low accomplishment, and the low alternatives dimension of continuance commitment. Career commitment correlated positively with perceived performance and life satisfaction, and the personal sacrifices dimension of continuance commitment (Cohen, 1999; Reilly & Orsak, 1991).

Factor analysis showed that career commitment was empirically distinct from affective organizational commitment, continuance commitment, and normative commitment (Cohen, 1996). Career commitment was also shown to be empirically distinct from job involvement and a measure of the Protestant work ethic (Cohen, 1999).

Source   Blau, G. (1989). Testing generalizability of a career commitment measure and its impact on employee turnover. *Journal of Vocational Behavior, 35,* 88-103. Items were taken from text, p. 92. Copyright © 1989 by Academic Press. Reproduced with permission.

Items   Response are obtained using a 5-point Likert-type scale where 1 = *strongly agree*, 3 = *unsure*, and 5 = *strongly disagree*.

1. I like this career too well to give it up
2. If I could go into a different profession which paid the same, I would probably take it (R)
3. If I could do it all over again, I would not choose to work in this profession (R)
4. I definitely want a career for myself in this profession
5. If I had all the money I needed without working, I would probably still continue to work in this profession
6. I am disappointed that I ever entered this profession (R)
7. This is the ideal profession for a life's work

Items denoted with (R) are reverse scored.

Commitment to a Parent Company Versus Local Operation

Description   This measure, developed by Gregersen and Black (1992), separates commitment to a parent company from commitment to a local operation. It was developed to differentiate commitment foci for expatriate managers. During both domestic and international assignments, employees are affiliated not only with the parent organization to which they will typically return but also become members of a local operation, which is distinguishable from the parent firm. As a consequence, employees may develop dual organizational commitments.

Reliability   In Gregersen and Black (1992), a factor analysis of organizational commitment items found two distinct factors each relating to the separate targets of commitment. The first factor was composed of four items focusing on commitment to a parent company, and the second factor reflected commitment to a local operation. Coefficient alpha for commitment to the parent company was .84. Alpha for commitment to the local operation was .72.

Validity   Commitment to the parent organization correlated positively with role conflict and ambiguity. Commitment to local/foreign operation correlated positively with role discretion. International experience correlated positively with commitment to a foreign operation, but not with commitment to the parent organization (Gregersen & Black, 1992).

Source   Gregersen, H. B., & Black, J. S. (1992). Antecedents to commitment to a parent company and a foreign operation. *Academy of Management Journal, 35*(1), 65-71. © 1992 by Academy of Management. Items were taken from Table 1, p. 75. Reproduced with permission of Academy of Management in the format textbook via Copyright Clearance Center.

Items   Responses are obtained on a 5-point Likert-type scale where 1 = *strongly disagree* and 5 = *strongly agree*.

Parent company items:

1. The reason I prefer this parent company to others is because of its values, or what it stands for
2. I really care about the fate of this parent company
3. I talk up this parent company to my friends as a great place to work
4. What this parent company stands for is important to me

Local operation items:

1. What my local firm stands for is important to me
2. I really care about the fate of my local firm
3. I talk up my local firm to my friends as a great group to work with
4. The reasons I prefer this local company to others is because of its values, or what it stands for

Supervisor-Related Commitment

Description This measure, developed by Becker, Billings, Eveleth, and Gilbert (1996), describes employee commitment to a supervisor. The measure has one dimension that describes identification with a supervisor and a second describing internalization of the same values as the supervisor. The same items can be used to measure and compare organizational identification, and internalization by substituting *organization* as the referent target (Becker et al., 1996).

Reliability Coefficient alpha was .85 for supervisor-related commitment based on identification. Alpha was .89 for supervisor-related commitment based on internalization (Becker et al., 1996).

Validity Supervisor-related identification and internalization were positively correlated (Becker et al., 1996). Confirmatory factor analysis suggested that commitment to a supervisor and commitment to the organization are empirically distinct. In multivariate analyses, both supervisor-related identification and internalization were positively correlated with employee performance ratings, but organizational commitment was not (Becker et al., 1996).

Source Becker, T. E., Billings, R. S., Eveleth, D. M., & Gilbert, N. L. (1996). Foci and bases of employee commitment: Implications for job performance. *Academy of Management Journal, 39*(2), 464-482. © 1996 by Academy of Management. Items were taken from text, p. 469. Reproduced with permission of Academy of Management in the format textbook via Copyright Clearance Center.

Items Responses are obtained using a 7-point Likert-type scale where 1 = *strongly disagree* and 7 = *strongly agree.*

Supervisor-related identification items:

1. When someone criticizes my supervisor, it feels like a personal insult
2. When I talk about my supervisor, I usually say "we" rather than "they"
3. My supervisor's successes are my successes
4. When someone praises my supervisor, it feels like a personal compliment
5. I feel a sense of "ownership" for my supervisor

Supervisor-related internalization items:

6. If the values of my supervisor were different, I would not be as attached to my supervisor
7. My attachment to my supervisor is primarily based on the similarity of my values and those represented by my supervisor

8. Since starting this job, my personal values and those of my supervisor have become more similar

9. The reason I prefer my supervisor to others is because of what he or she stands for, that is, his or her values

3

Job Characteristics

The Construct

The demand for valid measures of job characteristics is driven by continuing efforts in organizations to determine the features of jobs that induce employees to work harder and perform better. One of the most widely used perspectives of how aspects of jobs affect employee willingness to consistently perform better is the job characteristics model (JCM) developed by Hackman and Oldham (1980). This model predicts that if a job is well designed, it leads to higher levels of three critical psychological states. These are *experienced meaningfulness* of the work, such as results from the job that are meaningful within the employee's system of values; *experienced responsibility* for the outcomes of the work, or belief that the employee has personal accountability for the outcomes; and *knowledge of the results* of the work activities, including judgments of others about the quality or quantity of the work performed (Hackman & Oldham, 1980).

The JCM predicts that jobs that are well designed have five key characteristics:

1. Skill variety, which is the extent to which a job requires the use of different skills and talents

2. Task identity, which describes the extent to which a job involves completing a whole identifiable outcome
3. Task significance, which is the degree to which a job has impact on the lives of people in an organization or society in general
4. Autonomy, which describes the extent to which a job provides the employee with discretion to choose how the work is done and to set the schedule for completing the work activities
5. Job feedback, which indicates the extent to which carrying out the work activities provides the employee with clear information about his or her performance

Jobs with these characteristics create higher levels of the critical psychological states, which in turn leads to higher levels of internal work motivation (Hackman & Oldham, 1980). Research on the JCM has generally found that employees in jobs that score higher on variety, identity, significance, autonomy, and feedback have more internal motivation and better performance (Hochwarter, Zellars, Perrewé, & Harrison, 1999; Renn & Vandenberg, 1995). Individual differences among employees (personality, age, etc.) may affect the relationship between job dimensions, the psychological states, and internal motivation (Spector, Jex, & Chen, 1995).

The JCM has provided the framework from which to view the effects that job characteristics have on employee outcomes such as satisfaction, organizational commitment, and intention to remain with an organization (Hochwarter, Zellars, et al., 1999). Other approaches to describing and assessing job characteristics have been developed that provide an expanded view of jobs including engineering and biological perspectives (Campion, 1988). Many studies have attempted to isolate particular aspects of jobs, such as control, interdependence, and complexity that may have significant effects on workers (Dean & Snell, 1991; Karasek, 1979). An increasing amount of attention has been paid to the role that contextual variables play in the perceptions that employees form about their jobs. For example, perceptions of the extent to which employees believe they are empowered in their jobs and the extent to which employees believe the organization appreciates their efforts may affect the way that employees view the identity, significance, variety, autonomy, and feedback in their jobs (Eisenberger, Huntington, Hutchinson, & Sowa, 1986; Gagne, Senecal, & Koestner, 1997; Spreitzer, 1995).

The Measures

The issues in measurement of job characteristics for research revolve around three concerns. First, should we rely on incumbent workers' assessments of their jobs or use ratings about jobs provided by external sources? Second, if incumbent reports are used to describe jobs, should the focus be on the full range of dimensions of a job or only on selected features such as autonomy, control, and so on? Third, can a job be fully understood without consideration of the work environment surrounding the job?

The significance of the first question is brought into focus by a study in which Spector and Jex (1991) examined the same jobs using (a) incumbent perceptions of jobs obtained using the Job Diagnostic Survey, (b) descriptions of the same dimensions (autonomy, identity, variety, significance, feedback, and scope/complexity) obtained from a group of independent raters who reviewed job descriptions, and (c) ratings of control and complexity developed using descriptions of jobs provided in the *Dictionary of Occupational Titles* (*DOT*). The correlations of the job characteristics across the three methods averaged .20. All of the incumbent perceptions correlated significantly with job satisfaction, and most correlated significantly with incumbent reports of frustration, anxiety, and intentions to leave their job. However, none of the ratings based on job descriptions or the *DOT* correlated with satisfaction and anxiety. On one hand, these results could suggest that the measures of incumbent perceptions of their jobs may include items that share some content with the measures of the employee outcomes, thus inflating the relationship. On the other hand, the results may suggest that job ratings based on descriptions of a class of jobs such as job descriptions or the *DOT* fail to capture important aspects of a job within its particular context. Although most of the measures of job characteristics included in this chapter are based on employee perceptions of their job, I have included two validated measures that rate jobs based on aspects provided in the *DOT*.

A few of the measures of job characteristics describe jobs in terms of a range of dimensions including autonomy, variety, feedback (both from the job itself and from others), significance, identity, scope, dealing with others and opportunities of friendship, motivational elements, biological demands, and physical working conditions. However, numerous other validated measures focus only on selected aspects of jobs that may be stressful, demanding, or unusual. These selected aspects include overload, routinization, formalization, monotony, control, cognitive demands, production pressures, complexity, uncertainty, interdependence, and extent of computer use. Although these measures of selected job attributes have sound psychometrics, have been validated, and are included in this chapter, it is pertinent to ask if it is appropriate to focus attention only on selected aspects of a job and not include measures of the other aspects. That is, it is possible that employees may answer questions about control in their job based on a general job-related cognitive schema that is based on aspects of the job other than control (Feldman & Lynch, 1988).

The third question reflects a growing realization that employee perceptions of their jobs may reflect in part some aspects of the work context in which the job is located. For example, it is likely that the nature of supervision experienced by an employee, the extent to which the employee's work assignments include developmental experiences, the employee's understanding of the performance appraisal system, expectation that greater effort will be recognized and rewarded, social support received from supervisors and peers, appreciation felt by the employee, and a worker's general sense of empowerment will affect how an employee describes the nature of his or her job. In this chapter, I have also included validated measures of these aspects of the work environment.

Job Diagnostic Survey, With Revisions

Description
The Job Diagnostic Survey (JDS) was developed by Hackman and Oldham (1974) in conjunction with the theory of job characteristics and continues to be the most widely used measure of the nature of jobs. The measure includes separate subscales that describe employee perceptions of skill variety, task identity, task significance, autonomy, and feedback from the job itself, feedback from agents (supervisors, customers), and dealing with others in their jobs. The five dimensions most frequently used in studies that I reviewed from the 1990s were skill variety, task identity, task significance, autonomy, and feedback from the job itself. The original scales for these five dimensions have been subjected to extensive analyses, which resulted in revisions to some of the items by Idaszak and Drasgow (1987). I have included both the original and revised items. In some studies, the subscales for the five major dimensions have been combined to form a single measure of job complexity or job scope (Hochwarter, Zellars, et al., 1999; Siegall & McDonald, 1995).

Reliability
Coefficient alpha values for skill variety ranged from .65 to .78. Alpha values ranged from .74 to .83 for task identity, from .72 to .83 for task significance, from .68 to .77 for autonomy, and from .65 to .81 for feedback (Munz, Huelsman, Konold, & McKinney, 1996; Renn & Vandenberg, 1995; Siegall & McDonald, 1995; Spector et al., 1995; Steel & Rentsch, 1997; Taber & Taylor, 1990). Across several studies, the estimated portion of "true variance" accounted for by the JDS measures were 69% for skill variety, 63% for autonomy, 48% for task identity, 47% for task significance, and 59% for feedback The test-retest reliability of the JDS was $r = .62$ (Taber & Taylor, 1990).

Validity
Across several studies (16 to 20 depending on JDS dimension), the JDS dimensions correlated positively with job satisfaction and growth and correlated negatively with absenteeism (Renn & Vandenberg, 1995; Taber & Taylor, 1990). In Pearson (1991), more extensive and detailed job feedback correlated positively with internal motivation.

Using structural equation models, Renn and Vandenberg (1995) found that the five job dimensions were empirically distinct. Although responses to the items are affected by social cues, they are affected most by differences in objective job characteristics (Taber & Taylor, 1990). Munz et al. (1996) found that employee negative affectivity and positive affectivity were empirically distinct from the job dimensions and have minimal affects on the measurement of job characteristics with the JDS. Other confirmatory analyses have shown that the JDS dimensions fit the data better when an additional factor representing measurement artifacts associated with negatively worded items was included (Taber & Taylor, 1990). In Idaszak and Drasgow (1987), factor analysis in two independent samples showed the presence of a sixth factor corresponding to the negative wording of five items. This led to revision of the JDS to include only positively worded items (Idaszak & Drasgow, 1987). Subsequent analysis showed that this revision eliminated the sixth factor.

Sources   Original items: Hackman, J. R., & Oldham, G. R. (1974). *The Job Diagnostic Survey: An instrument for the diagnosis of jobs and the evaluation of job redesign projects* (Tech. Rep. No. 4). New Haven, CT: Yale University, Department of Administrative Sciences. Prepared in connection with research sponsored by the Office of Naval Research (Contract No. N00014-67A-0097-0026, NR170-744) and the U.S. Department of Labor (Manpower Administration, Grant No. 21-09-74-14).

Revised items: Idaszak, J. R., & Drasgow, F. (1987). A revision of the Job Diagnostic Survey: Elimination of a measurement artifact. *Journal of Applied Psychology, 72*(1), 69-74. Items were taken from Table 3, p. 71. Copyright © 1987 by the American Psychological Association. Reprinted with permission.

Items   The JDS has two types of questions related to job dimensions. Some are drawn from Section 1 of the survey, and others are drawn from Section 2. Each section of the JDS has separate instructions. I have grouped the items by job dimension for ease in visualizing what each scale actually describes. Rather than repeat the instructions for each type of question, I provide the directions once and then indicate the section of the JDS from which each item is drawn

Instructions for items in Section 1:

This part of the questionnaire asks you to describe your job, as objectively as you can. Please do not use this part of the questionnaire to show how much you like or dislike your job. Questions about that will come later. Instead, try to make your descriptions as accurate and as objective as you possibly can. The responses are on a continuum from 1 to 7. Circle the number that most accurately describes your job. (The anchors differ from item to item in Section 1 and are provided with each item below.)

Instructions for the items from Section 2:

Listed below are a number of statements which could be used to describe a job. You are to indicate whether each statement is an accurate or inaccurate description of your job. Please try to be as objective as you can in deciding how accurately each statement describes your job—regardless of whether you like or dislike your job. How accurate is the statement in describing your job? (The same response scale is applied to all Section 2 items: 1 = *very inaccurate*, 2 = *mostly inaccurate*, 3 = *slightly inaccurate*, 4 = *uncertain*, 5 = *slightly accurate*, 6 = *mostly accurate*, 7 = *very accurate.*)

Skill variety items:

Circle the number that most accurately describes your job.

1. (From Section 1) How much variety is there in your job? That is, to what extent does the job require you to do many different things at work, using a variety of your skills and talents?

    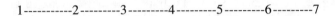
    1-----------2---------3---------4---------5---------6---------7

    Anchors: 1 = Very little: The job requires me to do the same routine things over and over again; 4 = Moderate variety; 7 = Very much: The job requires me to do many different things using a number of different skills and talents.

2. (From Section 2) The job requires me to use a number of complex or high-level skills.
3. (From Section 2) The job is quite simple and repetitive. (Reverse scored—subtract the number entered by the respondent from 8.)

Task identity items:

1. (From Section 1) To what extent does your job involve doing a "whole" and identifiable piece of work? That is, is the job a complete piece of work that has an obvious beginning and end? Or is it only a small part of the overall piece of work, which is finished by other people or by automatic machines?

    1-----------2---------3---------4---------5---------6---------7

    Anchors: 1 = My job is only a tiny part of the overall piece of work: The results of my activities cannot be seen in the final product or service; 4 = My job is a moderate-sized "chunk" of the overall piece of work: My own contribution can be seen in the final outcome; 7 = My job involves doing the whole piece of work, from start to finish: The results of my activities are easily seen in the final product or service.

2. (From Section 2) The job provides me the chance to completely finish the pieces of work I begin.
3. (From Section 2) The job is arranged so that I do not have the chance to do an entire piece of work from beginning to end. (This item is reverse scored.)

    Revised item: This item was positively worded by Idaszak and Drasgow's (1987) revisions to read: The job is arranged so that I can do an entire piece of work from beginning to end.

Task significance items:

1. (From Section 1) In general, how significant or important is your job? That is, are the results of your work likely to significantly affect the lives or well-being of other people?

    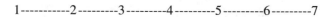

    Anchors: 1 = Not very significant: The outcomes of my work are not likely to have important effects on other people; 4 = Moderately significant; 7 = Highly significant: The outcomes of my work can affect other people in very important ways.

2. (From Section 2) This job is one where a lot of other people can be affected by how well the work gets done.
3. (From Section 2) The job itself is not very significant or important in the broader scheme of things. (This item is reverse scored.)

    Revised item: This item was positively worded in Idaszak and Dragsow's (1987) revisions to read: The job itself is very significant and important in the broader scheme of things.

Autonomy items:

1. (From Section 1) How much autonomy is there in your job? That is, to what extent does your job permit you to decide on your own how to go about doing the work?

    Anchors: 1 = Very little: The job gives me almost no personal "say" about how and when the work is done; 4 = Moderate autonomy: Many things are standardized and not under my control, but I can make some decisions about the work; 7 = Very much: The job gives me almost complete responsibility for deciding how and when the work is done.

2. (From Section 2) The job gives me considerable opportunity for independence and freedom in how I do the work.
3. (From Section 2) The job denies me any chance to use my personal initiative or judgment in carrying out the work. (This item is reverse scored.)

    Revised item: This item was positively worded in Idaszak and Dragsow's (1987) revisions to read: The job gives me a chance to use my personal initiative and judgment in carrying out the work.

Feedback (job itself) items:

1. (From Section 1) To what extent does doing the job itself provide you with information about your work performance? That is, does the actual work itself provide clues about how well you are doing—aside from any "feedback" co-workers or supervisors may provide?

   Anchors: 1 = Very little: The job itself is set up so I could work forever without finding out how well I am doing; 4 = Moderately: Sometimes doing the job provides "feedback" to me, sometimes it does not; 7 = Very much: The job is set up so that I get almost constant "feedback" as I work about how well I am doing.

2. (From Section 2) Just doing the work required by the job provides many chances for me to figure out how well I am doing.
3. (From Section 2) The job itself provides very few clues about whether or not I am performing well. (This item is reverse scored.)

   Revised item: This item was positively worded by Idaszak and Dragsow's (1987) revision to read: After I finish a job, I know whether I performed well.

Feedback (agents) items:

1. (From Section 1) To what extent do managers or co-workers let you know how well you are doing on your job?

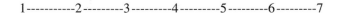

   Anchors: 1 = Very little: People almost never let me know how well I am doing; 4 = Moderately: Sometimes people may give me "feedback," other times they may not; 7 = Very much: Managers or co-workers provide me with almost constant "feedback" about how well I am doing.

2. (From Section 2) Supervisors often let me know how well they think I am performing the job.
3. (From Section 2) The supervisors and co-workers on this job almost never give me any "feedback" about how well I am doing in my work. (This item is reverse scored.)

Dealing with others items:

1. (From Section 1) To what extent does your job require you to work closely with other people (either "clients," or people in related jobs in your own organization)?

    1-----------2---------3---------4---------5---------6---------7

    Anchors: 1 = Very little: Dealing with other people is not at all necessary in doing the job; 4 = Moderately: Some dealing with others is necessary; 7 = Very much: Dealing with other people is an absolutely essential and crucial part of doing the job.

2. (From Section 2) The job requires a lot of cooperative work with other people.
3. (From Section 2) The job can be done adequately by a person working alone—without talking or checking with other people. (This item is reverse scored.)

Job Characteristics Inventory

Description   This measure was originally developed by Sims, Szilagyi, and Keller (1976) to describe employee perceptions about their jobs. The measure uses 30 items that can be grouped into six subscales indicating the extent to which a job involves variety, autonomy, feedback, interaction with others, task identity, and friendship. All 30 items have also been combined and used as a single measure of job complexity (Ganzach, 1998).

Reliability   Coefficient alphas of the six subscales for variety, autonomy, feedback, interaction with others, task identity, and friendship ranged from .76 to .84 (Aryee, Chay, & Chew, 1996; Dodd & Ganster, 1996; Ganzach, 1998; Mathieu, Hofmann, & Farr, 1993; Williams, Gavin, & Williams, 1996).

Validity   The subscales for autonomy, feedback, and identity correlated positively with satisfaction with growth and supervision. Autonomy correlated negatively with specialization. Variety was correlated negatively with standardization and specialization (Mathieu et al., 1993). Williams et al. (1996) examined the JDS with exploratory and confirmatory factor analysis and found that job complexity was a one-dimensional construct that was empirically distinct from job satisfaction, role overload, role ambiguity, and role conflict. Dodd and Ganster (1996) found that objective job measures correlated positively with employee perceptions of jobs obtained with the Job Characteristics Inventory.

Source   Sims, H. P., Szilagyi, A. D., & Keller, R. T. (1976). The measurement of job characteristics. *Academy of Management Journal, 19*, 195-212. © 1976 by Academy of Management. Items were taken from Figure 1, p. 200. Reproduced with permission of Academy of Management in the format textbook via Copyright Clearance Center.

Items   Responses are obtained on a 5-point Likert-type scale. For Items 1-13, the anchors are 1 = *very little*, 3 = *moderate amount*, and 5 = *very much*. For Items 14-30, the anchors are 1 = *minimum amount*, 3 = *moderate amount*, and 5 = *maximum amount*.

1. How much variety is there in your job?
2. How much are you left on your own to do your own work?
3. How often do you see projects or jobs through to completion?
4. To what extent do you find out how well you are doing on the job as you are working?
5. How much opportunity is there to meet individuals whom you would like to develop friendship with?
6. How much of your job depends upon your ability to work with others?
7. How repetitious are your duties?

8. To what extent are you able to act independently of your supervisor in performing your job function?
9. To what extent do you receive information from your superior on your job performance?
10. To what extent do you have the opportunity to talk informally with other employees while at work?
11. To what extent is dealing with other people a part of your job?
12. How similar are the tasks you perform in a typical work day?
13. To what extent are you able to do your job independently of others?
14. The feedback from my supervisor on how well I'm doing
15. Friendship from my co-workers
16. The opportunity to talk to others on my job
17. The opportunity to do a number of different things
18. The freedom to do pretty much what I want on my job
19. The degree to which the work I'm involved with is handled from beginning to end by myself
20. The opportunity to find out how well I am doing on my job
21. The opportunity in my job to get to know other people
22. The amount of variety in my job
23. The opportunity for independent thought and action
24. The opportunity to complete work I start
25. The feeling that I know whether I am performing my job well or poorly
26. The opportunity to develop close friendships in my job
27. Meeting with others in my work
28. The control I have over the pace of my work
29. The opportunity to do a job from the beginning to end (i.e., the chance to do a whole job)
30. The extent of feedback you receive from individuals other than your supervisor.

Items 1, 7, 12, 17, and 22 form a subscale for job variety.
Items 2, 8, 13, 18, 23, and 28 form a subscale for autonomy.
Items 4, 9, 14, 20, and 25 form a subscale for feedback.
Items 6, 11, and 30 form a subscale for dealing with others.
Items 3, 19, 24, and 29 form a subscale for task identity.
Items 5, 10, 15, 16, 21, 26, and 27 form a subscale for friendship.

Multimethod Job Design Questionnaire

Description   The Multimethod Job Design Questionnaire (MJDQ) was developed by Campion (1988) to more accurately describe a wide range of features of jobs. Other measures have focused on the motivational aspects of jobs and have included aspects such as autonomy, intrinsic feedback, extrinsic feedback, social interaction, goal clarity, participation, and recognition. The MJDQ also covers mechanistic, biological, and perceptual/motor aspects of jobs. These four dimensions (motivational, mechanistic, biological, and perceptual/motor aspects of jobs) represent a synthesis of alternative viewpoints about a job. That is, the traditional motivational perspective focuses on the psychological meaning of jobs and looks to enhance job aspects such as autonomy, skill variety, and task significance. Other disciplines such as industrial engineering focus more on the mechanistic aspects of jobs, whereas ergonomics focuses on the human factors or perceptual/motor aspects of jobs. The biological view focuses on work physiology and aims to minimize physical stress and strain on the worker (Campion, 1988).

Reliability   Coefficient alpha values for the motivational aspects of jobs ranged from .81 to .94 (Campion & McClelland, 1991; Wong & Campion, 1991). Alpha values for mechanistic aspects of jobs ranged from .75 to .89, from .72 to .88 for biological aspects of jobs, and from .85 to .93 for perceptual/motor aspects of jobs (Campion, 1988; Campion & McClelland, 1991). Correlations among job ratings provided by job incumbents, managers, and job analysts ranged from .76 to .86 for motivational, mechanistic, and perceptual/motor aspects of jobs. The correlations among ratings of biological aspects were small and not statistically significant (Campion, 1988).

Validity   Motivational job design correlated positively with an employee's affective view of the job, mental ability level required, mental demands, better customer service, and job efficiency (Campion & McClelland, 1991; Wong & Campion, 1991). Mechanistic and perceptual/motor design correlated negatively with mental demands of a job (Campion & McClelland, 1991).

Source   Campion, M. A. (1988). Interdisciplinary approaches to job design: A constructive replication with extensions. *Journal of Applied Psychology, 73*, 467-481. Items were taken from the appendix, pp. 480-481. Copyright © 1988 by the American Psychological Association. Reprinted with permission.

Items   Respondents indicate the extent to which each statement is descriptive of their job on a scale where 1 = *strongly agree*, 2 = *agree*, 3 = *neither agree nor disagree*, 4 = *disagree*, 5 = *strongly disagree*, and (blank) = *don't know or not applicable*. Scores for each scale are averages of the items.

Motivational scale items:

1. Autonomy. The job allows freedom, independence, or discretion in work scheduling, sequence, methods, procedures, quality control, or other decision making
2. Intrinsic job feedback. The work activities themselves provide direct and clear information as to the effectiveness (e.g., quality and quantity) of your job performance
3. Extrinsic job feedback. Other people in the organization, such as managers and co-workers, provide information as to the effectiveness (e.g., quality and quantity) of your job performance
4. Social interaction. The job provides for positive social interaction such as teamwork or co-worker assistance
5. Task/goal clarity. The job duties, requirements, and goals are clear and specific
6. Task variety. The job has a variety of duties, tasks, and activities
7. Task identity. The job requires completion of a whole and identifiable piece of work. It gives you a chance to do an entire piece of work from beginning to end
8. Ability/skill-level requirements. The job requires a high level of knowledge, skills, and abilities
9. Ability/skill variety. The job requires a variety of knowledge, skills, and abilities
10. Task significance. The job is significant and important compared with other jobs in the organization
11. Growth/learning. The job allows opportunities for learning and growth in competence and proficiency
12. Promotion. There are opportunities for advancement to higher-level jobs
13. Achievement. The job provides for feelings of achievement and task accomplishment
14. Participation. The job allows participation in work-related decision making
15. Communication. The job has access to relevant communication channels and information flows
16. Pay adequacy. The pay on this job is adequate compared with the job requirements and with the pay in similar jobs
17. Recognition. The job provides acknowledgment and recognition from others
18. Job security. People on this job have high job security

Mechanistic scale items:

19. Job specialization. The job is highly specialized in terms of purpose, tasks, or activities
20. Specialization of tools and procedures. The tools, procedures, materials, and so forth used on this job are highly specialized in terms of purpose

21. Task simplification. The tasks are simple and uncomplicated
22. Single activities. The job requires you to do only one task or activity at a time
23. Skill simplification. The job requires relatively little skill and training time
24. Repetition. The job requires performing the same activity(ies) repeatedly
25. Spare time. There is very little spare time between activities on this job
26. Automation. Many of the activities of this job are automated or assisted by automation

Biological scale items:

27. Strength. The job requires fairly little muscular strength
28. Lifting. The job requires fairly little lifting and/or the lifting is of very light weights
29. Endurance. The job requires fairly little muscular endurance
30. Seating. The seating arrangements on the job are adequate (e.g., ample opportunities to sit, comfortable chairs, good postural support, etc.)
31. Size differences. The work place allows for all size differences between people in terms of clearance, reach, eye height, legroom, and so forth
32. Wrist movement. The job allows the wrists to remain straight without excessive movement
33. Noise. The work place is free from excessive noise
34. Climate. The climate at the work place is comfortable in terms of temperature and humidity and it is free of excessive dust and fumes
35. Work breaks. There is adequate time for work breaks given the demands of the job
36. Shift work. The job does not require shift work or excessive overtime

Perceptual/motor items:

37. Lighting. The lighting in the work place is adequate and free from glare
38. Displays. The displays, gauges, meters, and computerized equipment on this job are easy to read and understand
39. Programs. The programs in the computerized equipment on this job are easy to learn and use
40. Other equipment. The other equipment (all types) used on this job is easy to learn and use
41. Printed job materials. The printed materials used on this job are easy to read and interpret
42. Work place layout. The work place is laid out so that you can see and hear well to perform the job

43. Information input requirements. The amount of information you must attend to in order to perform this job is fairly minimal

44. Information output requirements. The amount of information you must put out on this job, in terms of both action and communication, is fairly minimal

45. Information processing requirements. The amount of information you must process, in terms of thinking and problem solving, is fairly minimal

46. Memory requirements. The amount of information you must remember on this job is fairly minimal

47. Stress. There is relatively little stress on this job

48. Boredom. The chances of boredom on this job are fairly small

Job Demands and Decision Latitude

Description   This measure was developed by Karasek (1979) to assess the effects of stressful jobs on the physical health of employees. A job demand subscale that uses seven items describes psychological stressors such as workload and time pressures. Eight items describe job decision latitude. Four of these items relate to an employee's discretion in applying skills to do the job. Four items described an employee's authority to make job-related decisions. Job demands and decision latitude are constructs that can vary independently in a work environment (Fortunato, Jex, & Heinish, 1999; Xie, 1996).

Reliability   The coefficient alpha values for job demands ranged from .79 to .88, and the alpha values for job control or decision latitude ranged from .77 to .85 (Chay, 1993; Fortunato et al., 1999; Moyle & Parkes, 1999; Parkes, 1990; Westman, 1992; Xie, 1996; Zohar, 1995).

Validity   Work demands correlated positively with hours worked per week, psychological distress, being married, employee negative affectivity, and employee somatic complaints (Chay, 1993; Moyle & Parkes, 1999; Parkes, 1990). Work demand correlated negatively with social support from managers and job satisfaction (Moyle & Parkes, 1999). Decision latitude correlated positively with job level, hours worked per week, and job satisfaction (Chay, 1993; Moyle & Parkes, 1999; Xie, 1996). Decision latitude correlated negatively with employee somatic complaints (Chay, 1993; Xie, 1996).

Xie (1996) used factor analysis to examine the items and found that the items measuring job demands and decision latitude loaded on two factors exactly as suggested by Karasek (1979).

Source   Karasek, R. A. (1979). Job demands, job decision latitude, and mental strain: Implications for job redesign. *Administrative Science Quarterly, 24,* 285-308. The items were taken from Appendix A, p. 307. Reprinted with permission.

Items   Responses are obtained using a 5-point Likert-type scale where 1 = *never* and 5 = *extremely often.*

Job demand items:

1. To what extent does your job require your working fast?
2. To what extent does your job require your working hard?
3. To what extent does your job require a great deal of work to be done?
4. To what extent is there not enough time for you to do your job?
5. To what extent is there excessive work in your job?
6. To what extent do you feel there is not enough time for you to finish your work?
7. To what extent are you faced with conflicting demands on your job?

Skill discretion items:

1. To what extent is high skill level required?
2. To what extent are you required to learn new things?
3. To what extent is your work non-repetitious?
4. To what extent does your job require creativity?

Decision authority items:

1. To what extent do you have the freedom to decide how to organize your work?
2. To what extent do you have control over what happens on your job?
3. To what extent does your job allow you to make a lot of your own decisions?
4. To what extent are you assisted in making your own decisions?

Job Characteristics Based on the
Dictionary of Occupational Titles

Description   This measure, developed by Roos and Treiman (1980), uses information provided in the *Dictionary of Occupational Titles* (*DOT*) to describe substantive complexity, motor skills required, physical demands, and undesirable working conditions of an occupation. The *DOT*, developed by job analysts in the United States Department of Labor, describes 46 characteristics of 12,099 job titles. Roos and Treiman factor-analyzed these 46 characteristics and found four dimensions: substantive complexity, motor skills, physical demands, and undesirable working conditions. The *DOT* and perceptual measures such as the Job Diagnostic Survey (JDS) differ in many ways. The *DOT* ratings of job complexity are based on functional requirements of jobs and worker trait requirements, aspects not directly measured in the JDS. In addition, the *DOT* is a general index that applies to entire job titles, whereas the JDS assesses the unique perceptions held by individual jobholders toward their jobs.

Reliability   The coefficient alpha for the measure of job complexity was .90, alpha for motor skills was .95, and alpha for physical demands was .87 (Watson & Slack, 1993).

Validity   The motor skills rating was positively correlated with overall job satisfaction, the complexity rating correlated positively with satisfaction with the work itself, and the physical demands rating correlated negatively with satisfaction with co-workers (Watson & Slack, 1993). Job complexity correlated positively with employee age, job variety, identity, significance, autonomy, feedback, and scope. Job complexity correlated negatively with exhaustion and being female (Xie & Johns, 1995).

Source   Roos, P. A., & Treiman, D. J. (1980). DOT scales for the 1970 census classification. In A. Miller, D. Treiman, P. Cain, & P. Roos (Eds.), *Work, jobs, and occupations: A critical review of the* Dictionary of Occupational Titles. Washington, DC: National Academy Press. Items were taken from text, p. 339. Copyright © 1980 by National Academy Press. Reproduced with permission.

Items   The dimensions of substantive complexity, motor skills, physical demands, and undesirable working conditions are composed of 22 of the 46 characteristics reported for each job title in the *DOT*. The values for each of the *DOT* variables listed below each dimension are averaged to calculate the score for each dimension.

Substantive complexity:

        DATA (worker function)
        GED (training time)
        SVP (training time)
        INTELL (aptitude)
        VERBAL (aptitude)
        NUMER (aptitude)
        ABSTRACT (interest)
        REPCON (temperament for repetitive or continuous process)

Motor skills:

        THINGS (worker function)
        MOTOR (aptitude)
        FINGDEX (aptitude)
        MANDEX (aptitude)
        COLORDIS (aptitude)
        SEE (physical demand)

Physical demands:

        EYEHAND (aptitude)
        CLIMB (physical demand)
        STOOP (physical demand)
        LOCATION (working condition)
        HAZARDS (working condition)

Undesirable working conditions:

        COLD (working condition)
        HEAT (working condition)
        WET (working condition)

Job Complexity Based on the
Dictionary of Occupational Titles

Description   This measure, originally developed by Hunter (1980), uses information in the DATA dimension of the *Dictionary of Occupational Titles (DOT)* to rate job complexity. Although perceptual measures of job characteristics tend to focus on the psychological complexity of jobs, this measure focuses on the extent to which a job makes mental demands that require skill and training on the part of the job incumbent. Occupations are rated as high in task-person complexity when great aptitude, skill, and creativity are required of their incumbents. Schaubroeck, Ganster, and Kemmerer (1994) expanded the rating scheme for complexity to include complex relationships to people, required general intelligence, and abstract and creative activities.

Reliability   In Schaubroeck et al. (1994), coefficient alpha for the combined scale (four *DOT*-based characteristics) was .90. In Hunter, Schmidt, and Judiesch (1990), 15 of 18 studies of low-complexity jobs reported coefficient alpha values larger than .70. Fourteen of 15 studies of medium- and high-complexity jobs reported coefficient alpha values of .70 or larger.

Validity   In Robie, Ryan, Schmieder, Parra, and Smith (1998), job complexity correlated positively with satisfaction with pay, satisfaction with the work itself, satisfaction with supervision, and requirements for specific vocational preparation. Job complexity based on the *DOT* correlated positively with cardiovascular disorder at a later time (Schaubroeck et al., 1994). The level and variation in job output correlated positively with levels of job complexity (Hunter et al., 1990).

Source   Hunter, J. E., Schmidt, E. L., & Judiesch, M. K. (1990). Individual differences in output variability as a function of job complexity. *Journal of Applied Psychology, 75,* 28-42. Items were taken from text and footnote 1, p. 30. Copyright © 1990 by the American Psychological Association. Reprinted with permission.

Items   In Hunter's original system, the two highest-complexity levels contain jobs with a code of 0 or 1 on the DATA dimension in the *DOT* (example jobs include scientists and executives) and jobs with a code of 0 on the THINGS dimension in the *DOT* classification (an example job is computer trouble shooters). Jobs with codes on the DATA dimension of 2, 3, and 4 are rated in the third level of complexity. The fourth level of complexity contains jobs with codes of 5 or 6 on the DATA dimension of the *DOT.* Lowest-complexity jobs are those with code of 6 on the THINGS dimension of the *DOT.* This rating approach was modified by Hunter et al. (1990) so that the first two levels (managerial/professional and complex technical setup work) were combined into high-complexity jobs. Skilled crafts, technician jobs, first-line supervisors, and lower-level administrative jobs were combined into moderate-complexity jobs, and semiskilled and unskilled jobs were grouped into low-complexity jobs. In Schaubroeck et al. (1994), the rating scheme was expanded to cover additional characteristics included in the *DOT*. Besides the DATA and THINGS scores, the modified complexity rating includes a "worker function characteristic" for complex relationships to People, an "aptitude characteristic" for required intelligence, and an "interest characteristic" for Abstract and creative versus routine, concrete activities (Schaubroeck et al., 1994).

Job Cognitions

Description   The measure, developed by Williams and Anderson (1991), asks employees to describe the extent to which 20 statements are accurate descriptions of the nature of a job. The statements cover a broad range of job characteristics and leave unstated the specific referent an employee should use in responding. This approach allows respondents to naturally select reference group(s) they consider appropriate.

Reliability   In Williams and Anderson (1991), a subscale measuring extrinsic job cognitions had a coefficient alpha of .71, and a subscale measuring intrinsic job cognitions had a coefficient alpha of .78.

Validity   A factor analysis of the 20 items extracted two factors on which 15 items loaded (Williams & Anderson, 1991). One subscale measured cognitions about extrinsic aspects of the job (seven items). The other subscale describes intrinsic aspect of the job (eight items).

Source   Williams, L. J., & Anderson, S. E. (1991). Job satisfaction and organizational commitment as predictors of organizational citizenship and in-role behaviors. *Journal of Management, 17*(3), 601-617. Items were taken from Table 2, p. 608. Copyright © 1991 by *Journal of Management*. Reproduced with permission.

Items   The full 20 items are listed below. Items in the intrinsic subscale are labeled with (I), and those in the extrinsic subscale are labeled with (E). Responses to the items are obtained on a 5-point Likert-type scale where 1 = *never true* and 5 = *always true*.

1.   Am able to keep busy (I)
2.   Have the chance to work alone
3.   Have the chance to do different things (I)
4.   Have the chance to be somebody (I)
5.   My manager understands employees (E)
6.   My manager makes competent decisions (E)
7.   Can do things that do not go against conscience
8.   My job provides for steady employment
9.   Have chance to do things for other people (I)
10.   Have chance to tell other people what to do (I)
11.   Have chance to make use of abilities (I)
12.   Am informed about company policy
13.   Pay is reasonable for amount of work (E)
14.   Have chances for advancement (E)
15.   Have freedom to use my own judgment (I)
16.   Have chance to try my own methods (I)
17.   Working conditions are pleasant (E)

18. Co-workers get along well with each other (E)
19. Get praise for doing a good job (E)
20. Get a feeling of accomplishment

Job Overload

Description   This measure, developed by Caplan, Cobb, French, Van Harrison, and Pinneau (1980), uses 11 items to describe an employee's job overload. This focuses on the employee's perceptions of quantitative job overload (rather than mental strain or psychological pressure). It asks for description of the perceived pace and amount of work.

Reliability   Coefficient alpha values ranged from .72 to .81 (Dwyer & Ganster, 1991; Phelan, Bromet, Schwartz, Dew, & Curtis, 1993; Sargent & Terry, 1998; Wallace, 1997).

Validity   Job overload correlated positively with hours worked, competitiveness, firm size, and absenteeism and correlated negatively with work satisfaction, job satisfaction, and professional commitment (Dwyer & Ganster, 1991; Phelan et al., 1993; Sargent & Terry, 1998; Wallace, 1997).

Source   Caplan, R. D., Cobb, S., French, J. R. P., Van Harrison, R., & Pinneau, S. R. (1980). *Job demands and worker health.* Ann Arbor: University of Michigan, Institute for Social Research. Items were taken from Appendix E, pp. 238-239. Copyright © 1980. Reproduced with permission.

Items   Responses for items 1 to 4 are obtained on a 5-point Likert-type scale where 1 = *rarely*, 2 = *occasionally*, 3 = *sometimes*, 4 = *fairly often*, and 5 = *very often*.

1. How often does your job require you to work very fast?
2. How often does your job require you to work very hard?
3. How often does your job leave you with little time to get things done?
4. How often is there a great deal to be done?

Responses for items 5 to 11 are obtained on a 5-point Likert-type scale where 1 = *hardly any*, 2 = *a little*, 3 = *some*, 4 = *a lot*, and 5 = *a great deal*.

5. How much slowdown in the workload do you experience?
6. How much time do you have to think and contemplate?
7. How much workload do you have?
8. What quantity of work do others expect you to do?
9. How much time do you have to do all your work?
10. How many projects, assignments, or tasks do you have?
11. How many lulls between heavy workload periods do you have?

Job Routinization and Formalization

Description   This measure was developed by Bacharach, Bamberger, and Conley (1990) to capture the elements often used in organizations to assert indirect control on workers. The preferences of employees are often in conflict with the needs of organizations to reduce uncertainty and variation in performance through routinization, formal documentation, establishment of rules, and record-keeping requirements for jobs. Collectively, these efforts to structure jobs may have positive effects by reducing employee ambiguity and negative effects by making jobs less appealing (Bacharach & Bamberger, 1995). The measure uses 12 items to describe the routinization, formalization, pervasiveness of rules, and record-keeping requirements of a job.

Reliability   Coefficient alpha values for routinization ranged from .71 to .83 (Bacharach & Bamberger, 1995; Bacharach et al., 1990). Coefficient alpha values were .70 for formalization, .70 for pervasiveness of rules, and .72 for record keeping (Bacharach et al., 1990).

Validity   Routinization was negatively correlated with role overload and challenge/opportunities for growth. Pervasiveness of rules and record keeping were positively correlated with formal communication and formalization and negatively correlated with autonomy. Formalization was positively correlated with role conflict and the pervasiveness of rules for a job and negatively correlated with role overload and autonomy (Bacharach et al., 1990).

Source   Bacharach, S. B., Bamberger, P. R., & Conley, S. C. (1990). Work processes, role conflict, and role overload: The case of nurses and engineers in the public sector. *Work and Occupations*, *17*(2), 199-229. Copyright © 1990 by Sage Publications, Inc. Items were taken from portions of the appendix, pp. 223-224. Reprinted by permission of Sage Publications, Inc.

Items   Routinization items:
   Responses to items 1 and 2 are obtained on a 4-point Likert-type scale where 1 = *definitely true* and 4 = *definitely false*.

1.   There is something different to do here every day
2.   For almost every job I do, there is something new happening almost every day

   Responses to item 3 are obtained on a 4-point Likert-type scale where 1= *very non-routine* and 4 = *very routine*.

3.   How routine would you say the work here is?

Pervasiveness of rules items:

Responses are obtained on a 4-point Likert-type scale where 1 = *definitely false* and 4 = *definitely true*.

1. We have procedures here for every situation
2. I have to follow strict operating procedures at all times
3. I always check to see that I'm following the rules.

Record-keeping items:

Responses are obtained on a 4-point Likert-type scale where 1 = *definitely false* and 4 = *definitely true*.

1. In case of a crisis, I always refer to written records for accountability
2. I keep accurate records of every situation
3. I frequently use the records to check for information on an issue

Formalization items:

Responses are obtained on a 4-point Likert-type scale where 1 = *definitely false* and 4 = *definitely true*.

1. There exists a document indicating the general procedure to follow
2. There is a complete written description for my job
3. There is a handbook or manual for my facility
4. There is a chart showing the chain of command
5. There are well-defined procedures specifying the proper channels of communication in most matters
6. The organization keeps a written record of everyone's job performance

Subjective Monotony

Description   This measure, developed by Melamed, Ben-Avi, Luz, and Green (1995), assesses employee perceptions of the extent to which their work is monotonous, using an adjective checklist. The four adjectives used in the scale are *routine, boring, monotonous*, and *not varied enough*. Objective job monotony, which is typically rated by independent observers, is defined as relatively short cycle time, monotonous motor demands, or operations that do not require sustained attention (Shirom, Westman, & Melamed, 1999).

Reliability   Coefficient alpha values for subjective monotony ranged from .68 to .76 (Melamed et al., 1995; Shirom et al., 1999).

Validity   Subjective monotony correlated negatively with education level, age, and job satisfaction. It correlated positively with individual and piece-rate pay incentives, psychological distress, anxiety, and somatic complaints (Melamed et al., 1995; Shirom et al., 1999). In Shirom et al. (1999), subjective monotony correlated positively with objective monotony.

Source   Melamed, S., Ben-Avi, I., Luz, J., & Green, M. S. (1995). Objective and subjective work monotony: Effects on job satisfaction, psychological distress, and absenteeism in blue-collar workers. *Journal of Applied Psychology, 80,* 29-42. Items were taken from text, p. 32. Copyright © 1995 by the American Psychological Association. Reprinted with permission.

Items   Employees respond by indicating the extent to which each adjective describes their job using responses of yes (scored with value 3), ? (scored with value 1) or no (scored with value 0). The adjectives are as follows:

1. Routine
2. Boring
3. Monotonous
4. Not varied enough

Work Control

Description   This measure, developed by Dwyer and Ganster (1991), describes the extent to which workers perceive they have control over numerous aspects of their work environment. These aspects include control over the variety of tasks performed, the order of task performance, the pace of tasks, task scheduling, task procedures, and arrangement of the physical layout/environment.

Reliability   In Dwyer and Ganster (1991), coefficient alpha was .87.

Validity   Control over aspects of a job correlated positively with sick days taken, job workload, and work satisfaction. In multivariate analysis, control moderated the relationship of workload with work satisfaction (Dwyer & Ganster, 1991).

Source   Dwyer, D. J., & Ganster, D. C. (1991). The effects of job demands and control on employee attendance and satisfaction. *Journal of Organizational Behavior, 12,* 595-608. Items were taken from the appendix, p. 608. Reprinted with permission.

Items   *Instructions and items:* Below are listed a number of statements which could be used to describe a job. Please read each statement carefully and indicate the extent to which each is an accurate or an inaccurate description of your job by writing a number in front of each statement. The response options are 1 = *very little*, 2 = *little*, 3 = *a moderate amount*, 4 = *much*, and 5 = *very much*.

1. How much control do you have over the variety of methods you use in completing your work?
2. How much can you choose among a variety of tasks or projects to do?
3. How much control do you have personally over the quality of your work?
4. How much can you generally predict the amount of work you will have to do on any given day?
5. How much control do you personally have over how much work you get done?
6. How much control do you have over how quickly or slowly you have to work?
7. How much control do you have over the scheduling and duration of your rest breaks?
8. How much control do you have over when you come to work and leave?
9. How much control do you have over when you take vacation or days off?
10. How much are you able to predict what the results of decisions you make on the job will be?

11. How much are you able to decorate, rearrange, or personalize your work area?
12. How much can you control the physical condition of your work station (lighting, temperature)?
13. How much control do you have over how you do your work?
14. How much can you control when and how much you have to interact with others at work?
15. How much influence do you have over the policies and procedures in your work unit?
16. How much control do you have over the sources of information you need to do your job?
17. How much are things that affect you at work predictable, even if you can't directly control them?
18. How much control do you have over the amount of resources (tools, material) that you get?
19. How much can you control the number of times you are interrupted while you work?
20. How much control do you have over how much you earn at your job?
21. How much control do you have over how your work is evaluated?
22. In general, how much overall control do you have over work and work-related matters?

Job Control, Cognitive Demand, and Production Responsibility

Description   This measure, developed by Jackson, Wall, Martin, and Davids (1993), assesses the extent of job control, cognitive demand, and production responsibility an employee experiences in a job. The measure covers timing control, defined as the extent to which a job gives an employee the freedom to determine the scheduling of his or her work behavior, and method control, defined as the extent to which an employee has the freedom to choose how to carry out tasks. Cognitive demand is also assessed on two dimensions. The first is monitoring demand, defined as the extent to which a job requires an employee to perform passive monitoring tasks. The second is problem-solving demand, defined as the extent to which a job involves active, cognitive processing to prevent or detect errors. Production responsibility is defined as the extent to which a job involves responsibility for avoiding lost output and damage to expensive equipment.

Reliability   Coefficient alpha values ranged from .79 to .85 for timing control, .77 to .80 for method control, .73 to .75 for monitoring demand, .50 to .67 for problem-solving demand, and .86 to .90 for production responsibility (Jackson et al., 1993). In Wall, Jackson, Mullarkey, and Parker (1996), method and timing control were combined into a single scale with a coefficient alpha of .86. In Jackson et al. (1993), test-retest reliabilities were $r = .50$ for timing control, $r = .57$ for method control, $r = .51$ for monitoring demand, $r = .43$ for problem-solving demand, and $r = .42$ for production responsibility.

Validity   The structure of the five dimensions of the measure was confirmed with both exploratory and confirmatory factor analysis in two separate samples (Jackson et al., 1993). Both monitoring and problem-solving demands correlated positively with job control, job decision latitude, and employee anxiety. Job control correlated positively with employee length of service, job decision latitude, and job satisfaction. Job control correlated negatively with employee depression and employee anxiety (Wall et al., 1996).

In Jackson et al. (1993), the five subscales were used to compare employees in different job roles working on the same process in a production environment as well as employees in the same roles in processes differing in the extent of computerization. The scales described significant differences between job roles and technology. For example, monitoring demand and production responsibility scores were both higher in a fully computerized process compared to a noncomputerized process.

Source   Jackson, P. R., Wall, T. D., Martin, R., & Davids, K. (1993). New measures of job control, cognitive demand, and production responsibility. *Journal of Applied Psychology, 78*(5), 753-762. Items were taken from Table 2, p. 757. Copyright © 1993 by the American Psychological Association. Reprinted with permission.

Items

Responses are obtained on 5-point Likert-type scale where 1 = *not at all*, 2 = *just a little*, 3 = *a moderate amount*, 4 = *quite a lot*, and 5 = *a great deal*.

Timing control items:

1. Do you decide on the order in which you do things?
2. Do you decide when to start a piece of work?
3. Do you decide when to finish a piece of work?
4. Do you set your own pace of work?

Method control items:

1. Can you control how much you produce?
2. Can you vary how you do your work?
3. Do you plan your own work?
4. Can you control the quality of what you produce?
5. Can you decide how to go about getting your job done?
6. Can you choose the methods to use in carrying out your work?

Monitoring demand items:

1. Does your work need your undivided attention?
2. Do you have to keep track of more than one process at once?
3. Do you have to concentrate all the time to watch for things going wrong?
4. Do you have to react quickly to prevent problems arising?

Problem-solving demand items:

1. Do you have to solve problems which have no obvious correct answer?
2. Do the problems you deal with require a thorough knowledge of the production process in your area?
3. Do you come across problems in your job you have not met before?

Production responsibility items:

1. Could a lapse of attention cause a costly loss of output?
2. Could an error on your part cause expensive damage to equipment or machinery?
3. Could your alertness prevent expensive damage to equipment or machinery?
4. Could your alertness prevent a costly loss of output?
5. If you failed to notice a problem, would it result in a costly loss of production?

Control and Complexity

Description   This measure, developed by Frese, Kring, Soose, and Zempel (1996), assesses control and complexity in a job in terms of an employee's ability to influence working conditions and work strategies. It measures complexity of work in terms of how difficult an individual's job decisions are (Frese et al., 1996). If employees have low levels of control at work and expect that nothing can be done because they lack control, they are unlikely to persist in the face of setbacks. On the other hand, decision-making power enhances a worker's feeling of empowerment and sense of responsibility for a job. In addition, work complexity generally leads to the development and practice of a high degree of skills and knowledge, which help to overcome barriers and setbacks.

Reliability   Coefficient alpha was .67 for complexity and .78 for job control (Frese et al., 1996). In Frese, Teng, and Wijnin (1999), coefficient alpha for the complexity and control subscales combined was .81.

Validity   The combined measure of job control and complexity correlated positively with employee aspirations, proactivity, and self-efficacy (Frese et al., 1999). Control at work correlated positively with work complexity, self-efficacy, willingness of employee to take an active approach, and tendency of employees to overcome barriers (Frese et al., 1996).

Source   Frese, M., Kring, W., Soose, A., & Zempel, J. (1996). Personal initiative at work: Differences between East and West Germany. *Academy of Management Journal, 39*(1), 37-64. © 1996 by Academy of Management. Items were taken from the appendix, p. 64. Reproduced with permission of Academy of Management in the format textbook via Copyright Clearance Center.

Items   Responses are obtained using a 5-point Likert-type scale. The anchors vary among items. The end-point anchors are provided with each item. An example response scale is 1 = *very little*, 2 = *rather little*, 3 = *somewhat*, 4 = *rather much*, and 5 = *very much*.

Complexity of work items:

1. Do you receive tasks that are extraordinary and particularly difficult? (End-point anchors are 1 = *never*, 5 = *several times a week*)
2. A must make very complicated decisions in his/her work; B only has to make very simple decisions. (End-point anchors are 1 = *exactly like A*, 5 = *exactly like B*)
3. Can you use all your knowledge and skills in your work? (End-point anchors are 1 = *very little*, 5 = *very much*)

4. Can you learn new things in your work? (End-point anchors are 1 = *very little*, 5 = *very much*)

Control at work items:

(End-point anchors for all these items are 1 = *very little*, 5 = *very much*)

1. If you look at your job as a whole: how many decisions does it allow you to make?
2. Can you determine how you do your work?
3. Can you plan and arrange your work on your own (e.g., calculate which material/ tools you need)?
4. How much can you participate in decisions of your superior (e.g., the superior asks you for your opinion and asks for suggestions)?

Job Uncertainty, Complexity, Variety, and Interdependence

Description   These measures were developed by Dean and Snell (1991). The components of uncertainty include job complexity, defined as the extent a job involves mental processes such as problem solving, applying discretion, and using technical knowledge (three items); job variety, defined as the extent to which a job involves performing a number of different tasks and frequently encountering exceptional circumstances requiring flexibility (seven items); and job interdependence, defined as the extent to which people performing a job must rely on or collaborate with others to complete their work (seven items). The three dimensions may also be combined into a single measure of job uncertainty.

Reliability   The coefficient alpha values for job uncertainty (combination of the three dimensions) and for each dimension ranged from .69 to .80 across different types of jobs (Dean & Snell, 1991; Snell & Dean, 1994).

Validity   Job uncertainty in operations correlated positively with job uncertainty in quality and production. Job uncertainty was positively correlated with implementation of advanced manufacturing techniques, job interdependence, organization size, and salary level. Interdependence correlated positively with organization size, and skill-based pay (Dean & Snell, 1991; Snell & Dean, 1994).

Source   Dean, J. W., & Snell, S. A. (1991). Integrated manufacturing and job design: Moderating effects of organizational inertia. *Academy of Management Journal, 34*(4), 776-804. © 1991 by Academy of Management. Items were taken from the appendix, pp. 803-804. Reproduced with permission of Academy of Management in the format textbook via Copyright Clearance Center.

Items   Responses are obtained on a 7-point Likert-type scale. The anchors vary and are provided with each item.

Complexity items:

1. How much technical knowledge do the jobs in this unit require?

   (Anchors are 1= *very little*, 4 = *a moderate amount*, 7 = *a great deal*)

2. To what extent do the jobs involve solving problems?

   (Anchors are 1= *very little*, 4 = *a moderate amount*, 7 = *a great deal*)

3. How complicated are the jobs in this unit?

   (Anchors are 1= *not at all*, 4 = *a moderate amount*, 7 = *very complicated*)

Variety items:

1. How much variety in tasks, clients, or things do members of your work unit generally encounter in a working day?

   (Anchors are 1= *very little*, 4 = *a moderate amount*, 7 = *a great deal*)

2. How routine is the work of members in your unit?

   (Anchors are 1= *not routine*, 4 = *moderately routine*, 7 = *very routine*) (R)

3. How much opportunity do members have in this unit to do a number of different things?

   (Anchors are 1= *very little*, 4 = *a moderate amount*, 7 = *a great deal*)

4. How similar are the tasks members perform in a typical day?

   (Anchors are 1= *very similar*, 4 = *moderately different*, 7 = *very different*)

5. People in this unit do the same job in the same way most of the time.

   (Anchors are 1 = *completely true*, 7 = *completely false*)

6. In doing their jobs from day to day, unit members generally have to adopt different methods or procedures.

   (Anchors are 1 = *completely true*, 7 = *completely false*) (R)

7. There are different types or kinds of work to do every day in this job.

   (Anchors are 1 = *completely true*, 7 = *completely false*) (R)

Interdependence items:

1. How much do people in this unit have to coordinate work with others?

   (Anchors are 1 = *very little*, 4 = *a moderate amount*, 7 = *a great deal*)

2. How often do members start work that is finished by others?

   (Anchors are 1 = *rarely*, 4 = *occasionally*, 7 = *frequently*)

3. How often do members finish work that is started by others?

   (Anchors are 1 = *rarely*, 4 = *occasionally*, 7 = *frequently*)

4. To what extent is dealing with other people part of jobs in this unit?

   (Anchors are 1= *very little*, 4 = *a moderate amount*, 7 = *a great deal*)

5. How often do individuals in this unit work by themselves?

   (Anchors are 1= *very little*, 4 = *a moderate amount*, 7 = *a great deal*)

6. How much does success in this unit depend on cooperation with other people?

    (Anchors are 1= *very little*, 4 = *a moderate amount*, 7 = *a great deal*)

7. How much do people in this unit rely on people in other units?

    (Anchors are 1= *very little*, 4 = *a moderate amount*, 7 = *a great deal*)

Job Interdependence

Description   This measure, developed by Pearce and Gregersen (1991), describes the interdependence of a job along two dimensions. The first dimension reflects reciprocal interdependence with other jobs (measured with five items). The second dimension reflects the extent to which an employee works independently of other employees to complete their tasks (measured with three items). The two subscales can also be combined into a single measure of job interdependence (Anderson & Williams, 1996).

Reliability   Coefficient alpha was .76 for interdependence and .61 for independence (Pearce & Gregersen, 1991). Coefficient alpha for the subscales combined into a single measure was .85 (Anderson & Williams, 1996).

Validity   Reciprocal interdependence correlated negatively with independence and with the cost of seeking help. Interdependence correlated positively with felt responsibility, help-seeking behavior, and quality of exchange relationship with other workers (Anderson & Williams, 1996; Pearce & Gregersen, 1991). In Anderson and Williams (1996), ratings of interdependence between pairs of co-workers were positively correlated.

Source   Pearce, J. L., & Gregersen, H. B. (1991). Task interdependence and extra-role behavior: A test of the mediating effects of felt responsibility. *Journal of Applied Psychology, 76*(6), 838-844. Items were taken from Table 1, p. 841. Copyright © 1991 by the American Psychological Association. Reprinted with permission.

Items   Response are obtained using a Likert-type scale where 1 = *strongly disagree* and 5 = *strongly agree.*

Interdependence items:

1. I work closely with others in doing my work
2. I frequently must coordinate my efforts with others
3. My own performance is dependent on receiving accurate information from others
4. The way I perform my job has a significant impact on others
5. My work requires me to consult with others fairly frequently

Independence items:

6. I work fairly independently of others in my work
7. I can plan my own work with little need to coordinate with others
8. I rarely have to obtain information from others to complete my work

Extent of Computer Use

Description   This measure, developed by Medcof (1996), describes the proportion of the workday spent in computer activities. It also measures the percentage of time that an employee spends engaged in computer tasks that are high, medium, and low in cognitive demands.

Reliability   In Medcof (1996), coefficient alpha was .77.

Validity   For low cognitive demand computer-related activities (data entry, data read, read and change data), extent of computer use was positively related to skill variety and autonomy measured by the Job Diagnostic Survey (JDS). For high cognitive demand tasks (end user programming and professional system use), extent of computer use was related to skill variety. For medium cognitive demand computer activities (word processing and data analysis using systems such as Lotus 1-2-3), extent of use was not related to the JDS job dimensions.

Source   Medcof, J. W. (1996). The job characteristics of computing and non-computing work activities. *Journal of Occupational and Organizational Psychology*, *69*, 199-212. Items were taken from text, pp. 203-204. Copyright © 1996. Reproduced with permission.

Items   Extent of computer use items:

The measures uses four questions:

1. On a typical working day how many hours do you spend seated at and using the computer?
2. On a typical working day, how many hours do you spend at work?

   The response to the first questions is divided by the response to the second and the quotient multiplied by 100 to provide a percentage of the day at the computer.

3. On a typical working day what percentage of your work time do you spend seated at and using the computer?
4. How would you describe the degree to which you use the computer to carry out your job functions?

   Responses to question 4 are obtained using a 5-point Likert-type scale where 1 = *rarely* and 5 = *always*.

   The response to question 4 is multiplied by 20 and averaged with the percentages obtained from questions 1, 2, and 3.

Type of computer use items:

In a single question, respondents are given a list of various types of computer use and asked to indicate what percentage of their time spent on the computer they did each. The list of types of computer use is as follows: data entry, data read, read and change data, word processing, data analysis using systems such as Lotus 1-2-3 and D-base III, end-user programming, professional system use, and other. The percentages for the first three categories (data entry, data read, read and change data) were summed to give the percentage of computer time spent at uses with low cognitive demands. The percentages for word processing and data analysis using systems such as Lotus 1-2-3 and D-base III were summed to give the percentage of computer time spent at uses with medium cognitive demands. The percentages for end-user programming and professional systems use were summed to give the percentage of computer time spent at uses with high cognitive demands.

Supportive and Non-Controlling Supervision

Description   This measure, developed by Oldham and Cummings (1996), uses 12 items to describe employee perceptions of the extent to which they receive supervisory support (eight items) and are subject to a non-controlling supervisory approach (four items). When supervisors are supportive, they show concern for employees' feelings and needs; encourage them to voice their own concerns; provide positive, chiefly informational feedback; and facilitate employee skill development (Deci, Connell, & Ryan, 1989). When supervisors are controlling, they closely monitor employee behavior; make decisions without employee involvement; provide feedback in a controlling manner; and generally pressure employees to think, feel, or behave in prescribed ways (Oldham & Cummings, 1996).

Reliability   Coefficient alpha for supportive supervision was .86. Alpha for non-controlling supervision was .67 (Oldham & Cummings, 1996).

Validity   Exploratory factor analysis of the 12 items found two factors. The first factor was composed of the eight items that reflected supportive supervision. The second factor was composed of the remaining four items and reflected non-controlling supervision (Oldham & Cummings, 1996). Non-controlling supervision correlated positively with job complexity, employee creativity, and employee performance ratings. Supportive supervision correlated positively with job complexity, non-controlling supervision, and employee performance ratings. Supportive supervision correlated negatively with intentions to quit (Oldham & Cummings, 1996).

Source   Oldham, G. R., & Cummings, A. (1996). Employee creativity: Personal and contextual factors at work. *Academy of Management Journal, 39*(3), 607-634. © 1996 by Academy of Management. Items were taken from the appendix, p. 634. Reproduced with permission of Academy of Management in the format textbook via Copyright Clearance Center.

Items   Responses are obtained using a 7-point Likert-type scale where 1 = *strongly disagree* and 7 = *strongly agree*.

Supportive supervision items:

1. My supervisor helps me solve work-related problems
2. My supervisor encourages me to develop new skills
3. My supervisor keeps informed about how employees think and feel about things
4. My supervisor encourages employees to participate in important decisions
5. My supervisor praises good work

6. My supervisor encourages employees to speak up when they disagree with a decision
7. My supervisor refuses to explain his or her actions (R)
8. My supervisor rewards me for good performance

Non-controlling supervision items:

1. My supervisor always seems to be around checking on my work (R)
2. My supervisor tells me what shall be done and how it shall be done (R)
3. My supervisor never gives me a chance to make important decisions on my own (R)
4. My supervisor leaves it up to me to decide how to go about doing my job

Items denoted with (R) are reverse scored.

Supervisory Support

Description   This measure was developed by Greenhaus, Parasuraman, and Wormley (1990) to assess employee perceptions of the extent to which they receive supervisory support in their job. In general, supervisory support may include career guidance, performance feedback, challenging work assignments, and work opportunities that promote employee development and visibility.

Reliability   Coefficient alpha was .93 (Greenhaus et al., 1990).

Validity   In Greenhaus et al. (1990), supervisory support correlated positively with perceptions of acceptance, job discretion, job performance in terms of both tasks and relationships, employee promotability, and career satisfaction.

Source   Greenhaus, J. H., Parasuraman, A., & Wormley, W. M. (1990). Effects of race on organizational experiences, job performance evaluations, and career outcomes. *Academy of Management Journal, 33*(1), 64-86. © 1990 by Academy of Management. Items were taken from the appendix, pp. 85-86. Reproduced with permission of Academy of Management in the format textbook via Copyright Clearance Center.

Items   Responses are obtained using a 5-point Likert-type scale where 5 = *strongly disagree*, 4 = *disagree to some extent*, 3 = *uncertain*, 2 = *agree to some extent*, and 1 = *strongly agree*.

1. My supervisor takes the time to learn about my career goals and aspirations
2. My supervisor cares about whether or not I achieve my goals
3. My supervisor keeps me informed about different career opportunities for me in the organization
4. My supervisor makes sure I get the credit when I accomplish something substantial on the job
5. My supervisor gives me helpful feedback about my performance
6. My supervisor gives me helpful advice about improving my performance when I need it
7. My supervisor supports my attempts to acquire additional training or education to further my career
8. My supervisor provides assignments that give me the opportunity to develop and strengthen new skills
9. My supervisor assigns me special projects that increase my visibility in the organization

Developmental Experiences

Description   This measure, developed by Wayne, Shore, and Liden (1997), describes the formal and informal developmental experiences a job affords employees. The measure focuses on the extent to which an organization makes discretionary investments in formal and informal training and development of an employee.

Reliability   Coefficient alpha was .87 (Wayne, Shore, & Liden, 1997).

Validity   In a factor analysis of the items used to measure developmental experiences, perceived organizational support, leader-member exchange (LMX), affective commitment, intentions to quit, and employee favor-doing, the four items measuring development experiences loaded on a single factor by themselves. Development experiences were correlated positively with the number of promotions an employee has received, perceived organizational support, affective commitment to the organization, and organizational citizenship behavior (Wayne, Shore, & Liden, 1997).

Source   Wayne, S. J., Shore, L. M., & Liden, R. C. (1997). Perceived organizational support and leader-member exchange: A social exchange perspective. *Academy of Management Journal, 40*(1), 82-111. © 1997 by Academy of Management. Items were taken from text, p. 93. Reproduced with permission of Academy of Management in the format textbook via Copyright Clearance Center.

Items   Responses for items 1 and 2 are obtained on a 7-point Likert-type scale where 1 = *strongly disagree* and 7 = *strongly agree*. Responses for items 3 and 4 are obtained on a 7-point scale where 1 = *not at all* and 7 = *a very large extent*.

1. In the positions that I have held at [company name], I have often been given additional challenging assignments.
2. In the positions that I have held at [company name], I have often been assigned projects that have enabled me to develop and strengthen new skills.
3. Besides formal training and development opportunities, to what extent have your managers helped to develop your skills by providing you with challenging job assignments?
4. Regardless of [company's name]'s policy on training and development, to what extent have your managers made a substantial investment in you by providing formal training and development opportunities?

Performance Appraisal System Knowledge

Description   This measure, developed by Williams and Levy (1992), describes the extent to which employees perceive they understand important aspects of the performance appraisal system related to their job. Performance appraisal system knowledge has been found to explain the extent of agreement between employee and supervisor ratings of work performance.

Reliability   Coefficient alpha values ranged from .85 to .89 (Kacmar & Ferris, 1991; Levy & Williams, 1998).

Validity   In Levy and Williams (1998), performance appraisal system knowledge correlated positively with job satisfaction, organizational commitment, and perceptions of fairness.

Source   Williams, J. R., & Levy, P. E. (1992). The effects of perceived system knowledge on the agreement between self-ratings and supervisor ratings. *Personnel Psychology, 45*, 835-847. Items were taken from Table 1, p. 841. Copyright © 1992. Reproduced with permission.

Items   Responses are obtained using a 7-point Likert-type scale where 1 = *strongly disagree* and 7 = *strongly agree*.

1. I understand the performance appraisal system being used in my agency
2. My supervisor and I concur on the meaning of the criteria used in the performance appraisal system
3. I understand the objectives of the present performance appraisal system
4. I have a real understanding of how the performance appraisal system works
5. I do not understand how my last performance appraisal rating was determined (R)
6. I know the criteria used by my employer to evaluate my performance
7. I understand the standards of performance my employer expects
8. My employer clearly communicates to me the objectives of the performance appraisal system
9. I would benefit from additional training in the process of the appraisal system (R)
10. Procedures regarding the performance appraisal system are not generally understood by the employees (R)
11. An attempt should be made to increase employees' understanding of the performance appraisal system (R)

Items denoted with (R) are reverse scored.

Work-Related Expectancies

Description   This measure was developed by Eisenberger, Fasolo, and Davis-LaMastro (1990) to describe the extent to which employees believe that higher levels of job performance will be rewarded. The measure assesses employee expectancies about the relationship of better performance with increased pay, promotions, and job security. It also assesses employee expectancies that better performance will lead to increased influence, supervisory approval, and recognition.

Reliability   Coefficient alpha values for the subscales for pay/promotion reward expectancies and approval/recognition expectancies ranged between .77 and .89 (Eisenberger et al., 1990; Smith & Brannick, 1990).

Validity   Factor analysis of the nine items found two factors for work-related expectancies. One dimension captures expectancies about pay and promotion rewards. The other dimension describes expectancies about approval and recognition. The two factors were consistent across samples of hourly workers and managers (Eisenberger et al., 1990). Expectancies for pay/promotion rewards and approval/recognition/influence both correlated positively with perceived organizational support, job satisfaction, participation in decisions, and job involvement. Expectancies for rewards and influence both correlated negatively with role conflict and ambiguity (Eisenberger et al., 1990; Smith & Brannick, 1990).

Source   Eisenberger, R., Fasolo, P., & Davis-LaMastro, V. (1990). Perceived organizational support and employee diligence, commitment, and innovation. *Journal of Applied Psychology, 75*(1), 51-59. Items were taken from Table 2, p. 56. Copyright © 1990 by the American Psychological Association. Reprinted with permission.

Items   Responses are obtained on a 5-point Likert-type scale where 1 = *definitely not part of my job* and 5 = *extremely true of my job*.

Pay/promotion expectancy items:

1. It is more likely that I will be given a pay raise or promotion at [company name] if I finish a large amount of work
2. It is more likely that I will be given a pay raise or promotion at [company name] if I do high-quality work
3. Getting work done quickly at [company name] increases my chances for a pay raise or promotion
4. Getting work done on time is rewarded with high pay at [company name]

Approval/recognition/influence expectancy items:

1. Completing my work on time gets me greater approval from my immediate supervisor at [company name]
2. My immediate supervisor at [company name] gives me more recognition when I get a lot of work done
3. If I get my job done on time, I have more influence with my immediate supervisor at [company name]
4. My immediate supervisor at [company name] pays added attention to the opinions of the best workers
5. When I finish my job on time, my job is more secure at [company name]

Empowerment at Work Scale

Description   This measure, developed by Spreitzer (1995), describes the extent to which employees believe they are empowered in their jobs. Empowerment has been defined as the intrinsic motivation resulting from four cognitions reflecting an individual's orientation to his or her work role. The four cognitions are meaning, competence, self-determination, and impact (Spreitzer, 1995). Meaning involves a fit between the requirements of a work role and a person's beliefs, values, and behaviors. Competence refers to self-efficacy specific to work, a belief in one's capability to perform work activities with skill, analogous to personal mastery. Self-determination reflects autonomy over the initiation and continuation of work processes and making decisions about work methods, pace, and effort. Impact is the degree to which a person can influence strategic, administrative, or operating outcomes at work.

Reliability   Coefficient alpha values ranged from .81 to. 87 for meaning, 76 to .84 for competence, .79 to .85 for self-determination, and .83 to .88 for impact. Alpha for a combined scale for overall empowerment was .72 in an industrial sample and .62 in an insurance sample (Gagne et al., 1997; Markel & Frone, 1998; Spreitzer, 1995, 1996; Spreitzer, Kizilos, & Nason, 1997).

Validity   A factor analysis showed that the 12 items all loaded on four factors corresponding to the dimensions of meaning, competence, self-determination, and impact (Gagne et al., 1997). In Spreitzer (1995), confirmatory factor analysis showed the items loaded on the appropriate subscales and found evidence for an underlying second-order factor of overall empowerment. In Kraimer, Seibert, and Liden (1999), confirmatory factor analysis in two samples collected at different points in time showed that the four empowerment dimensions were distinct from one another.

The meaning, competence, self-determination, and impact dimensions all correlated positively with job satisfaction (Spreitzer et al., 1997). In addition, all of the dimensions except meaning correlated negatively with strain and positively with self-reported job effectiveness. Additional analysis in Spreitzer (1995) showed that self-esteem and information about an organization's mission were both antecedents of empowerment. In addition, both perceived managerial effectiveness and innovative behaviors were consequences of empowerment. Using structural equation models, Kraimer et al. (1999) found that job meaningfulness was related positively with meaning, job autonomy was related positively with self-determination, and task feedback related positively with competence and impact. Both meaning and competence were related positively with career intentions and impact was related directly with organizational commitment.

Source   Spreitzer, G. M. (1995). Psychological empowerment in the workplace: Dimensions, measurement, and validation. *Academy of Management Journal, 38*(5), 1442-1465. © 1995 by Academy of Management. Items were taken from the appendix, pp. 1464-1465. Reproduced with permission of Academy of Management in the format textbook via Copyright Clearance Center.

Items   Responses are obtained on a 7-point Likert-type scale where 1 = *strongly disagree* and 7 = *strongly agree*.

Meaning items:

1. The work I do is very important to me
2. My job activities are personally meaningful to me
3. The work I do is meaningful to me

Competence items:

1. I am confident about my ability to do my job
2. I am self-assured about my capabilities to perform my work activities
3. I have mastered the skills necessary for my job

Self-determination items:

1. I have significant autonomy in determining how I do my job
2. I can decide on my own how to go about doing my work
3. I have considerable opportunity for independence and freedom in how I do my job

Impact items:

1. My impact on what happens in my department is large
2. I have a great deal of control over what happens in my department
3. I have significant influence over what happens in my department

Social Support

Description   This measure, developed by Caplan et al. (1975), includes subscales that describe the support an employee perceives is available from his or her co-workers, supervisor, spouse, and family/friends. It describes the extent to which these three sources go out of their way to help an employee, are easy to talk to, can be relied on when things get tough on the job, and are willing to listen to an employee's personal problems. These types of support have been characterized as emotional (easy to talk to and willing to listen to personal problems) and instrumental (make things easier and can be relied on). This measure has been widely used and has remained one of the most established scales used to measure social support in a job (Lim, 1996).

Reliability   Coefficient alpha for the supervisor support subscale ranged from .86 to .91 (Lee & Ashforth, 1993; Repeti & Cosmas, 1991;). Alpha for co-worker support was .79 (Repeti & Cosmas, 1991). Lim (1996) combined respondents' scores on the supervisor and co-workers support subscales into a measure of work-based support. This eight-item scale had a coefficient alpha of .80.

Validity   Supervisor and co-worker support correlated positively with overall job satisfaction and work group cohesiveness (Repeti & Cosmas, 1991). Lim (1996) found that work-based support correlated negatively with job insecurity, job dissatisfaction, and noncompliant job behaviors. Scheck, Kinicki, and Davy (1995) found through confirmatory factor analysis that combining the measures of instrumental and emotional social support into a single measure fit the data best.

Source   Caplan, R. D., Cobb, S., French, J. R. P., Van Harrison, R., & Pinneau. S. R. (1980). *Job demands and worker health.* Ann Arbor: University of Michigan, Institute of Social Research. Items were taken from text, pp. 251-252. Copyright © 1980. Reproduced with permission.

Items   Responses are obtained on a 5-point Likert-type scale where 4 = *very much*, 3 = *somewhat*, 2 = *a little*, 1 = *not at all*, and 0 = *don't have any such person.*

1. How much does each of these people go out of their way to do things to make your work life easier for you?

   A. Your immediate supervisor
   B. Other people at work.
   C. Your wife [husband], friends and relatives

2. How easy is it to talk with each of the following people?

   A. Your immediate supervisor
   B. Other people at work
   C. Your wife [husband], friends and relatives

3. How much can each of these people be relied on when things get tough at work?

    A. Your immediate supervisor (boss)
    B. Other people at work
    C. Your wife [husband], friends and relatives

4. How much is each of the following people willing to listen to your personal problems?

    A. Your immediate supervisor
    B. Other people at work
    C. Your wife [husband], friends and relatives

The items labeled A (1A, 2A, 3A, 4A) constitute the Social Support from Supervisor Index. Similarly, the items labeled B and C constitute the Social Support from Others at Work Index and the Social Support from Wife, Friends and Relatives Index.

Perceived Organizational Support

Description   This measure, developed by Eisenberger et al. (1986), describes employee perceptions about the extent to which an organization is willing to reward greater efforts by the employee because the organization values the employee's contribution and cares about his or her well-being. The measure includes eight items that measure an employee's perceptions of the degree to which the organization values the worker's contributions and nine items about actions that the organization might take that would affect the well-being of the employee. Some studies have used an abbreviated version consisting of the nine items with the highest factor loadings in the original scale development study (Moorman, Blakely, & Niehoff, 1998; Wayne, Shore, & Liden, 1997).

Reliability   Coefficient alpha values ranged from .74 to .95 (Cropanzano, Howes, Grandey, & Toth, 1997; Eisenberger, Cummings, Armeli, & Lynch, 1997; Eisenberger et al., 1990; Hutchinson, Valentino, & Kirkner, 1998; Lee & Ashforth, 1993; Lynch, Eisenberger, & Armeli, 1999; Moorman et al., 1998; Wayne, Shore, & Liden, 1997).

Validity   Perceived organizational support correlated positively with overall job satisfaction, organizational commitment, direct and indirect control at work, job discretion, interpersonal helping, affective attachment to the organization, pay/promotion expectancies, approval/recognition expectancies, and employee performance ratings (Cropanzano et al., 1997; Eisenberger et al., 1997; Eisenberger et al., 1990; Hutchinson et al., 1998; Lee & Ashforth, 1993; Moorman et al., 1998). Perceived organizational support correlated negatively with perceived organizational politics, turnover intentions, days absent, role stress, and emotional exhaustion (Cropanzano et al., 1997; Eisenberger et al., 1990; Lee & Ashforth, 1993).

     Wayne, Shore, and Liden (1997) found through factor analysis that perceived organizational support was empirically distinct from developmental experiences, leader-member exchange (LMX), affective commitment, and intentions to quit. Eisenberger et al. (1997) found through confirmatory factor analysis that perceived organizational support and overall job satisfaction were empirically distinct.

Source   Eisenberger, R., Huntington, R., Hutchinson, S., & Sowa, D. (1986). Perceived organizational support. *Journal of Applied Psychology, 71*, 500-507. Items were taken from Table 1, p. 502. Copyright © 1986 by the American Psychological Association. Reprinted with permission.

Items   Responses are obtained on a 7-point Likert-type scale where 1 = *strongly disagree* and 7 = *strongly agree*.

Instructions:

Listed below is a series of statements that represent possible feelings that individuals might have about the company or organization for which they work. With respect to your own feelings about the particular organization for which you are now working—[name of organization]—please indicate the degree of your agreement or disagreement with each statement by checking one of the seven alternatives below each statement.

Items denoted with (S) are used in the shortened nine-item version of the measure. Items denoted with (R) are reverse scored.

1.   The organization values my contribution to its well-being
2.   If the organization could hire someone to replace me at a lower salary it would do so (R)
3.   The organization fails to appreciate any extra effort from me (R)
4.   The organization strongly considers my goals and values (S)
5.   The organization would ignore any complaint from me (R)
6.   The organization disregards my best interests when it makes decisions that affect me (R)
7.   Help is available from the organization when I have a problem (S)
8.   The organization really cares about my well-being (S)
9.   The organization is willing to extend itself in order to help me perform my job to the best of my ability (S)
10. Even if I did the best job possible, the organization would fail to notice (R) (S)
11. The organization is willing to help me when I need a special favor
12. The organization cares about my general satisfaction at work (S)
13. If given the opportunity, the organization would take advantage of me (R)
14. The organization shows very little concern for me (R) (S)
15. The organization cares about my opinions (S)
16. The organization takes pride in my accomplishments at work (S)
17. The organization tries to make my job as interesting as possible

Perceptions of Organizational Politics Scale

Description   The Perceptions of Organizational Politics Scale (POPS), developed by Kacmar and Ferris (1991), assesses employee perceptions of the extent to which a job setting is political in nature including politics in the organization, behavior of supervisors, and actions of co-workers. Twelve items are used in the measure to describe general political behavior, political behavior to "get ahead," and ambiguity in pay and promotion policies and rules.

Reliability   Coefficient alpha values ranged from .87 to .91 (Cropanzano et al., 1997; Kacmar, 1999; Kacmar & Ferris, 1991).

Validity   Perceived organizational politics correlated negatively with perceived organizational support, job satisfaction, and job involvement. Perceived organizational politics correlated positively with turnover intentions (Cropanzano et al., 1997; Kacmar, 1999; Kacmar & Ferris, 1991).

Kacmar and Ferris (1991) factor analyzed the POPS items with the items of the Job Descriptive Index (JDI). The politics items loaded on a single factor separate from the JDI items.

Source   Kacmar, K. M., & Ferris, G. R. (1991). Perceptions of Organizational Politics Scale (POPS): Development and construct validation. *Educational and Psychological Measurement, 51,* 193-205. Copyright © 1991 by Sage Publications, Inc. Items were taken from Table 3, p. 203. Reprinted by permission of Sage Publications, Inc.

Items   Responses are obtained using a 5-point Likert-type scale where 1 = *strongly disagree* and 5 = *strongly agree.*

General political behavior items:

1. One group always gets their way
2. Influential group no one crosses
3. Policy changes help only a few
4. Build themselves up by tearing others down
5. Favoritism not merit gets people ahead
6. Don't speak up for fear of retaliation

Get ahead items:

1. Promotions go to top performers (R)
2. Rewards come to hard workers (R)
3. Encouraged to speak out (R)
4. No place for yes men (R)

Pay and promotion policies items:

1. Pay and promotion policies are not politically applied
2. Pay and promotion decisions are consistent with policies

Items denoted with (R) are reverse scored.

4

Job Stress

The Construct

In general, the study of job stress has focused on the belief that prolonged exposure to stressful conditions within a job leads to mental and/or physical disorders (Ganster & Schaubroeck, 1991). In terms of defining stress, difficulties can arise because operational definitions may fail to reflect the transactional nature of the stress process. That is, stress does not reside solely in the environment or solely in the individual but is established when the interactions between the two are appraised as demanding enough to threaten well-being (Dewe, 1992).

Two models have been frequently used to describe the process by which aspects of a job and its environment lead to worker stress and strain. One model focuses on the fit between the stressors, such as demands and requirements of the job, and an employee's coping resources, such as his or her skills, abilities, and needs/preferences (Ganster & Schaubroeck, 1991). Job stressors are defined as those aspects of a job that produce excessive and undesirable constraints or demands on the individual (Scheck, Kinicki, & Davy, 1995). A positive or negative appraisal of a stressor affects the outcomes to the employee differently (Scheck et al., 1995).

The second model is known as the job demands-control perspective (Karasek, 1979). This model suggests that when the psychological demands of a job are high and control over the job is low, health status and well-being are lowered. However, when both demands and control are high, an individual will experience an increased motivation to perform. A major hypothesis of this model is that high job demands produce a state of physical arousal in a worker that would normally be channeled into coping responses such as altering the schedule of work or changing procedures. If a worker is not allowed sufficient control to implement stress-reducing changes, the physical and mental impacts of job demands are increased. To a degree, this model predicts that some job conditions may buffer the negative effects of other job dimensions of employees. For example, larger amounts of control at work may buffer the effects of very high job demands (Daniels & Guppy, 1994).

Both models indicate that some variables such as social support from an employee's supervisor and co-workers may reduce the effects of stressors on well-being. Social support is defined as a flow of communication between people involving emotional concern, caring, information, as well as instrumental help (Viswesvaran, Sanchez, & Fisher, 1999). In essence, social support may provide resources that lessen the impact of job stressors.

A general presumption of the occupational stress literature is that personal work stress and strain ultimately lead to failing individual health and illness. Some empirical support exists for this relationship (Manning, Jackson, & Fusilier, 1996). Ganster and Schaubroeck (1991) conducted a review of work stress and employee health and concluded that strong indirect evidence exists that stress causes illness.

The Measures

Stress measurement has been criticized for having too much focus on identification and classification of job and work characteristics that may act on and affect the individual. Social structures and perceptions that give meaning to such characteristics are rarely integrated into measurement. As a result, various situations have been identified as being intrinsically stressful (Dewe, 1992). However, this approach may oversimplify stressor measurement because the perceived presence of a stressor is not necessarily a condition for stress (Duckworth, 1986). The meaning individuals give to events may be missing. It is difficult for existing measures to capture the appraisal process through which individuals give meaning to events

and evaluate coping alternatives (Dewe, 1992). The result has been one group of job stress measures that focuses on outcomes of the appraisal process and a second group of measures that focuses on antecedents of the appraisal process.

The first group of measures assesses employee perceived outcomes such as tension, frustration, burnout, anxiety, and depression. The second group of measures assesses the presence of stressors, through inventories that cover aspects of jobs and work environments such as role conflict, role ambiguity, job overload, lack of control, job responsibility pressures, and conflict between work and nonwork responsibilities. Rush, Schoel, and Barnard (1985) have noted that the feelings expressed about the presence of stressors most likely reflect an individual employee's sensitivity to the conditions and events presented by the stressors. In presenting validated measures in this chapter, I first provide information about measures that focus on employee outcomes, such as burnout and frustration. These are followed by measures that inventory various types of work stressors and those that assess the presence of a single type of job stressor. I intended to include the Maslach Burnout Inventory in this chapter. It is a widely used measure of employee burnout. However, the copyright holder refused permission to reprint the items comprising the measure, and therefore it is excluded from this book.

Work Tension Scale

Description   This measure, developed by House and Rizzo (1972), describes an employee's psychological or psychosomatic symptoms associated with tension experienced at work. It includes the extent to which tension from work tends to keep employees awake at night and be constantly on an employee's mind.

Reliability   Coefficient alpha values ranged from .71 to .89 (Bunce & West, 1996; Cropanzano, Howes, Grandey, & Toth, 1997; Grandey & Cropanzano, 1998; Kacmar, 1999; Netemeyer, Johnston, & Burton, 1990; Sanchez & Brock, 1996).

Validity   Job tension correlated positively with work role ambiguity, work role conflict, work role stress, family role stress, work-family conflict, family distress, turnover intentions, and poor physical health (Grandey & Cropanzano, 1998; Netemeyer et al., 1990; Sanchez & Brock, 1996). Job tension correlated negatively with organizational commitment, job satisfaction, age, and self-esteem (Grandey & Cropanzano, 1998; Netemeyer et al., 1990; Sanchez & Brock, 1996).

Source   Cook, J. D., Hepworth, S. J., Wall, T. D., & Warr, P. B. (1981) *The experience of work: A compendium of 249 measures and their use.* London: Academic Press. Items were taken from text, p. 104. Copyright © 1981 by Academic Press. Reproduced with permission.

Items   Responses are obtained as true, coded 2, or false, coded 1.

1. My job tends to directly affect my health
2. I work under a great deal of tensions
3. I have felt fidgety or nervous as a result of my job
4. If I had a different job, my health would probably improve
5. Problems associated with my job have kept me awake at night
6. I have felt nervous before attending meetings in the company
7. I often "take my job home with me" in the sense that I think about it when doing other things

Job-Related Tension Index

Description   This measure was developed by Kahn, Wolfe, Quinn, and Snoek (1964). It describes employee perceptions of job stress using 15 items asking about the frequency of stressful occurrences and the extent of role overload. This measure assesses psychological symptoms of stress, such as feelings of having too much work, not having the means and materials to accomplish assignments or projects, and generally being unable to handle all of the work. In some studies, the items have been used to form subscales for role ambiguity, role overload, and resource inadequacy (Jamal, 1990; Shirom & Mayer, 1993).

Reliability   Coefficient alpha values ranged from .80 to .89 (Abraham & Hansson, 1996; Bennett, Lehman, & Forst, 1999; Duxbury & Higgins, 1991; Iverson, 1997; Rush et al., 1985; Seibert, 1999). Coefficient alpha values for the subscales were .76 for role ambiguity and .74 for resource inadequacy and ranged from .65 to .82 for role overload (Jamal, 1990; Shirom & Mayer, 1993).

Validity   Job-related tension correlated positively with control problems at work, work involvement, work expectations, lack of psychosocial support from a mentor, and family expectations (Abraham & Hansson, 1996; Duxbury & Higgins, 1991; Seibert, 1999). Job tension correlated negatively with quality of work life, job satisfaction, goal attainment, organizational commitment, self-esteem at work, quality of family life, and life satisfaction (Abraham & Hansson, 1996; Duxbury & Higgins, 1991; Seibert, 1999). In Jamal (1990), the job tension subscales for role ambiguity, role overload, and resource inadequacy all correlated positively with psychosomatic problems. All the subscales except role overload correlated negatively with job satisfaction. In Shirom and Mayer (1993), role overload correlated positively with parent-teacher conflict, teacher-principal conflict, and work-home conflict.

Source   Kahn, R. L., Wolfe, D. M., Quinn, R. P., & Snoek, J. D. (with Rosenthal, R. A.). (1964). *Organizational stress: Studies in role conflict and ambiguity.* New York: John Wiley. Items were taken from pp. 424-425. Reproduced with permission of the author.

Items   Response options are 1 = *never*, 2 = *rarely*, 3 = *sometimes*, 4 = *rather often*, and 5 = *nearly all the time*. It is optional to use "doesn't apply" and this response is coded with score of 0.

Items and instructions:

All of us occasionally feel bothered by certain kinds of things in our work. How frequently do you feel bothered by each of these?

1. Feeling that you have too little authority to carry out the responsibilities assigned to you
2. Being unclear on just what the scope and responsibilities of your job are
3. Not knowing what opportunities for advancement or promotion exist for you
4. Feeling that you have too heavy a work load, one that you can't possibly finish during an ordinary workday
5. Thinking that you'll not be able to satisfy the conflicting demands of various people over you
6. Feeling that you're not fully qualified to handle your job
7. Not knowing what your supervisor thinks of you, how he [she] evaluates your performance
8. The fact that you can't get information needed to carry out your job
9. Having to decide things that affect the lives of individuals, people that you know
10. Feeling that you may not be liked and accepted by the people you work with
11. Feeling unable to influence your immediate supervisor's decisions and actions that affect you
12. Not knowing just what the people you work with expect of you
13. Thinking that the amount of work you have to do may interfere with how well it gets done
14. Feeling that you have to do things on the job that are against your better judgment
15. Feeling that your job tends to interfere with your family life

Burnout Measure

Description   This measure, developed by Pines and Aronson (1988), assesses physical and emotional states by asking respondents to rate how frequently they experience 21 stress-related occurrences. The Burnout Measure focuses on exhaustion, shown to be a central aspect of burnout. The Burnout Measure is considered the second most widely used burnout measure after the Maslach Burnout Inventory (MBI; Etzion, Eden, & Lapidot, 1998). It is considered the better of the two measures for use outside the human service professions, because the MBI focuses on burnout of professionals who work with people (Westman & Eden, 1997). The Burnout Measure has also been translated into Hebrew (Etzion et al., 1998).

Reliability   Coefficient alpha values ranged from .88 to .95 (Cropanzano et al., 1997; Etzion et al., 1998; Melamed, Kushnir, & Meir, 1991; Schaufeli & Van Dierendonck, 1993; Westman & Eden, 1997).

Validity   The Burnout Measure correlated negatively with job satisfaction, perceived control at work, and social support. Burnout correlated positively with job demands and the presence of job stressors (Etzion et al., 1998; Melamed et al., 1991). Westman and Eden (1997) factor analyzed the Burnout Measure and found that it is unidimensional. Confirmatory factor analysis showed that the Burnout Measure measures the affective nature of burnout, which is often expressed as exhaustion (Schaufeli & Van Dierendonck, 1993).

Source   Pines, A., & Aronson, E. (1988) *Career burnout: Causes and cures.* New York: Free Press. Copyright © 1988 by Ayala M. Pines and Elliot Aronson. Items from text (p. 219) were adapted with the permission of The Free Press, a Division of Simon & Schuster, Inc.

Items   Responses are obtained on a 7-point Likert-type scale where 1 = *never*, 2 = *once in a great while*, 3 = *rarely*, 4 = *sometimes*, 5 = *often*, 6 = *usually*, and 7 = *always*.

1. Being tired
2. Feeling depressed
3. Having a good day
4. Being physically exhausted
5. Being emotionallyexhausted
6. Being happy
7. Being "wiped out"
8. "Can't take it anymore"
9. Being unhappy
10. Feeling run-down
11. Feeling trapped
12. Feeling worthless
13. Being weary
14. Being troubled
15. Feeling disillusioned and resentful
16. Being weak and susceptible to illness
17. Feeling hopeless
18. Feeling rejected
19. Feeling optimistic
20. Feeling energetic
21. Feeling anxious

Work-Related Depression, Anxiety, and Irritation

Description   This measure, developed by Caplan, Cobb, French, Van Harrison, and Pinneau (1980), assesses three dimensions of employee stress and strain. These include the extent to which employees felt depressed (unhappy, sad, blue), anxious (nervous, jittery), and irritated (annoyed, angry) while working in their job.

Reliability   Coefficient alpha values ranged from .81 to .86 (Begley & Czajka, 1993; Jalajas, 1994).

Validity   Work-related depression correlated negatively with being married, organizational commitment, and job satisfaction. Work-related depression correlated positively with intentions to quit (Begley & Czajka, 1993). Jalajas (1994) factor analyzed the items and found that the subscales for depression and anxiety were empirically distinct.

Source   Caplan, R. D., Cobb, S., French, J. R. P., Van Harrison, R., & Pinneau, S. R. (1980). *Job demands and worker health.* Ann Arbor: University of Michigan, Institute for Social Research. Items were taken from text, p. 274. Copyright © 1980. Reproduced with permission.

Items   Responses are obtained on a 4-point response scale where 1 = *never or a little of the time*, 2 = *some of the time*, 3 = *a good part of the time*, and 4 = *most of the time*.

Depression items:

1. I feel sad
2. I feel unhappy
3. I feel good (R)
4. I feel depressed
5. I feel blue
6. I feel cheerful (R)

Anxiety items:

7. I feel nervous
8. I feel jittery
9. I feel calm (R)
10. I feel fidgety

Irritation items:

11. I get angry
12. I get aggravated
13. I get irritated or annoyed

Items denoted with (R) are reverse scored.

Frustration With Work

Description   This measure, developed by Peters, O'Connor, and Rudolf (1980), uses three items to assess the extent to which employees find their job frustrating.

Reliability   Coefficient alpha values ranged from .67 to .84 (Fortunato, Jex, & Heinish, 1999; Jex, 1999; Jex, Beehr, & Roberts, 1992; Jex & Gudanowski, 1992; Spector & O'Connell, 1994).

Validity   Job frustration correlated positively with work anxiety, role conflict, role ambiguity, workload, situational constraints, anxiety, conflict at work, perceived workload, interpersonal conflict, and intent to quit. Job frustration correlated negatively with job satisfaction (Jex & Gudanowski, 1992; Spector & O'Connell, 1994; Jex et al., 1992).

Source   Peters, L. H., O'Connor, E. J., & Rudolf, C. J. (1980). The behavioral and affective consequences of performance-relevant situational variables. *Organizational Behavior and Human Performance, 25,* 79-96. Copyright © 1980 by Academic Press. Items were taken from text, p. 88. Reproduced with permission.

Items   Responses are obtained on a 7-point Likert-type scale where 1 = *strongly disagree* and 7 = *strongly agree.*

Items:

1. Trying to get this job done was a very frustrating experience
2. Being frustrated comes with this job
3. Overall, I experienced very little frustration on this job (R)

Items denoted with (R) are reverse scored.

Stress Diagnostic Survey

Description This measure, developed by Ivancevich and Matteson (1980), describes employee tension due to role ambiguity (five items), role conflict (five items), quantitative role overload (five items), qualitative role overload (five items), concerns about career development (five items), and responsibility for people (five items). The measure can also be used as a composite indicator of the presence of job stressors (Nelson & Sutton, 1990).

Reliability Coefficient alpha values for the six subscales for role ambiguity, role conflict, quantitative overload, qualitative overload, concerns about career development, and responsibility for people ranged from .68 to .85 (Deluga, 1991; Rush et al., 1985). Coefficient alpha for the composite stress survey was .93 (Nelson & Sutton, 1990).

Validity Job tension correlated positively with pressure for change, "hard" upward-influence strategies by subordinates, and intention to quit. Job tension correlated negatively with job satisfaction, job involvement, and job challenge (Deluga, 1991; Rush et al., 1985). The composite measure correlated negatively with employee job mastery and positively with concurrent and future period distress symptoms (Nelson & Sutton, 1990).

Source Ivancevich, J., & Matteson, M. (1980). *Stress and work: A managerial perspective.* Glenview, IL: Scott, Foresman. Items were taken from text, pp. 118-120. Reprinted with permission.

Items Instructions and items:

The following questionnaire is designed to provide you with an indication of the extent to which various individual-level stressors are sources of stress to you. For each item you should indicate the frequency with which the condition described is a source of stress.

Next to each item write the appropriate number which best describes how frequently the condition described is a source of stress.

Write 1 if the condition described is never a source of stress.

Write 2 if it is rarely a source of stress.

Write 3 if it is occasionally a source of stress.

Write 4 if it is sometimes a source of stress.

Write 5 if it is often a source of stress.

Write 6 if it is usually a source of stress.

Write 7 if it is always a source of stress.

1. My job duties and work objectives are unclear to me
2. I work on unnecessary tasks or projects
3. I have to take work home in the evenings or on weekends to stay caught up
4. The demands for work quality made upon me are unreasonable
5. I lack the proper opportunities to advance in this organization
6. I am held accountable for the development of other employees
7. I am unclear about whom I report to and/or who reports to me
8. I get caught in the middle between my supervisors and my subordinates
9. I spend too much time in unimportant meetings that take me away from my work
10. My assigned tasks are sometimes too difficult and/or complex
11. If I want to get promoted, I have to look for a job with another organization
12. I am responsible for counseling with my subordinates and/or helping them solve their problems
13. I lack the authority to carry out my job responsibilities
14. The formal chain of command is not adhered to
15. I am responsible for an almost unmanageable number of projects or assignments at the same time
16. Tasks seem to be getting more and more complex
17. I am hurting my career progress by staying with this organization
18. I take action or make decisions that affect the safety or well-being of others
19. I do not fully understand what is expected of me
20. I do things on the job that are accepted by one person and not by others
21. I simply have more work to do than can be done in an ordinary day
22. The organization expects more of me than my skills and/or abilities provide
23. I have few opportunities to grow and learn new knowledge and skills in my job
24. My responsibilities in this organization are more for people than for things
25. I do not understand the part my job plays in meeting overall organizational objectives
26. I receive conflicting requests from two or more people
27. I feel that I just don't have time to take an occasional break
28. I have insufficient training and/or experience to discharge my duties properly
29. I feel that I am at a standstill in my career
30. I have responsibility for the future (careers) of others

Scoring:

Each item is associated with a specific individual-level stressor. The item numbers and the appropriate categories are listed below.

Role ambiguity: items 1, 7, 13, 19, 25

Role conflict: items 2, 8, 14, 20, 26

Role overload–quantitative: items 3, 9, 15, 21, 27

Role overload–qualitative: items 4, 10, 16, 22, 28

Career development: items 5, 11, 17, 23, 29

Responsibility for people: items 6, 12, 18, 24, 30

The significance of the total score in each of the stressor categories will, of course, vary from individual to individual. In general, however, the following guidelines may be used to provide a perspective for each total score:

Total scores in a category of less than 10 are indicators of low stress levels.

Total scores between 10 and 24 are indicative of moderate stress levels.

Total scores of 25 and greater are indicative of high stress levels.

Job Stress Scale

Description   This measure was developed by Parker and Decotiis (1983). The measure uses 13 items to measure job stress along two dimensions. One dimension is time stress (feelings of being under constant pressure) and the second dimension is anxiety (job-related feelings of anxiety). Jamal and Baba (1992) used a shortened version of the Job Stress Scale consisting of nine of the items.

Reliability   Coefficient alpha values ranged from .71 to .82 (Jamal, 1990; Schaubroeck & Merritt, 1997; Xie & Johns, 1995). In Jamal and Baba (1992), alpha for the nine-item version was .83.

Validity   Job stress was negatively correlated with organizational commitment and job satisfaction and positively correlated with role ambiguity and overload (Jamal & Baba, 1992). Factor analyses have shown that time stress and anxiety are empirically distinct dimensions (Melamed et al., 1991; Xie & Johns, 1995).

Source   Parker, D. F., & Decotiis, T. A. (1983). Organizational determinants of job stress. *Organizational Behavior and Human Performance, 32*, 160-177. Items were taken from Table 2, p. 169. Copyright © 1983 by Academic Press. Reproduced with permission.

Items   Responses are obtained using a 5-point Likert-type scale where 1 = *strong disagreement* and 5 = *strong agreement* with the following statements. Items denoted with (9) were used in the nine-item version (Jamal & Baba, 1992).

Time stress items:

1.   Working here makes it hard to spend enough time with my family
2.   I spend so much time at work, I can't see the forest for the trees
3.   Working here leaves little time for other activities
4.   I frequently get the feeling I am married to the company
5.   I have too much work and too little time to do it in (9)
6.   I sometimes dread the telephone ringing at home because the call might be job-related (9)
7.   I feel like I never have a day off (9)
8.   Too many people at my level in the company get burned out by job demands (9)

Anxiety items:

1.   I have felt fidgety or nervous as a result of my job (9)
2.   My job gets to me more than it should (9)
3.   There are lots of times when my job drives me right up the wall (9)
4.   Sometimes when I think about my job I get a tight feeling in my chest (9)
5.   I feel guilty when I take time off from job (9)

Inventory of Stressful Events

Description   This measure, developed and validated by Motowidlo, Packard, and Manning (1986), uses 45 items to measure the frequency of stressful occurrences in a job. The instrument was originally developed for nurses and the items were derived from interviews in a variety of clinical areas in several hospitals. Thus, they contain wording specific to the hospital context. Respondents are asked to indicate how often stressful things happen in performing a job.

Reliability   Coefficient alpha value was .88 (Fox & Dwyer, 1995; Fox, Dwyer, & Ganster, 1993).

Validity   The frequency of stressful events was positively correlated with psychological distress, quantitative workload, qualitative workload, self-monitoring, and somatic complaints. The frequency of stressful events correlated negatively with job satisfaction, job performance, and job control (Fox & Dwyer, 1995; Fox et al., 1993).

Source   Motowidlo, S. J., Packard, J. S., & Manning, M. R. (1986). Occupational stress: Its causes and consequences for job performance. *Journal of Applied Psychology, 71,* 618-629. Items were taken from the appendix, p. 629. Copyright © 1986 by the American Psychological Association. Reprinted with permission.

Items   Respondents are asked, "How often does this generally happen to you?" Responses are obtained on a 4-point Likert-type scale where 1 = *never* and 4 = *fairly often.* Responses can also be obtained for the same 45 items asking the question "How stressful is or would this be for you?" and obtaining responses from 1 = *not at all stressful* to 5 = *extremely stressful.*

How often do these things generally happen to you in your job?

1. You fall behind in your regular duties because you have extra work that is not part of your daily routine
2. You are so busy you have to pass up a chance to talk to a patient and give him or her some emotional support
3. Another nurse calls you away from important work for a trivial matter
4. A patient complains to you about the food or other things not under your control
5. Your head nurse or supervisor disagrees with your judgment about a patient's treatment or condition
6. A doctor is verbally abusive toward you
7. You perform work that should have been done by your head nurse
8. Your regular head nurse is temporarily absent from the unit when you need help
9. A doctor becomes angry at you for something that is not your fault

10. Your work is interrupted by delays caused by other units or departments
11. You have so much to do that you have to leave some things undone
12. You are unable to contact a doctor in an emergency
13. You have to make an extra trip for special supplies because a doctor changed his or her mind about a medical procedure
14. A doctor wastes your time by having you perform non-nursing tasks
15. A doctor becomes upset with you for taking too long to do something
16. Your unit is short-staffed because someone called in sick
17. A doctor does not accept your suggestions regarding a patient's condition or treatment
18. Your head nurse or supervisor assigns a lighter workload to a co-worker
19. A doctor contradicts hospital rules or standard nursing procedures which you were following with a patient
20. A patient under your care refuses to accept medication or other treatment
21. You have to explain the behavior of a doctor to a patient or the patient's family
22. A patient criticizes your nursing care
23. You have to do extra work because another unit or department did not do their own work properly
24. A patient becomes verbally abusive with you
25. Another nurse is angry or rude with you
26. You disagree with the patient care ordered by a doctor
27. You see a doctor act rudely or inconsiderately toward a patient
28. You see another nurse relaxing and taking it easy while you are very busy
29. A patient under your care refuses to eat a meal
30. Another nurse's negligence makes it difficult for you to perform your own work properly
31. Visitors are verbally abusive or rude toward a patient under your care
32. Your head nurse or supervisor gives you incorrect information pertaining to patient care
33. Another nurse will not fill in for you so you can take a day off
34. Your head nurse or supervisor refuses your request for time off or a change in your schedule
35. A patient under your care refuses to stay in bed
36. A patient under your care purposely removes his or her dressings
37. You have so much to do that you have to work overtime
38. You need medical equipment or supplies that are not available in your unit
39. A doctor publicly criticizes your nursing care
40. A patient tries to harm himself or herself while under your care
41. You hear another nurse complaining about the workload
42. Another nurse criticizes your nursing care
43. You have to use a piece of equipment or perform a nursing procedure that is new to you
44. A patient's family or visitors criticize your nursing care
45. A patient reports you to a doctor or a nursing supervisor

Occupational Stress Scale

Description   The Occupational Stress Scale (OSS) was developed by House, McMichael, Wells, Kaplan, and Landerman (1979). It measures the frequency with which employees are bothered by stressful occurrences. The measure contains five subscales that assess the extent of occupational stress due to job responsibilities, quality concerns, role conflict, job vs. non-job conflict, and workload.

Reliability   Coefficient alpha values ranged from .59 to .76 for responsibility pressure, and from .56 to .76 for job vs. non-job conflict (Holder & Vaux, 1998; House et al., 1979). Alpha for quality concerns was .72. Alpha was .70 for role conflict and .73 for workload stress (House et al., 1979).

Validity   Occupational stress was correlated negatively with social support at work, internal locus of control, and job satisfaction. Stress was correlated positively with role ambiguity, role conflict, and personal discrimination (Holder & Vaux, 1998). The five stress dimensions (responsibility pressure, role conflict, work load, quality concerns, and job vs. non-job conflict) intercorrelated positively. The five dimensions all correlated negatively with job satisfaction and extrinsic job rewards. The five dimensions all correlated positively with employee Type A personality. Work load, quality concerns, and job vs. non-job conflict all correlated negatively with intrinsic job rewards (House et al., 1979).

Source   House, J. S., McMichael, A. J., Wells, J. A., Kaplan, B. H., & Landerman, L. R. (1979). Occupational stress and health among factory workers. *Journal of Health and Social Behavior, 20*, 139-160. Items were taken from text, pp. 157-158. © American Sociological Association. Reprinted with permission.

Items   Responses to the items for responsibility pressure, quality concerns, role conflict, and job vs. non-work conflict are obtained using a 5-point Likert-type scale where 0 = *not at all*, 1 = *rarely*, 2 = *sometimes*, 3 = *rather often*, and 4 = *nearly all the time*.

Responsibility pressure items:

How often are you bothered by each of the following in your work?

1. Feeling you have too much responsibility for the work of others
2. Having to do or decide things where mistakes could be quite costly
3. Not having enough help or equipment to get the job done well

Quality concerns items:

How often are you bothered by each of the following in your work?

1. Thinking that the amount of work you have to do may interfere with how well it gets done
2. Feeling that you have to do things that are against your better judgment
3. Feeling unable to influence your immediate supervisor's decisions and actions that affect you

Role conflict items:

How often are you bothered by each of the following in your work?

1. Thinking that you'll not be able to meet the conflicting demands of various people you work with
2. Not knowing what the people you work with expect of you
3. Having to deal with or satisfy too many people

Job vs. non-job conflict items:

How often are you bothered by each of the following in your work?

1. Feeling that your job tends to interfere with your family life
2. Being asked to work overtime when you don't want to
3. Feeling trapped in a job you don't like but can't get out of

Workload items:

(Responses to the following questions code 0 = *never*, 1 = *rarely*, 2 = *sometimes*, 3 = *fairly often*, and 4 = *very often*.)

1. How often does your job require you to work very fast?
2. How often does your job require you to work very hard (physically or mentally)?
3. How often does your job leave you with little time to get everything done?

Perceived Job Stressors

Description   This measure was developed by Kanner, Kafry, and Pines (1978). Many job stress measures focus on the presence of negative conditions. However, work or life stress may also result from the cumulative absence of positive experiences in daily life. The daily hassles and problems may lead to tedium defined as emotional and attitudinal exhaustion (Kanner et al., 1978). This measure of perceived job stressors assesses both the lack of positive features in work and life, associated with tedium, and the presence of negative features, associated with stress. The measure asks employees to describe the frequency with which they experience 17 positive conditions and 14 negative stressors. In Etzion et al. (1998), the measure was reduced to 23 items (11 positive and 12 negative). After reverse scoring, the 23 negative and positive items were combined to form a single measure of job stress.

Reliability   Coefficient alpha values ranged from .72 to .84 (Etzion et al., 1998; Melamed et al., 1991).

Validity   Job stressors were positively correlated with burnout and negatively correlated with social support, perceived control at work, and quality of the job experience (Etzion et al., 1998; Melamed et al., 1991).

Source   Kanner, A., Kafry, D., & Pines, A. (1978) Conspicuous in its absence: The lack of positive conditions as a source of stress. *Journal of Human Stress, 4,* 33-39. Items were taken from text, p. 36. Reprinted with permission of the Helen Dwight Reid Educational Foundation. Published by Heldref Publications, 1319 Eighteenth St., NW, Washington, DC 20036-1802. Copyright © 1978.

Items   Responses are obtained on a 7-point Likert-type scale where 1 = *very infrequently*, 2 = *infrequently*, 3 = *somewhat infrequently*, 4 = *neither*, 5 = *somewhat frequently*, 6 = *frequently*, and 7 = *very frequently*. Respondents are asked to indicate how frequently they experience these life events.

Lack of positive work and life items:

1. Variety
2. Complexity
3. Autonomy
4. Significance
5. Success
6. Feedback
7. Self-expression
8. Self-actualization
9. Policy influence
10. Tangible rewards

11. Appreciation
12. Opportunity to take time off
13. Personal relations
14. Unconditional support
15. Sharing
16. Emotional reciprocity
17. Comfortable environment

Negative work and life items:

1. Negative consequences
2. Demands for innovation
3. Under-load
4. Overload
5. Demands for proving oneself
6. Decision load
7. Physical danger
8. Environmental pressures
9. Bureaucratic interference
10. Administrative hassles
11. Experience of guilt
12. Emotional overextension
13. Overextension of commitments and deadlines
14. Conflicting demands from other people

Commute Strain Scale

Description   This measure, developed by Kluger (1998), assesses the degree to which employees are strained by the length and hassles of their commute to and from work. It taps both the employee's cognitive evaluation of the commute to work and his or her affective reactions to the commute.

Reliability   In Kluger (1998), coefficient alpha was .92.

Validity   Cognitive and affective commute strains correlated positively with commute length and variability, tardiness, and somatic symptoms. Commute strain correlated negatively with alternatives for commuting and enjoyment of the commute to work (Kluger, 1998).

Source   Kluger, A. N. (1998). Commute variability and strain. *Journal of Organizational Behavior, 19,* 147-165. Items were taken from text, p. 155. Copyright © 1998. Reproduced by permission of John Wiley & Sons Limited.

Items   Responses are obtained on a 6-point Likert-type scale where 1 = *strongly disagree* and 6 = *strongly agree.*

Strain items:

1. I resent the length of my commute
2. I resent the hassles my commute causes me
3. My commute affects my productivity on the job in the following ways: It takes work time out of my day
4. In general, how do you feel about your commute? (Responses to this item were obtained on a 7-point Likert-type scale where 1 = *extremely negative* and 7 = *extremely positive*, which was recalibrated to a 6-point scale for combination of this item with the others preceding it.)

I often fear for my personal safety during my commute due to:

5. seeing accidents
6. roads in disrepair
7. driving near bad or drunk drivers
8. bad weather
9. having car trouble

My commute causes me to worry about:

10. constantly being under time pressure
11. stress
12. accidents

13. body aches/pains
14. hostility, negative feelings
15. being harmed or killed
16. my mental health
17. traffic violation ticket

Work-Specific Control Problems

Description   This measure, developed by Remondet and Hansson (1991), assesses employee control problems in the areas of workplace demands, limited growth opportunities, personal/family crises, and working conditions. The measure asks respondents to rate both the frequency with which stressful events occur and the degree to which the occurrence of each event results in loss of control over the employee's job. The four subscales (demands, limited growth, personal/family, and working conditions) also combine into a composite measure of overall control problems at work.

Reliability   In Abraham and Hansson (1996), coefficient alpha was .87 for the composite measure of work-related control problems.

Validity   In Abraham and Hansson (1996), work-related control problems correlated negatively with job satisfaction and positively with job-related anxiety.

Source   Remondet, J. H., & Hansson, R. O. (1991), Job-related threats to control among older employees. *Journal of Social Issues, 47*, 129-141. Items were taken from text, p. 134. Copyright © 1991. Reproduced with permission.

Items   Respondents are asked to rate each item in terms of (a) how frequently an incident of this type happens on the employee's job (1 = *never* to 5 = *very often*) and (b) the extent to which such an incident when it happens on the job would constitute a loss or threat to the employee's sense of personal control (1 = *very little* to 5 = *very much*). A score for control problems is developed by multiplying the frequency and severity responses together.

Workload demands items:

1. My supervisor makes poorly planned changes that directly affect me
2. My supervisor is unrealistic in the demands placed upon me
3. My supervisor places unfair demands upon me
4. My workload is too heavy
5. I have had unrealistic schedule demands
6. My supervisor places demands on me that aren't placed on co-workers
7. I've been forced to do another's work in addition to my own

Limited growth opportunity items:

1. My job is not challenging
2. My job is meaningless
3. I see no room for growth in my job
4. There is no future for me in my position

Personal/family crises items:

1. Family crises have required that I miss work
2. Personal concerns have interfered with my job performance
3. Family illnesses have affected my job performance

Working conditions/environment items:

1. The work environment is uncomfortable
2. I have limited space to complete my job
3. I work in a dangerous environment

Industrial Relations Event Scale

Description   This measure, developed by Kelloway, Barling, and Shah (1993), uses 25 items to describe stressful industrial relations events drawn from a larger measure originally developed by Bluen and Barling (1987). The measure uses a life events methodology and provides three scores: the occurrence of industrial relations events, the perceived negativity of such events, and the positive perception of industrial relations. Respondents are asked to score only the industrial relations stressors that had occurred on a selected day or period.

Reliability   The stressful industrial relations events recorded by each respondent for the day or time period specified and the nature of impact (negative or positive) may differ from individual to individual. Thus, different items may be scored for each respondent making customary measures of internal consistency inappropriate.

Validity   Positive industrial relations stress correlated positively with positive mood and job satisfaction. Negative industrial relations stress correlated negatively with positive mood and job satisfaction, while correlating positively with negative mood (Kelloway et al., 1993).

Source   Kelloway, E. K., Barling, J., & Shah, A. (1993). Industrial relations stress and job satisfaction: Concurrent effects and mediation. *Journal of Organizational Behavior, 14,* 447-457. Items were taken from the appendix, p. 456. Copyright © 1993. Reproduced by permission of John Wiley & Sons Limited.

Items   Instructions and items:

Listed below are a number of events sometimes experienced by individuals which bring about change in the work situation. Please respond to only those events which you experienced at work today. For those events that you experienced today, please indicate the extent to which you viewed the event as having either a positive or negative impact when it occurred. That is, indicate the type (positive or negative) and extent of impact that the event had. A rating of –3 would indicate an extremely negative impact. A rating of +3 would indicate an extremely positive impact. A rating of 0 would indicate that the event occurred to you, but that it had no impact on you.

List of events:

1. Change in work rules
2. Conflict with supervisor or subordinates
3. Unfair labor practices
4. Dealing with resistance to change

5. Being discriminated against
6. Failure to use industrial relations procedures
7. Being victimized
8. Being intimidated
9. Being disciplined
10. Shop steward or worker representative elections
11. Representing others
12. Injustice and inequality
13. Anticipating or being approached by the trade union
14. Being powerless to act in the face of corruption
15. Inter-group conflict
16. Management resistance to minority (e.g., women, black) advancement
17. Being called abusive names
18. Not knowing who to turn to
19. Problems with accommodation, transportation, schools, etc.
20. Not being treated with human dignity
21. Lack of trust
22. Making or handling complaints
23. Job insecurity
24. Change in working conditions
25. Not being represented adequately

5

Job Roles

The Construct

According to role theory, every position in an organization should have a clear set of responsibilities so that management can give appropriate guidance and employees can be held accountable for performance. If people do not know the extent of their authority and what is expected of them, they may hesitate to act and be fearful about the potential repercussions for making decisions (Jackson & Schuler, 1985). Clear job roles tend to increase employee feelings of competency because individuals understand what needs to be done (Spreitzer, 1996). However, job roles are seldom clearly specified in advance, and there typically is an episodic role-making process between role senders and role receivers (Schaubroeck, Ganster, Sime, & Ditman, 1993). Disruptions in the role definition process, limitations inherent in the nature of jobs or organizations, and differences in management styles may lead to job role conflict, role ambiguity, and role overload. These aspects of job roles in an organization may create job tension and stress for employees and negatively affect employee attitudes (Schaubroeck et al., 1993). Greater role discretion and the freedom to innovate in a job role may enhance employee views about

their job and positively affect attitudes (Gregersen & Black, 1992). Of course, role innovation in itself may be stressful and bring an employee into conflict with others in a similar role or with established practices in an organization (West, 1987). In general, fulfilling a job role may be an inherently stressful activity because some tension will always exist between the way an employee wants to do a job and the needs of an organization for conformity among persons filling similar job roles.

Most of the research about job roles has focused on role conflict and ambiguity. Role conflict is defined as incompatibility between the expectations of parties or between aspects of a single role. Role ambiguity is defined as uncertainty about what actions to take to fulfill a role. Role conflict, ambiguity, and overload may affect employees because they increase stress. Prolonged exposure to stressors increases demand on an employee's cognitive resources because individuals exert greater effort to cope and neutralize stressors. This leaves fewer cognitive resources available for performing assigned job duties and responsibilities effectively (Fried, Ben-David, Tiegs, Avital, & Yeverechyahu, 1998). Employees may find it more difficult to function effectively in a work environment where a number of role stressors such as role conflict, ambiguity, and overload are present concurrently. When stressful demands exceed an employee's capacity to cope, work attitudes and performance are likely to deteriorate (Erera-Weatherley, 1996).

However, it is also possible that role conflict, ambiguity, and overload have direct effects on key employee outcomes independent of stress. In a meta-analysis, Jackson and Schuler (1985) reported that role ambiguity and role conflict both correlated negatively with job satisfaction. However, Netemeyer, Burton, and Johnston (1995) evaluated alternative structural models and found that (a) role ambiguity and role conflict both had direct negative effects on job satisfaction, (b) role conflict had positive effects on job tension (role ambiguity did not), and (c) role overload covaried with both conflict and ambiguity, but did not directly affect job tension or job satisfaction. All three dimensions of role perceptions affected organizational commitment and intention to leave indirectly through their effects on job satisfaction.

The Measures

The major issues in measurement of the attributes of job roles have centered on (a) the distinction between measures of role conflict and role ambiguity and measures of job characteristics, job involvement, and job satisfaction; (b) the focus and dimensionality of measures of job roles; and (c) how best to capture the extent of sources, frequency and intensity of role conflict, ambiguity, and overload experiences. The first issue has been the subject of several studies I reviewed. These studies have generally found that the role conflict and ambiguity constructs are empirically distinct from job satisfaction, job tension, and job characteristics.

The second issue concerns which aspects of a job role cause perceptions of conflict and ambiguity. For example, should role conflict be defined in reference to other roles an employee must fulfill? Is the extent of role stress an employee experiences related to the way he or she is treated when things go wrong? I have included measures that describe inter-role conflict, measures that assess role justice (how an employee is treated by supervisors when problems arise), and measures that differentiate the conflict or ambiguity inherent to different facets of a job role.

The third measurement issue is whether the impact of role conflict, ambiguity, and overload may be misrepresented by measures that ask employees to provide "on average" descriptions of their job roles. Thus, I have included a measure that asks employees to respond in terms of the frequency and intensity of role tension-related events they have recently experienced in their job.

Role Conflict and Ambiguity

Description   This measure, developed by Rizzo, House, and Lirtzman (1970), was one of the first measures of role ambiguity and role conflict. A lack of necessary information regarding role expectation for a given organizational position has been defined as role ambiguity. Role conflict was defined as a condition of when employees have incompatible roles defined by supervisors or other members of an organization. This measure includes intrarole, interrole, and intersender conflict, as well as ambiguity due to lack of role predictability, role clarity, and role certainty (Bedeian, Mossholder, Kemery, & Armenakis, 1990).

Reliability   Coefficient alpha values for role conflict ranged from .71 to .87, and alpha values for role ambiguity ranged from .71 to .95 (Adkins, 1995; Bauer & Green 1994; Dobbins, Cardy, & Platz-Vieno, 1990; Fisher & Shaw, 1994; Fortunato, Jex, & Heinish, 1999; Fried, 1998; Fried & Tiegs, 1995; Gregersen & Black, 1992; Hemingway, 1999; Jex, 1999; Morrison, 1997; Netemeyer et al., 1995; Pearson, 1992; Schaubroeck et al., 1993; Siegall, 1992; Zellars, Perrewé, & Hochwarter, 1999).

Validity   Though the role conflict and role ambiguity measures have been used extensively, some scholars have raised concerns about the content validity, susceptibility to wording biases and factor structure of this measures (King & King, 1990; Smith, Tisak, & Schmieder, 1993). Netemeyer and colleagues (1995) evaluated alternative structural models and showed that role conflict and role ambiguity are distinct constructs (Netemeyer et al., 1995; Netemeyer, Johnston, & Burton, 1990). Harris and Bladen (1994) also found that role conflict and ambiguity were empirically distinct from role overload, job satisfaction, and job tension. Smith et al. (1993) also found that role conflict and ambiguity were empirically distinct in three samples.

Role conflict had direct effects on job tension and job satisfaction. Role ambiguity did not directly affect job tension or satisfaction. Neither role conflict nor role ambiguity directly affected propensity to leave (Netemeyer et al., 1990). In Fried (1998), both role conflict and ambiguity correlated negatively with job performance. Williams, Podsakoff, and Huber (1992) found that the role conflict measure distinguished between different groups of university administrators experiencing distinct levels of role stress.

Source   Rizzo, J., House, R. J., & Lirtzman, S. I. (1970). Role conflict and role ambiguity in complex organizations. *Administrative Science Quarterly, 15,* 150-163. Items were taken from Table 1, p. 156. Copyright © 1970. Reproduced with permission.

Items   Responses are obtained on a 7-point Likert-type scale where 1 = *strongly disagree* and 7 = *strongly agree.*

Role conflict items:

1. I have to do things that should be done differently
2. I have to buck a rule of a policy in order to carry out an assignment
3. I receive incompatible requests from two or more people
4. I do things that are apt to be accepted by one person and not accepted by others
5. I work on unnecessary things
6. I work with two or more groups who operate quite differently
7. I receive assignments without the manpower to complete them
8. I receive assignments without adequate resources and material to execute them

Role ambiguity items:

1. I know exactly what is expected of me (R)
2. I know that I have divided my time properly (R)
3. Explanation is clear of what has to be done (R)
4. I feel certain about how much authority I have (R)
5. I know what my responsibilities are (R)
6. Clear, planned goals and objectives exist for my job (R)

Items denoted by (R) are reverse scored.

Role Conflict and Ambiguity

Description   This measure was developed by House, Schuler, and Levanoni (1983) to address criticisms that other measures for role conflict and ambiguity were possibly confounded with stress and comfort. That is, other role conflict measures used items that were "stress worded," whereas other role ambiguity measures used items that were "comfort worded." In developing this measure of role conflict and ambiguity, House and colleagues (1983) developed and tested scales for both constructs using a pool of 43 items. These items loaded on two factors with ambiguity items containing a mix of stress/comfort and self/other worded statements. The conflict factor contained items worded in terms of stress caused by other parties.

Reliability   Coefficient alpha values for the role conflict and role ambiguity scales ranged from .79 to .86 (O'Driscoll & Beehr, 1994; Westman, 1992).

Validity   Role ambiguity correlated positively with role conflict, employee uncertainty, psychological strain, turnover intentions, job dissatisfaction, job decision latitude, and employee psychological distress (O'Driscoll & Beehr, 1994; Westman, 1992). Role ambiguity and conflict correlated negatively with job satisfaction (O'Driscoll & Beehr, 1994). Harris (1991) found evidence that employee role conflict and ambiguity may result only when the sources are perceived as external. Employees may categorize internal sources of role conflict and ambiguity differently.

Source   House, R. J., Schuler, R. S., & Levanoni, E. (1983). Role conflict and ambiguity scales: Reality or artifacts? *Journal of Applied Psychology, 68*(2), 334-337. Items were taken from Table 1, p. 336. Copyright © 1983 by the American Psychological Association. Reprinted with permission.

Items   Responses are scored on a 7-point Likert-type scale where 1 = *strongly disagree* and 7 = *strongly agree*.

Role ambiguity items:

1. My authority matches the responsibilities assigned to me (R)
2. I don't know what is expected of me
3. My responsibilities are clearly defined (R)
4. I feel certain about how much authority I have (R)
5. I know what my responsibilities are (R)
6. I have clear planned goals and objectives for my job (R)
7. The planned goals and objectives are not clear
8. I don't know how I will be evaluated for a raise or promotion
9. I know what is expected of me (R)
10. Explanations are clear of what has to be done (R)
11. My boss makes it clear how he will evaluate my performance (R)

Role conflict items:

1. I often get myself involved in situations in which there are conflicting requirements
2. There are unreasonable pressures for better performance
3. I am often asked to do things that are against my better judgment
4. I receive an assignment without adequate resources and materials to execute it
5. I have to buck a rule or policy in order to carry out an assignment
6. I receive incompatible requests from two or more people
7. I have to do things that should be done differently under different conditions

Items denoted with (R) are reverse scored.

Role Hassles Index

Description   This measure, developed by Zohar (1997), is designed to capture specific episodes over the past 2 weeks of role conflict, role ambiguity, and role overload. Burnout is thought to develop when emotional or physical resources are depleted at a rate that exceeds replenishment. It is possible that measures of role conflict and ambiguity that ask respondents to report the extent to which a condition is present may not capture the imbalance between expenditure and replenishment (Zohar, 1997). Respondents to this measure are asked to identify the date when the episode occurred and to rate the episode in terms of its degree of disruption. The disruption scores are summed to yield three subscales for hassles-conflict, hassles-ambiguity, and hassles-overload.

Reliability   In Zohar (1997), the composite Role Hassles Index had a coefficient alpha of .88. Coefficient alpha was .80 for the hassles-conflict subscale, .71 for the hassles-ambiguity subscale, and .82 for the hassles-overload subscale.

Validity   Zohar (1997) examined the 20 items with factor analysis and found three factors corresponding to conflict, ambiguity, and overload. The overall Role Hassles Index and the subscales for hassles-conflict, hassles-ambiguity, and hassles-overload correlated positively with role conflict, ambiguity, and overload. The hassles subscales also all correlated positively with exhaustion, depersonalization, and reduced accomplishment (Zohar, 1997).

Source   Zohar, D. (1997). Predicting burnout with a hassle-based measure of role demands. *Journal of Organizational Behavior, 18*(2), 101-115. Items were taken from Table 1, p. 107. Copyright © 1997. Reproduced by permission of John Wiley & Sons Limited.

Items   Instructions and items:

Employees are instructed to review the list of 20 events and to indicate which had occurred in the past 2 weeks. For an event to be marked, the subject is required to recall the date. Each event is then rated as to how emotionally or physically disruptive it was on the day it occurred using a 3-point Likert-type scale where 1 = *slightly disruptive* 2 = *quite disruptive*, and 3 = *very disruptive*.

The events are as follows:

Hassles conflict:

1. Had an argument or confrontation over differing views
2. Encountered an attempt to step into my territory
3. Encountered a lack of cooperation or an inconsideration
4. Had difficulty convincing a superior of an important issue
5. Had to interact with an inconsiderate or disliked person

6. Received a negative or critical comment
7. Had to deal with conflicting expectations from different people
8. Had difficulties receiving feedback from superiors

Hassles overload:

9. Felt under time pressure, had difficulty due to insufficient time
10. Had too much or too many things to take care of
11. Had to stay too many extra hours or do inconvenient shift-work schedule
12. Had difficulty in completing a task due to bureaucratic constraints
13. Had too few resources (help, equipment, budget) for dealing with a task
14. Had to waste time over some unimportant activity
15. Had insufficient formal authority to do things my way

Hassles ambiguity:

16. Had concerns about how to solve a problem
17. Had to take action without knowing exactly what was expected of me
18. Made a mistake or was concerned over making one
19. Had difficulty obtaining needed information
20. Had to respond without clear priorities or goals

Role Overload

Description   This measure, developed by Bacharach, Bamberger, and Conley (1990), assesses an employee's role overload. Role overload has been conceptualized as the inconsistency between activities or tasks demanded of an employee and the time or other resources available for completing these tasks. Time-focused incompatibilities, such as when an employee feels that he or she has too much to do in the time allocated, may be the primary source of perceived role overload. The sheer quantity of work events requiring attention can also generate perceived overload. Role overload can be measured separately from and seems to be a construct distinct from role conflict (Bacharach et al., 1990).

Reliability   Coefficient alpha values ranged from .60 to .64 (Bacharach, Bamberger, & Conley, 1990, 1991).

Validity   Role overload was correlated positively with role conflict and negatively with team efficacy, task feedback, and task identity (Bacharach et al., 1990). Role overload correlated positively with role conflict and work-family conflict. In addition, factor analysis showed that role overload and role conflict were empirically distinct (Bacharach et al., 1991).

Source   Bacharach, S. B., Bamberger, P. R., & Conley, S. C. (1990). Work processes, role conflict, and role overload: The case of nurses and engineers in the public sector. *Work and Occupations, 17*(2), 199-229. Copyright © 1990 by Sage Publications, Inc. Items were taken from the appendix, p. 223. Reprinted by permission of Sage Publications, Inc.

Items   Responses are obtained on a 4-point Likert-type scale where 1 = *definitely false* and 4 = *definitely true*.

1. I don't have time to finish my job
2. I'm rushed in doing my job
3. I have a lot of free time on my hands (R)

Items denoted with (R) are reverse scored.

Cross-Cultural Role Conflict, Ambiguity, and Overload

Description   In an international study spanning 21 countries, Peterson and colleagues (1995) investigated the posttranslation equivalency of measures of role conflict, ambiguity, and overload previously used in studies of American subjects. Because confirmatory factor models of this group of measures fit the cross-national data poorly, the measures were refined using exploratory factor analyses in each country. This step identified items that would form reliable scales equivalent in factor structures across countries. Five role ambiguity items, three role conflict items, and five role overload items retained their factor structure in the countries studied. Overall, the values of the fit indexes compare favorably to those reported in confirmatory analyses of the full set of role stress items in U.S. samples.

Reliability   Coefficient alpha values for the role ambiguity, role conflict, and role overload scales were .87, .93, and .93, respectively (Peterson et al., 1995; Van De Vliert & Van Yperen, 1996).

Validity   Across countries, role overload was correlated negatively with employee harmony, job satisfaction, and subjective well-being. Role ambiguity, role conflict, and role overload were positively correlated (Peterson et al., 1995).

Source   Peterson, M. F., Smith, P. B., Akande, A., Ayestaran, S., Bochner, S., Callan, V., Cho, N. G., Jesuino, J. C., D'Amorim, M., Francois, P., Hofmann, K., Koopman, P. L., Leung, K., Lim, T. K., Mortazavi, S., Munene, J., Radford, M., Ropo, A., Savage, G., Setiadi, B., Sinha, T. N. Sorenson, R., & Viedge, C. (1995). Role conflict, ambiguity, and overload: A 21-nation study, *Academy of Management Journal, 38*(2), 429-452. © 1995 by Academy of Management. The items were taken from text, p. 440. Reproduced with permission of Academy of Management in the format textbook via Copyright Clearance Center.

Items   Responses are obtained on a 5-point Likert-type scale where 1 = *strongly disagree* and 5 = *strongly agree*.

Role conflict items:

1. I often get involved in situations in which there are conflicting requirements
2. I receive incompatible requests from two or more people
3. I have to do things that should be done differently under different conditions.

Role ambiguity items:

1. I have clear planned goals and objectives for my job
2. I know exactly what is expected of me
3. I know what my responsibilities are
4. I feel certain about how much responsibility I have
5. My responsibilities are clearly defined

Role overload items:

1. There is a need to reduce some parts of my role
2. I feel overburdened in my role
3. I have been given too much responsibility
4. My workload is too heavy
5. The amount of work I have to do interferes with the quality I want to maintain

Inter-Role Conflict

Description   This measure, developed by Thompson and Werner (1997), assesses the extent to which different roles that an employee fills at work and in nonwork settings are in conflict or are supportive. A work/nonwork total score is obtained for each employee by summing the ratings made by the individual for potential conflict/facilitation between their work role and all their other reported roles. A negative total score indicates high levels of perceived conflict between work and other roles, while a positive score suggests greater overall facilitation.

Reliability   Internal consistency (coefficient alpha) is not applicable for this scoring method. No test-retest reliability information is available.

Validity   Thompson and Werner (1997) found that interrole conflict correlated positively with an independent measure of job and off-job interference.

Source   Thompson, H. B., & Werner, J. M. (1997). The impact of role conflict/ facilitation on core and discretionary behaviors: Testing a mediated model. *Journal of Management, 23*(4), 583-602. Items were taken from text, pp. 588-589. Copyright © 1997. Reprinted with permission from Elsevier Science.

Items   A list of 10 roles is given to each individual. These roles are student, employee, spouse, primary care giver, volunteer, home maintainer, friend, religious participant, hobbyist/amateur, and other. No restrictions are given as to the number of roles a person can report about, although subjects are instructed to check only those roles where they are involved at least once a week. Respondents are asked to write the different roles they currently occupy down the left-hand side of a matrix and to replicate that list across the top of the matrix. Participants are then asked to compare each role with each other role and report the degree to which participation in one role facilitated the achievement of success in the comparison role, did not affect the comparison role, or participation in that role conflicted with the comparison role. Respondents answer on a scale from –2 to +2. The numerical values reflect the following responses: –2 = participation in one activity had a harmful or conflicting effect on the other, –1 = a somewhat harmful/conflicting effect, 0 = no effect, +1 = a somewhat facilitative or helpful effect, and +2 = a very facilitative or helpful effect.

Role Justice

Description   This measure, developed by Zohar (1995), describes employee perceptions of role justice. Role justice perceptions represent an employee's appraisal of fairness when a role sender's (e.g., supervisor, client) expectations are not met by the employee due to limiting conditions associated with a job. Perceptions of injustice or unfair reactions may be a source of role stress. Alternately, perceptions of justice may moderate the effects of role conflict and overload. That is, role senders who react fairly when an employee is unable to meet all role demands may help reduce the effects of overload. And role senders who react unfairly may increase the salience and discomfort employees feel when overloaded.

Reliability   The measure had a coefficient alpha of .87 (Zohar, 1995).

Validity   In Zohar (1995), the construct correlated negatively with role conflict and ambiguity and positively with social support.

Source   Zohar, D. (1995). The justice perspective of job stress. *Journal of Organizational Behavior, 16*(5), 487-495. Items were taken from text, p. 489. Copyright © 1995. Reproduced by permission of John Wiley & Sons Limited.

Items   Employees are asked to think about their current situation at work and indicate how fairly their significant role senders would respond in four different scenarios. Responses are obtained using a 9-point Likert-type scale where 9 = *the affected individual would respond very fairly* and 1 = *the affected individual would respond very unfairly.*

The scenarios are as follows:

1. One of your role senders is negatively affected because you were not informed of your responsibilities, or you were not told what exactly was expected of you
2. One of your role senders is negatively affected because you had to satisfy contradictory requests, or to work with guidelines which were incompatible with one another
3. One of your role senders is negatively affected because your job required you to work too fast, or to complete an assignment without the needed time to do it properly
4. One of your role senders is negatively affected because you did not have the freedom to decide how to organize your work, or the authority to control what was happening

Job Role Ambiguity

Description   This measure, developed by Breaugh and Colihan (1994), uses nine items to measure role ambiguity in three areas: (1) work methods, defined as employee uncertainty about the methods to use to perform a job; (2) work scheduling, defined as uncertainty about the sequence in which tasks should be performed, the allocation of their time, and the sequence for performing certain tasks; and (3) performance evaluation, defined as employee uncertainty concerning the standards that are used for measuring and assessing whether job performance is satisfactory.

Reliability   Coefficient alpha values ranged from .81 to .92 for ambiguity in work methods, .80 to .91 for ambiguity in scheduling, and .93 to .97 for performance criteria ambiguity (Breaugh & Colihan, 1994). The internal consistency reliability of the combined scale was .89 (Fortunato et al., 1999). In a series of four studies, the measures showed average test-retest reliabilities of $r = .65$ for work method ambiguity, .73 for scheduling ambiguity, and .80 for performance criteria (Breaugh & Colihan, 1994).

Validity   In four studies by Breaugh and Colihan (1994), all three dimensions of ambiguity correlated negatively with satisfaction with work and satisfaction with supervision. The correlations for performance criteria ambiguity were the largest in absolute size. Both work methods ambiguity and performance criteria ambiguity were negatively correlated with supervisory performance ratings of employees. Overall job ambiguity was also negatively related to employee tenure with the company and tenure with the employee's supervisor (Fortunato et al., 1999).

Source   Breaugh, J. A., & Colihan, J. P. (1994). Measuring facets of job ambiguity: Construct validity evidence. *Journal of Applied Psychology, 79*(2), 191-203. Items were taken from the appendix, p. 202. Copyright © 1994 by the American Psychological Association. Reprinted with permission.

Items   Responses are obtained using a 7-point Likert-type scale where 1 = *strongly disagree* and 7 = *strongly agree* (lower scores indicate higher levels of ambiguity).

Work method ambiguity items:

1. I am certain how to go about getting my job done (the methods to use)
2. I know what is the best way (approach) to go about getting my work done
3. I know how to get my work done (what procedures to use)

Scheduling ambiguity items:

1. I know when I should be doing a particular aspect (part) of my job
2. I am certain about the sequencing of my work activities (when to do what)
3. My job is such that I know when I should be doing a given work activity

Performance criteria ambiguity items:

1. I know what my supervisor considers satisfactory work performance
2. It is clear to me what is considered acceptable performance by my supervisor
3. I know what level of performance is considered acceptable by my supervisor

Goal and Process Clarity

Description   This measure was developed and tested by Sawyer (1992). It describes two dimensions thought to make up role ambiguity. One dimension describes clarity about a job's outcome goals and objectives. The other dimension describes clarity or certainty about a job's process or how it should be performed.

Reliability   Composite reliability estimates (analogous to coefficient alpha) were .92 for goal clarity and .90 for process clarity (Sawyer, 1992).

Validity   Exploratory factor analysis found the items loaded on two distinct factors. Confirmatory factor analysis indicated that the two factors were empirically distinct (Sawyer, 1992). In a structural equation model, autonomy, task feedback, and feedback from others (supervisors and co-workers) were antecedents to process clarity. Recognition was positively related to goal clarity, goal clarity was directly related to satisfaction, and process clarity was indirectly related to job satisfaction through goal clarity (Sawyer, 1992).

Source   Sawyer, J. E. (1992). Goal and process clarity: Specification of multiple constructs of role ambiguity and a structural equation model of their antecedents and consequences. *Journal of Applied Psychology, 77*(2), 130-143. Items were taken from Table 1, p. 135. Copyright © 1992 by the American Psychological Association. Reprinted with permission.

Items   Responses are obtained using a 6-point Likert-type scale where 1 = *very uncertain* and 6 = *very certain*. Respondents are asked to indicate the degree of certainty about each of the following items:

Goal clarity items:

1. My duties and responsibilities
2. The goals and objectives for my job
3. How my work relates to the overall objectives of my work unit
4. The expected results of my work
5. What aspects of my work will lead to a positive evaluation

Process clarity items:

1. How to divide my time among the tasks required of my job
2. How to schedule my work day
3. How to determine the appropriate procedures for each work task
4. The procedures I use to do my job are correct and proper
5. Considering all your work tasks, how certain are you that you know the best ways to do these tasks

Job Role Discretion

Description   This measure, developed by Gregersen and Black (1992), assesses the extent to which employees believe their job role gives them discretion to make choices about how and when things are done. The greater an individual's discretion as to what work gets done, how it gets done, and by whom, the greater the empowering sense of responsibility the individual would feel for those decisions. Thus, regardless of the job, role discretion is likely to increase felt responsibility. Role discretion may be particularly relevant to internationally assigned employees who are in autonomous roles away from a parent company's headquarters (Gregersen & Black, 1992).

Reliability   Coefficient alpha values ranged from .80 to .87 (Aryee, Chay, & Tan, 1994; Gregersen & Black, 1992; Gregersen & Stroh, 1997).

Validity   Role discretion was negatively correlated with role conflict and ambiguity. Role discretion was positively correlated with role clarity, having an organizational sponsor, organizational commitment to both the parent company and a foreign operation, and work adjustment. (Gregersen & Black, 1992; Gregersen & Stroh, 1997).

Source   Gregersen, H. B., & Black, J. S. (1992). Antecedents to commitment to a parent company and a foreign operation. *Academy of Management Journal, 35*(1), 65-71. © 1992 by Academy of Management. Items were taken from text, p. 68. Reproduced with permission of Academy of Management in the format textbook via Copyright Clearance Center.

Items   Responses are obtained on a 5-point Likert-type scale where 1 = *strongly disagree* and 5 = *strongly agree*.

1. I have discretion as to what work gets done
2. I have discretion as to how work gets done
3. I have authority to decide what tasks to delegate
4. I have freedom to choose what to become an expert in
5. I have discretion as to what tasks subordinates do
6. I have authority to decide what work gets shared
7. I have freedom to decide how much of a generalist or expert to become
8. I have discretion as to what I am responsible for

Role Innovation

Description   This measure, developed by West (1987), asks employees to indicate the ways in which they are doing their job differently from the person(s) who did the job previously or from others doing this job in the organization. Although employees taking on an organizational role will tend to stay close to the approach observed in previous role holders, role innovation may occur when the old behaviors do not seem to have as much benefit as alternative new behaviors.

Reliability   Coefficient alpha values ranged from .88 to .90 (Ashforth & Saks, 1996; Morrison, 1997). Role innovation test-retest reliability was $r = .77$ (Munton & West, 1995).

Validity   Role innovation correlated negatively with collective, formal, sequential, fixed, and serial approaches to socialization at 4 months and 10 months after role assumption. Role innovation correlated positively with intentions to quit and job performance at 4 months and positively with role conflict and job performance at 10 months (Ashforth & Saks, 1996). Role innovation correlated positively with personal change and job discretion within and across time periods, and negatively with self-esteem across periods (Munton & West, 1995).

Source   West, M. A. (1987). A measure of role innovation at work. *British Journal of Social Psychology, 26*, 83-85. Items were taken from text, p. 85. Copyright © 1987. Reproduced with permission.

Items   Responses are obtained on a 4-point Likert-type scale where 1 = *I do the job much the same as other people have done it*, 2 = *I do the job somewhat differently than others have done it*, 3 = *I do the job very differently than others have done it*, and 4 = *I do the job completely differently than others have done it*. If the respondent is the first person to do the job, he or she is instructed to use a "Not applicable" response. If a respondent has absolutely no idea how the job has been done, he or she is instructed to respond "Don't know." Responses are obtained for the following six areas of job role:

1. Setting work targets/objectives
2. Deciding the methods used to achieve work targets/objectives
3. Deciding the order in which different parts of the job are done
4. Choosing whom you deal with in order to carry out your work duties
5. Initiating new procedures or information systems
6. Developing innovative ways of accomplishing targets/objectives

6

Organizational Justice

The Construct

Organizational justice research starts from the premise that employees focus on the fairness in organizational systems in determining their commitment, satisfaction, and intent to turn over. One view is that employees determine their perception of fairness in the workplace by comparing the equity of the ratio of their inputs to their outcomes in comparison to those of their co-workers. This results in a judgment about distributive justice. It is a summary judgment about the fairness of managerial decisions concerning the distribution of outcomes such as pay and promotions (Dailey & Kirk, 1992). Another aspect of organizational fairness is procedural justice that focuses on how such decisions are made. The process for making organizational decisions may be just as important to the employees as their perception of outcome fairness. These two types of justice have different effects on the perception of organizational fairness. For example, Folger and Konovsky (1989) found that distributive justice has a much greater impact on pay satisfaction than procedural justice, whereas procedural justice tends to affect an employee's organizational commitment and trust in his or her supervisor or boss (Dailey & Kirk, 1992).

Generally, fair distributions—those in which input-output ratios are perceived to be equal to those of a comparison other—result in positive psychological and behavioral outcomes (Ball, Trevino, & Sims, 1994). For example, an employee who works 80 hours of overtime during the holiday season to complete a project on time and then receives no bonus and an unfavorable performance evaluation for that period is likely to perceive the organization as unfair. The perception of injustice would be particularly strong if the employee knew that another employee in the work unit was asked to but did not work the overtime and subsequently received a bonus and more favorable performance rating (Joy & Witt, 1992).

Procedural justice examines the impact of the process of decision making on the quality of exchange relationships. Individuals may value just procedures because they provide a means of indirect control over a decision when direct control is not possible. Thus, even when a particular decision has adverse outcomes for an individual, just procedures assure the individual that, over time, he or she will receive what is due from the exchange relationship (Sapienza & Korsgaard, 1996). The basic premise of justice theories is that fair treatment is central to people and a major determinant of their reactions to decisions. In fact, people are affected by the perceived fairness of such procedures regardless of the perceived fairness of a decision itself (Folger & Konovsky, 1989; McFarlin & Sweeney, 1992).

Three principles may affect employee perceptions of procedural justice: (a) Procedures should increase employee inputs into the decision process or "voice," (b) procedures should enhance the accuracy of information used in the decision process, and (c) procedures should discourage supervisor motivations to be biased in their decisions (Joy & Witt, 1992). In addition, three other factors in the organization-person relationship—standing, neutrality, and trust—may be determinants of perceptions of fairness. Information about individuals' standing may be conveyed by their interpersonal treatment during social interactions. Rude treatment conveys a message that the group or authority regards the individual as being of low status. Neutrality concerns the authority or institution's tendency to create a neutral playing field on which all affected parties will benefit fairly from the application of fair decision processes. Finally, trust is the individual's belief that the authority or institution intends to treat people in a fair and reasonable way (Taylor et al., 1995).

The Measures

Across most situations, when individuals perceive a fair outcome, they are likely to assume that fair procedures led to that outcome. However, when employees perceive a lack of congruence between perceived procedural and distributive justice, they tend to experience a cognitive inconsistency that tends to produce some sort of stress. In fact, the correlation between measures of distributive and procedural justice is often large enough to question whether they are indeed distinct constructs. Generally, distributive and procedural justice are measured separately be-

cause there are good theoretical reasons to evaluate them on separate grounds and because exploratory and confirmatory factor analyses both tend to show they are empirically distinct (Gilliland, 1994; Sweeney & McFarlin, 1997).

As the discussion above illustrates, there are numerous alternative views about the critical components of procedural justice. Consequently, there is great variety in alternative measures for procedural justice and process fairness. One frequently included dimension is voice, allowing individuals affected by the decision to present information relevant to it. Having input into a decision also makes people feel the decision maker or leader values them and affirms their status in the group or organization. Of course, the extent to which a decision maker acknowledges and shows consideration of others' input is also a part of employee perceptions of fairness. Thus, both the presence of procedures and the quality and nature of the interactions between employees and managers and supervisors are frequently incorporated into measures of procedural justice. That is, measures of procedural justice will frequently include a separate measure of voice or interactive justice.

The measures in this chapter include several alternative approaches to assessing employees' perceptions of both distributive and procedural justice from a "global" or overall organizational viewpoint. These are followed by measures that assess distributive and procedural justice as they relate to specific areas of operation in most organizations, such as pay and performance appraisal. Finally, several measures are included that assess perceived fairness with respect to some specialized decisions and policies, such as corporate relocations and parental leave. These specialized measures of justice and fairness may serve as validated examples that could be adapted or modified to capture justice perceptions with respect to other specialized areas of work.

Distributive and Procedural Justice

Description   These measures were developed by Sweeney and McFarlin (1997). The procedural justice subscale uses 13 items to assess the fairness of procedures within an organization, including procedures relevant to assessing and communicating performance feedback, solving work-related problems, and promotion processes. Eleven items describe employee perceptions of an organization's fairness in distributing rewards such as raises, promotions, performance ratings, and general recognition.

Reliability   Coefficient alpha for procedural justice was .84. Alpha for distributive justice was .81 (Sweeney & McFarlin, 1997).

Validity   Confirmatory factor analysis showed that distributive and procedural justice were empirically distinct (Sweeney & McFarlin, 1997). Distributive and procedural justice both correlated positively with employee pay level, intention to stay in a job, job satisfaction, supervisor's evaluation of the employee, and organizational commitment. Procedural justice also correlated positively with tenure and being male (Sweeney & McFarlin, 1997).

Source   Sweeney, P. D., & McFarlin, D. B. (1997). Process and outcome: Gender differences in the assessment of justice. *Journal of Organizational Behavior, 18*(1), 83-98. Items were taken from Appendix 1, pp. 97, 98. Copyright © 1997. Reproduced by permission of John Wiley & Sons Limited.

Items   Responses are obtained using a 5-point Likert-type scale where 1 = *strongly disagree* and 5 = *strongly agree*.

Procedural justice items:

1. I am not sure what determines how I can get a promotion in this organization (R)
2. I am told promptly when there is a change in policy, rules, or regulations that affects me
3. It's really not possible to change things around here (R)
4. There are adequate procedures to get my performance rating reconsidered if necessary
5. I understand the performance appraisal system being used in this organization
6. When changes are made in this organization, the employees usually lose out in the end (R)
7. Affirmative action policies have helped advance the employment opportunities in this organization
8. In general, disciplinary actions taken in this organization are fair and justified

9.   I am not afraid to "blow the whistle" on things I find wrong with my organization

10. If I were subject to an involuntary personnel action, I believe my agency would adequately inform me of my grievance and appeal rights

11. I am aware of the specific steps I must take to have a personnel action taken against me reconsidered

12. The procedures used to evaluate my performance have been fair and objective

13. In the past, I have been aware of what standards have been used to evaluate my performance

Distributive justice items:

1.   Promotions or unscheduled pay increases here usually depend on how well a person performs on his/her job

2.   Under the present system, financial rewards are seldom related to employee performance (R)

3.   There is a tendency for supervisors here to give the same performance ratings regardless of how well people perform their jobs (R)

4.   Under the present system, supervisors here get a few tangible rewards for excellent performance (R)

5.   Performance appraisals do influence personnel actions taken in this organization

6.   My supervisor evaluated my performance on things not related to my job (R)

7.   I will be demoted or removed from my position if I perform my job poorly

8.   My performance rating presents a fair and accurate picture of my actual job performance

9.   I will be promoted or given a better job if I perform especially well

10. My own hard work will lead to recognition as a good performer

11. I will get a cash award or unscheduled pay increase if I perform especially well

Items denoted with (R) are reverse scored.

Distributive and Procedural Justice

Description　　These measures were developed by Joy and Witt (1992). They are parsimonious in that they each use only three items to assess distributive and procedural justice. The procedural justice measure focuses on the extent to which employees believe they have a voice in negotiating their job assignment, job duties, and performance appraisal results. The distributive justice measure focuses on the fairness in the decisions made by the organization concerning job assignments, job duties, and performance appraisals.

Reliability　　Coefficient alpha for distributive justice was .70. The alpha for procedural justice was .86 (Joy & Witt, 1992).

Validity　　Distributive and procedural justice were positively correlated. The relationship between distributive and procedural justice was smaller for employees when delays in gratification were shorter (Joy & Witt, 1992).

Source　　Joy, V. L., & Witt, L. A. (1992). Delay of gratification as a moderator of the procedural justice-distributive justice relationship. *Group & Organization Management, 17*(3), 297-308. Copyright © 1992 by Sage Publications, Inc. Items were taken from text, p. 301. Reprinted by permission of Sage Publications, Inc.

Items　　Responses are obtained on a 5-point Likert-type scale where 1 = *definitely disagree* and 5 = *definitely agree.*

Procedural justice items:

1. I have considerable voice in determining my performance evaluation
2. I have considerable voice in determining my job duties
3. I have considerable voice in determining my job assignment

Distributive justice items:

1. Most of my job assignments have been fair
2. The treatment that I have generally received here at [company name] has been fair
3. I have received fair performance evaluations

Distributive and Procedural Justice

Description   This measure was developed by Parker, Baltes, and Christiansen (1997). The measure uses three items to assess employee perceptions of fairness in the allocation of rewards and recognition as an indicator of distributive justice. It uses four items to assess employee perceptions of the extent to which employees have input and involvement in decisions as an indicator of both the "voice" and "choice" aspects of procedural justice. The measures assess judgments about the organization overall, rather than policies or practices in a specific area.

Reliability   Coefficient alpha for distributive justice was .88. Coefficient alpha for procedural justice was .74 (Parker et al., 1997).

Validity   Across four subsamples, distributive and procedural justice correlated positively. Both procedural and distributive justice correlated positively with career development opportunities, satisfaction with work, and loyalty to the organization (Parker et al., 1997). Confirmatory analysis showed that distributive justice, procedural justice, judgments about career opportunities, satisfaction with work, organizational loyalty, and judgments about organizational support for affirmative action/equal employment opportunity (EEO) programs were empirically distinct (Parker et al., 1997).

Source   Parker, C. P, Baltes, B. B., & Christiansen, N. D. (1997). Support for affirmative action, justice perceptions, and work attitudes: A study of gender and racial-ethnic group differences. *Journal of Applied Psychology, 82*(3), 376-389. Items were taken from Table 1, p. 381. Copyright © 1997 by the American Psychological Association. Reprinted with permission.

Items   Responses are obtained using a 5-point Likert-type scale where 1 = *strongly disagree* and 5 = *strongly agree*.

Procedural justice items:

1. People involved in implementing decisions have a say in making the decisions
2. Members of my work unit are involved in making decisions that directly affect their work
3. Decisions are made on the basis of research, data, and technical criteria, as opposed to political concerns
4. People with the most knowledge are involved in the resolution of problems

Distributive justice items:

5. If a work unit performs well, there is appropriate recognition and rewards for all
6. If one performs well, there is appropriate recognition and reward
7. If one performs well, there is sufficient recognition and rewards

Distributive, Procedural, and Interactive Justice

Description   These measures were developed by Niehoff and Moorman (1993). A distributive justice subscale (five items) describes the extent to which an employee believes that his or her work outcomes, such as rewards and recognition, are fair. The outcomes include pay level, work schedule, workload, and job responsibilities. A procedural justice subscale (six items) describes the extent to which formal procedures exist and whether these procedures are implemented in a way that takes employees' needs into consideration. The formal procedures cover the degree to which job decisions are based on complete and unbiased information and that employees have opportunities to ask questions and challenge decisions. An interactive justice subscale (nine items) covers the extent to which employees perceive that their needs are taken into account in making job decisions and that employees are provided with adequate explanations when decisions are finalized.

Reliability   Coefficient alpha for distributive justice ranged from .72 to 74 (Aquino, Lewis, & Bradfield, 1999; Niehoff & Moorman, 1993). Coefficient alpha for formal procedures was .85 and alpha for interactive justice was .92. A 12-item measure combining items for formal procedures and interactive justice had a coefficient alpha of .98 (Moorman, Blakely, & Niehoff, 1998).

Validity   Formal procedures correlated positively with distributive justice and interactive justice. Distributive justice, procedural justice, and interactive justice correlated positively with the five organizational citizenship behaviors of altruism, courtesy, sportsmanship, conscientiousness, and civic virtue (Niehoff & Moorman, 1993). Procedural justice and interactive justice correlated positively with supervisor observations of employee work. Interactive justice correlated positively with formal meetings (Niehoff & Moorman, 1993). In Moorman et al. (1998), procedural justice correlated positively with perceived organizational support, interpersonal helping, personal industry, and loyal boosterism for an organization. Aquino, Lewis, and Bradfield (1999) and Niehoff and Moorman (1993) examined the measures with confirmatory factor analysis and found that distributive, procedural, and interactive justices were empirically distinct. Distributive justice correlated positively with procedural and interactive justice. Distributive justice also correlated negatively with deviant behaviors toward other employees and employee negative affect (Aquino, Lewis, & Bradfield, 1999).

Source   Niehoff, B. P., & Moorman, R. H. (1993). Justice as a mediator of the relationship between methods of monitoring and organizational citizenship behavior. *Academy of Management Journal, 36*(3), 527-556. © 1993 by Academy of Management. Items were taken from Table 1, p. 541. Reproduced with permission of Academy of Management in the format textbook via Copyright Clearance Center.

Items   Responses are obtained on a 7-point Likert-type scale where 1 = *strongly disagree* and 7 = *strongly agree*.

Distributive justice items:

1. My work schedule is fair
2. I think that my level of pay is fair
3. I consider my workload to be quite fair
4. Overall, the rewards I receive here are quite fair
5. I feel that my job responsibilities are fair

Formal procedures items:

1. Job decisions are made by the general manager in an unbiased manner
2. My general manager makes sure that all employee concerns are heard before job decisions are made
3. To make formal job decisions, my general manager collects accurate and complete information
4. My general manager clarifies decisions and provides additional information when requested by employees
5. All job decisions are applied consistently across all affected employees
6. Employees are allowed to challenge or appeal job decisions made by the general manager

Interactive justice items:

1. When decisions are made about my job, the general manager treats me with kindness and consideration
2. When decisions are made about my job, the general manager treats me with respect and dignity
3. When decisions are made about my job, the general manager is sensitive to my personal needs
4. When decisions are made about my job, the general manager deals with me in a truthful manner
5. When decisions are made about my job, the general manager shows concern for my rights as an employee
6. Concerning decisions about my job, the general manager discusses the implications of the decisions with me
7. The general manager offers adequate justification for decisions made about my job
8. When making decisions about my job, the general manager offers explanations that make sense to me
9. My general manager explains very clearly any decision made about my job

Distributive Justice Index

Description   This measure was developed by Price and Mueller (1986). It focuses on assessment of the degree to which rewards received by employees are perceived to be related to performance inputs. Performance inputs from an employee include effort, experience, and education. Distributive justice is judged high in an organization when effort, experience, good work, and dealing with stresses and strains of a job are rewarded and their absence punished. The original items were modified by Mansour-Cole and Scott (1998) to assess the degree of perceived fairness in an employee's work situation compared with co-workers.

Reliability   Coefficient alpha values ranged from .75 to .94 (Mansour-Cole & Scott, 1998; McFarlin & Sweeney, 1992; Moorman, 1991; Sweeney & McFarlin, 1993).

Validity   Distributive justice correlated positively with job satisfaction, procedural justice, interactive justice, and the organizational citizenship behaviors of courtesy, altruism, sportsmanship, and conscientiousness (Moorman, 1991). Distributive justice also correlated positively with employee sense of control, extent to which an employee benefited personally from a structuring and layoff, leader-member exchange (LMX) with his or her manager, pay satisfaction, employee age, job satisfaction, subordinate's evaluation of his or her supervisor, and organizational commitment (Mansour-Cole & Scott, 1998; McFarlin & Sweeney, 1992; Sweeney & McFarlin, 1993). Sweeney and McFarlin (1993) found through confirmatory factor analysis that distributive justice was one dimensional with the items loading as expected. These analyses also found that distributive and procedural justice were empirically distinct. DeConinck, Stilwell, and Brock (1996) found through confirmatory factor analysis that distributive justice was empirically distinct from four dimensions of the Pay Satisfaction Questionnaire (satisfaction with benefits, last raise, pay level and structure, and administration of the pay plan).

Source   Original items: Price J., & Mueller, C. (1986). *Handbook of organizational measurement.* Marshfield, MA: Pittman. Items were taken from text, p. 124. © Pittman Publishing. Reprinted with permission.

Modified items: Mansour-Cole, D. M., &. Scott, S. G. (1998). Hearing it through the grapevine: The influence of source, leader-relations, and legitimacy on survivors' fairness perceptions. *Personnel Psychology, 51*(1), 25-54. Items were taken from text, p. 37. Copyright © 1998. Reproduced with permission.

Items   Original items and instructions: Fairness in the following questions means the extent to which a person's contributions to [the organization] are related to the rewards received. Money, recognition, and physical facilities are examples of rewards. Responses are obtained on a 5-point Likert-type scale where 1 = *rewards are not distributed at all fairly*, 2 = *very little fairness*, 3 = *some fairness*, 4 = *quite fairly distributed*, and 5 = *rewards are very fairly distributed*.

1. To what extent are you fairly rewarded considering the responsibilities that you have?
2. To what extent are you fairly rewarded taking into account the amount of education and training that you have had?
3. To what extent are you fairly rewarded in view of the amount of experience that you have?
4. To what extent are you fairly rewarded for the amount of effort that you put forth?
5. To what extent are you fairly rewarded for the work that you have done well?
6. To what extent are you fairly rewarded for the stresses and strains of your job?

Modified items and instructions:

In this section, we are interested in how fair you feel your current work situation is as compared to your co-workers. Responses are obtained using a 5-point Likert-type scale where 1 = *strongly disagree* and 5 = *strongly agree*.

1. I feel that my current job responsibilities are fair
2. Overall, the rewards I receive here now are quite fair
3. I consider my current workload to be quite fair
4. I think that my current level of pay is fair
5. My current work schedule is fair

Procedural Justice

Description   This measure, developed by McFarlin and Sweeney (1992), uses similar items and response format to the Distributive Justice Index to describe employee perceptions of procedural justice. Procedural justice is an assessment of the fairness of the means or process used to determine employee rewards. The measure asks employees about the fairness of procedures used to communicate performance feedback, determine pay raises, evaluate performance, and determine who is promoted. Aquino, Lewis, and Bradfield (1999) added two items asking about the fairness of procedures used to terminate or discipline employees and the fairness of procedures used to express grievances

Reliability   Coefficient alpha values ranged from .73 to .85 (Aquino, Lewis, & Bradfield, 1999; McFarlin & Sweeney, 1992; Sweeney & McFarlin, 1993).

Validity   Perceptions of procedural justice were negatively correlated with deviant behaviors against other employees and were positively correlated with distributive justice, interactive justice, age, pay level satisfaction, job satisfaction, subordinate's evaluation of his or her supervisor, organizational commitment, and distributive justice (Aquino, Lewis, & Bradfield, 1999; McFarlin & Sweeney, 1992; Sweeney & McFarlin, 1993). Structural models evaluated by Sweeney and McFarlin (1993) showed that distributive justice best predicts job satisfaction, whereas procedural justice best predicts organizational commitment. Aquino, Lewis, and Bradfield (1999) used confirmatory factor analysis to find that procedural justice was one dimensional and was empirically distinct from distributive justice.

Source   Sweeney, P. D., & McFarlin, D. B. (1993). Workers' evaluations of the "ends" and the "means": An examination of four models of distributive and procedural justice. *Organizational Behavior & Human Decision Processes, 55*(1), 23-40. Copyright © 1993 by Academic Press. Items were taken from text, p. 27. Reproduced with permission.

Items   Responses are obtained on a 5-point Likert-type scale where 1 = *very unfair* and 5 = *very fair.*

1. How fair or unfair are the procedures used to communicate performance feedback?
2. How fair or unfair are the procedures used to determine pay raises?
3. How fair or unfair are the procedures used to evaluate performance
4. How fair or unfair are the procedures used to determine promotions?

Procedural and Interactive Justice

Description   This measure, developed by Moorman (1991), assesses the extent to which formal procedures are established that ensure fairness, as well as the nature of the interactions that supervisors and managers have with employees in implementing the procedures. The formal procedures items describe the degree to which fair procedures are established in the organization. The interactive items describe the perceptions that the interactions that accompanied an organization's formal procedures are fair and considerate. The two subscales have also been used in combination to assess fairness in treatment of employees and overall procedural justice (Skarlicki & Folger, 1997; Skarlicki & Latham, 1996).

Reliability   Coefficient alpha for the formal procedures subscale was .94. Alpha for the interactive justice subscale ranged from .93 to .94 (Moorman, 1991; Skarlicki & Folger, 1997). Coefficient alpha for the combined procedural and interactive justice measure ranged from .95 to .96 (Mansour-Cole & Scott, 1998; Skarlicki & Latham, 1996).

Validity   Formal procedures and interactive justice both correlated positively with job satisfaction, distributive justice, and the organizational citizenship behaviors of courtesy, sportsmanship, and conscientiousness (Moorman, 1991). Interactive justice correlated positively with the organizational citizenship behavior of altruism and correlated negatively with retaliatory behavior (Skarlicki & Folger, 1997). The combined procedural and interactive justice items correlated positively with trust of manager, distributive fairness, job satisfaction, organizational commitment, and organizational citizenship behaviors (Mansour-Cole & Scott, 1998; Skarlicki & Latham, 1996).

Source   Moorman, R. H. (1991). Relationship between organizational justice and organizational citizenship behaviors: Do fairness perceptions influence employee citizenship? *Journal of Applied Psychology, 76*(6), 845-855. Items were taken from Table 1, p. 850. Copyright © 1991 by the American Psychological Association. Reprinted with permission.

Items   Responses are obtained on a 7-point Likert-type scale where 1 = *strongly disagree* and 7 = *strongly agree*.

Formal procedures items:

1. Collect accurate information necessary for making decisions
2. Provide opportunities to appeal or challenge the decision
3. Have all sides affected by the decision represented
4. Generate standards so that decisions could be made with consistency
5. Hear the concerns of all those affected by the decision

6. Provide useful feedback regarding the decision and its implementation
7. Allow for requests for clarification or additional information about the decision

Interactive justice items:

1. Your supervisor considered your viewpoint
2. Your supervisor was able to suppress personal biases
3. Your supervisor provided you with timely feedback about the decision and its implications
4. Your supervisor treated you with kindness and consideration
5. Your supervisor showed concern for your rights as an employee
6. Your supervisor took steps to deal with you in a truthful manner

Procedural Justice

Description   This measure was developed by Folger and Konovsky (1989). The measure contains 23 items designed to describe procedural justice in performance appraisal and pay raise decisions. The 23 items form subscales that describe the effectiveness of the feedback an employee receives (11 items), the extent of planning that went into a performance appraisal and pay raise decision (six items), the extent to which an employee had recourse after a pay raise decision (five items), and the degree to which a supervisor observed the employee's performance (one item). Skarlicki, Folger, and Tesluk (1999) and Skarlicki and Folger (1997) used an eight-item version based on items that measure the extent to which company procedures are consistent, suppress bias, require accuracy, are correctable, ensure representation, and are ethical.

Reliability   Coefficient alpha for the full 23-item measure ranged from .93 to .95 (Lee & Farh, 1999). Alpha values for the subscales were .88 for interactive justice and .86 for planning and ranged from .90 to .94 for feedback (Mossholder, Bennett, Kemery, & Wesolowski, 1998; Skarlicki & Folger, 1997; Skarlicki & Latham, 1997). Test-retest reliability of the feedback subscale was .84 (Skarlicki & Latham, 1997). Coefficient alpha for the eight-item subscale was .88 (Skarlicki & Folger, 1997; Skarlicki et al., 1999).

Validity   Procedural justice correlated positively with distributive justice, interactive justice, pay satisfaction, trust, bonus amount, commitment, and pay raise. Procedural justice correlated negatively with negative affectivity and retaliatory behavior (Lee & Farh, 1999; Skarlicki et al., 1999; Skarlicki & Folger, 1997). Interactive justice correlated positively with organizational citizenship behaviors. Interactive justice also correlated positively with distributive justice and participation (Farh, Earley, & Lin, 1997). Mossholder, Bennett, Kemery, and Wesolowski (1998) found through confirmatory analysis that procedural justice, five types of social power, job satisfaction, and organizational commitment were empirically distinct.

Source   Folger, R., & Konovsky, M. A. (1989). Effects of procedural and distributive justice on reactions to pay raise decisions. *Academy of Management Journal, 32*(1), 115-130. © 1989 by Academy of Management. Items were taken from Table 1, pp. 120-121. Reproduced with permission of Academy of Management in the format textbook via Copyright Clearance Center.

Items   Responses are obtained using a 9-point Likert-type scale where 1 = *very little* and 9 = *very much*.

Feedback items:

Indicate the extent to which your supervisor did each of the following:

1. Was honest and ethical in dealing with you
2. Gave you an opportunity to express your side
3. Used consistent standards in evaluating your performance
4. Considered your views regarding your performance
5. Gave you feedback that helped you learn how well you were doing
6. Was completely candid and frank with you
7. Showed a real interest in trying to be fair
8. Became thoroughly familiar with your performance
9. Took into account factors beyond your control
10. Got input from you before a recommendation
11. Made clear what was expected of you

Planning items:

12. Discussed plans or objectives to improve your performance

Indicate how much of an opportunity existed, after your last raise decision, for you to do each of the following things:

13. Review, with your supervisor, objectives for improvement
14. With your supervisor, resolve difficulties about your duties and responsibilities

Indicate the extent to which your supervisor did each of the following:

15. Obtained accurate information about your performance
16. Found out how well you thought you were doing your job
17. Asked for your ideas on what you could do to improve company performance

Recourse items:

Indicate how much of an opportunity existed, after your last raise decision, for you to do each of the following things:

18. Find out why you got the size of raise that you did
19. Make an appeal about the size of a raise
20. Express your feelings to your supervisor about salary decisions
21. Discuss, with your supervisor, how your performance was evaluated
22. Develop, with your supervisor, an action plan for future performance

Observation item:

Indicate the extent to which your supervisor did each of the following:

23. Frequently observed your performance.

Procedural Fairness, Employee Voice, and Justification

Description This measure, developed by Daly and Geyer (1994), assesses the extent to which employees perceive that the company has used fair procedures and incorporated employee input when making decisions that affect employees. The measure was developed to measure these attributes surrounding an organization's decision to relocate an employment location. The employee voice subscale assesses the extent to which employees were able or were invited to express their views and concerns to decision makers prior to a final decision being made. The voice measure also includes three items that describe the extent to which management provided adequate justification for the decision.

Reliability Coefficient alpha for procedural fairness was .88. Alpha for employee voice and justification was .77 (Daley & Geyer, 1994).

Validity Analysis of structural models showed that distributive fairness, procedural fairness, and voice/justification were empirically distinct. Procedural fairness correlated positively with intention to remain with the organization, distributive fairness, and voice/justification (Daly & Geyer, 1994).

Source Daly, J. P., & Geyer, P. D. (1994). The role of fairness in implementing large-scale change: Employee evaluations of process and outcome in seven facility relocations. *Journal of Organizational Behavior, 15*(7), 623-638. Items were taken from Table 1, p. 629. Copyright © 1994. Reproduced by permission of John Wiley & Sons Limited.

Items Responses are obtained using a 5-point Likert-type scale where 1 = *strongly disagree* and 5 = *strongly agree.*

Procedural fairness items:

1. The organization went about deciding to move in a way that was not fair to me (R)
2. The way that management made the relocation decision was not fair to me (R)
3. The organization was fair to me in the way that it made the decision to relocate
4. The steps that the company took to make the relocation decision were fair to me

Voice items:

1. People like myself had input into the decision to relocate
2. Management did not give me a chance to express my concerns before they made the decision to move (R)

3. The organization did not listen to my views about relocating before they decided to move (R)
4. Before management decided to move, they asked me what I thought about the idea

Justification items:

1. Management did not explain to me why the move was taking place (R)
2. Management fully explained to me why the company was relocating
3. Management never really explained why the company was moving (R)

Items denoted with (R) are reverse scored.

Perceived Injustice

Description   This measure, developed by Hodson, Creighton, Jamison, Rieble, and Welsh (1994), describes the extent to which employees perceive their employer treats them unfairly. The measure asks employees to describe the extent of injustice using four specific questions rather than generalized evaluations of injustice at their workplaces. The measure was originally developed to investigate the impact of modern forms of incorporating workers in the labor process on employee solidarity and resistance.

Reliability   Coefficient alpha was .70. The items were factor analyzed with four other items measuring workplace solidarity of employees. The four items assessing perceived injustice loaded on a single factor with no significant cross-loadings (Hodson et al., 1994).

Validity   In multivariate regression, perceived injustice was related positively to workplace participation, working in a physically demanding job, and working in a larger organization. Perceived injustice was negatively related with being married, being in a higher socioeconomic status, having more bureaucratic procedures, and having more solidarity.

Source   Hodson, R., Creighton, S., Jamison, C. S., Rieble, S., & Welsh, S. (1994). Loyalty to whom? Workplace participation and the development of consent. *Human Relations, 47*(8), 895-909. Items were taken from text, p. 905. © Sage Ltd. Reprinted with permission.

Items   Responses are obtained using a 4-point Likert-type scale where 4 = *strongly agree*, 3 = *somewhat agree*, 2 = *somewhat disagree*, and 1 = *strongly disagree*.

1. Some people at my workplace receive special treatment because they are friendly with supervisors
2. People at my workplace sometimes get credit for doing more than they actually do
3. People at my workplace sometimes put off finishing tasks so that they do not get assigned additional work
4. The work in my department is often more difficult than it needs to be because people in other departments do not do their jobs the best they could

Procedural and Interactive Justice

Description   The measure, developed by Farh et al. (1997), assesses employee perceptions about both formal procedures and informal interactions in an organization concerning pay decisions. It contains a subscale for participation, which
describes the extent to which formal procedures are present that ensure
employees have input into pay and performance appraisal decisions; appeal
mechanism, which describes the extent to which there are formal appeal procedures present and followed in the organization; and interactive justice,
which describes the extent to which supervisors enact the formal procedures
that are in place. The interactive justice subscale is based on previous evidence suggesting that actions taken by managers and supervisors as they
implement procedures and explain decisions are indicators to employees
that procedural justice exists.

Reliability   Coefficient alpha for the participation subscale was .71, alpha for the appeal
mechanism subscale was .81, and alpha for the interactive justice subscale
was .88 (Farh et al., 1997).

Validity   Employee participation correlated positively with distributive justice, interactive justice, existence of an appeal mechanism, pay satisfaction, organizational commitment, and organizational citizenship behaviors. Participation
correlated negatively with education level. Existence of an appeal mechanism correlated positively with organizational citizenship behaviors, pay
satisfaction, and organizational commitment. Interactive justice correlated
positively with organizational citizenship behaviors, pay satisfaction, and
organizational commitment (Farh et al., 1997).

Source   Farh, J. L., Earley, P. C., & Lin, S. C. (1997). Impetus for action: A cultural
analysis of justice and organizational citizenship behavior in Chinese society. *Administrative Science Quarterly, 42,* 421-444. Items were taken from
text, pp. 431-432. Copyright © 1997. Reproduced with permission.

Items   Responses are obtained on a 7-point Likert-type scale where 1 = *strongly
disagree* and 7 = *strongly agree.*

Participation items:

1. Managers at all levels participate in pay and performance appraisal
decisions
2. Through various channels, my company tries to understand
employees' opinions regarding pay and performance appraisal
policies and decisions
3. Pay decisions are made exclusively by top management in my
company; others are excluded from this process (R)

4. My company does not take employees' opinions into account in designing pay and performance appraisal policies (R)

Appeal mechanism items:

1. The company has a formal appeal channel
2. The company imposes a time limit within which the responsible parties must respond to the employee's appeal
3. Employees' questions concerning pay or performance appraisal are usually answered promptly and satisfactorily

Interaction items:

1. My supervisor is thoroughly familiar with my job performance
2. My supervisor allows me to tell my side of the story in performance evaluation
3. My supervisor lets me know my appraisal outcomes and provides justification
4. My supervisor lets me know my pay raise and annual bonus and provides justification
5. My supervisor reviews my performance with me and discusses plans or objectives to improve my performance

Items denoted with (R) are reverse scored.

Procedural Fairness

Description   This measure was developed by Scarpello and Jones (1996). The measure was designed to assess employee perceptions about the fairness of the proce- dure used for making pay-related decisions. It uses 15 items to describe the fairness of procedures used for pay determination (six items), such as the methods used for job evaluation and establishing criteria for pay raises; pay communication (three items), including judgments about the fairness of how pay issues are communicated and questions answered; performance appraisal (four items), which includes how performance-related informa- tion is gathered, evaluations are made, and how evaluations are appealed; and appeal (two items), which describes the fairness of mechanism for resolving disagreements about pay decisions.

Reliability   Coefficient alphas for the subscales were as follows: pay determination .88, pay communication .92, performance appraisal .87, and appeal .83. The composite measure obtained by summing the subscales had a coefficient alpha of .93 (Jones, Scarpello, & Bergmann, 1999).

Validity   Factor analysis by Scarpello and Jones (1996) showed that the items loaded on the four factors with no significant cross-loadings. All four procedural fairness subscales (pay determination, communication, performance appraisal, and appeal) were positively intercorrelated. The four subscales all correlated positively with pay outcome fairness, pay satisfaction, supervisor satisfaction, and organizational commitment. Perceptions of the fairness of performance appraisal procedures correlated negatively with job tenure (Jones et al., 1999).

Source   Scarpello, V., & Jones, F. F. (1996). Why justice matters in compensation decision making. *Journal of Organizational Behavior, 17,* 285-299. Items were taken from Table 1, p. 291. Copyright © 1996. Reproduced by permis- sion of John Wiley & Sons Limited.

Items   Responses are obtained using a 5-point Likert-type scale where 1 = *very unfair* and 5 = *very fair.*
    All items are introduced with "This is how I feel about the fairness of the procedures for . . ."

Pay determination items:

1. Determining the pay for my job
2. Determining pay raises
3. How my pay raises are determined
4. Determining the pay for my job relative to higher and lower level jobs than mine
5. The way performance is reflected in my pay
6. The frequency of pay raises

Pay communication items:

7. Communicating pay policies and procedures
8. Communicating pay issues of concern to me
9. Answering questions about how my pay is determined

Performance appraisal items:

10. Gathering information used to evaluate my performance
11. Evaluating my performance
12. Appealing performance evaluations
13. Monitoring my supervisor's pay decisions

Appeal items:

14. Appealing pay decisions
15. Resolving disagreements about my pay

Fairness in Skill-Based Pay

Description   This measure, developed by Lee, Law, and Bobko (1998), assesses perceived fairness in a skill-based pay program. Skill-based pay systems pay employees for the range, depth, and types of skills applied on jobs. Employee perceptions of the skill-based pay program are likely to be influenced by their perceptions that certification procedures are objective and consistent across people, times, and skills; include opportunities for employees to ask questions about the decisions made; and incorporate the use of accurate information.

Reliability   Coefficient alpha for the fairness measure was .80 (Lee et al., 1998).

Validity   Confirmatory factor analysis showed that measures of fairness, three skill-based pay system characteristics (training, understanding, and advancement), and perceived benefits of skill-based pay and pay satisfaction were empirically distinct. Perceived fairness of skill-based pay correlated positively with the amount of pay at risk, pay satisfaction, perceived benefits of skill-based pay, training/job rotation provided, understanding of the skill-based pay plan, and understanding of how to advance in the plan (Lee et al., 1998).

Source   Lee, C., Law, K. S., & Bobko, P. (1998). The importance of justice perceptions on pay effectiveness: A two-year study of a skill-based pay plan. *Journal of Management, 25*(6), 851-873. Items were taken from the appendix, p. 871. © 1998, reprinted with permission of Elsevier Science.

Items   Responses are obtained using a 7-point Likert-type scale where 1 = *strongly disagree*, 2 = *disagree*, 3 = *slightly disagree*, 4 = *neither agree nor disagree*, 5 = *slightly agree*, 6 = *agree*, and 7 = *strongly agree*.

1. Supervisors do a good job of certifying employees for skill-based pay raises
2. The skill-based pay certifications are a fair test of employee ability to perform a task
3. If an employee really knows how to perform the tasks that make up a skill level, the employee will be able to pass the certification tests for that skill level
4. The skill-based pay plan is fair to most employees

Procedural and Distributive Fairness of Gainsharing

Description   This measure, developed by Welbourne, Balkin, and Gomez-Mejia (1995), focuses on the issues relevant to gainsharing programs. Distributive justice covers the perceived fairness of the amount of the gainsharing bonuses. Procedural justice includes assessment of perceived consistency of the program, decision structure, rules, procedures to limit the effects of bias, accuracy, adequate explanation of decisions, feedback, and consideration of employee viewpoints. One subscale of procedural justice describes fairness due to rules and procedures. A second subscale describes justice due to fair actions by the suggestion committee.

Reliability   Coefficient alpha for procedural justice based on rules and administration ranged from .71 to .90. Alpha for distributive justice ranged from .73 to .86. Coefficient alpha for justice based on actions of the suggestion committee was .60 (Welbourne, 1998; Welbourne et al., 1995).

Validity   Confirmatory factor analysis showed that the factors for procedural justice based on rules, justice based on fair processes of the suggestion committee, and distributive justice were empirically distinct from one another and from measures of monitoring the behaviors of other employees and willingness to act based on the behavior of others (Welbourne et al., 1995). Distributive justice correlated positively with both types of procedural justice and with employee willingness to act based on the behavior of other employees who are performing in the gainsharing program according to expectations. Procedural justice based on rules and administration and actions of the suggestion committee were both correlated positively with employee monitoring and willingness to act based on the behavior of other employees in the gainsharing program (Welbourne, 1998; Welbourne et al., 1995). Both procedural and distributive fairness correlated positively with satisfaction with the gainsharing program, employee income level, pay satisfaction, and procedural fairness (Welbourne, 1998).

Source   Welbourne, T. M., Balkin, D. B., & Gomez-Mejia, L. R. (1995). Gainsharing and mutual monitoring: A combined agency-organizational justice interpretation. *Academy of Management Journal, 38*(3), 881-899. © 1995 by Academy of Management. Items were taken from Table 1, pp. 892-893. Reproduced with permission of Academy of Management in the format textbook via Copyright Clearance Center.

Items   Responses are obtained on a 5-point Likert-type scale where 1 = *strongly disagree* and 5 = *strongly agree*.

Procedural justice based on rules and administration:

1.   The design of the gainsharing plan seems fair
2.   The gainsharing formula is the same for all employees

3. The gainsharing plan is administered fairly
4. The rules used for sharing the gainsharing bonus with all employees are fair
5. The gainsharing plan developed by the company to reward employees for their performance is fair and impartial
6. When determining whether a gainsharing bonus will be paid, the company uses accurate information about the department's performance
7. The performance level required to receive a gainsharing bonus is clear to me

Procedural justice based on suggestion committee actions:

8. Suggestion committees provide an opportunity for me to express "my opinion"
9. People who provide suggestions are treated fairly
10. The suggestion committees and gainsharing program provide an opportunity for us to receive feedback and learn how well we are doing

Distributive justice:

11. The size of our bonus is fair
12. The bonus we receive is fair
13. All in all, the bonus payment is what it ought to be
14. Our bonus is fair compared to what others are getting
15. The extent to which the bonus gives us the full amount we deserve is fair

Procedural Fairness Standards in Pay

Description This measure, developed by Jones et al. (1999), assesses the standards or comparison points that employees use when assessing the fairness of procedures used by an organization in making pay decisions. The measure covers five dimensions. The first is supervisory support (nine items), which describes the extent to which supervisors support their employees' pay interests and are open in discussing pay matters with subordinates. The second dimension is accuracy (seven items), which describes the extent to which performance information used in pay decisions is accurate, consistent, and relevant. The third dimension is process control (six items), which describes the extent to which employees have the opportunity to express their opinions and possibly influence the pay decision process. The fourth dimension is justification (four items), which describes how the organization responds to questions about pay decisions and provides adequate explanation for the basis for pay decisions. The last dimension is bias suppression, which describes the extent to which pay decisions are made with neutrality. Supervisor support, accuracy, justification, and bias suppression were combined in Jones et al. (1999) to form a non-control index.

Reliability Supervisory support had a coefficient alpha of .92. Accuracy had an alpha of .96. Justification had an alpha of .91. Bias suppression had a coefficient alpha of .81. The process control dimension had an alpha of .92. The combined non-control index had a coefficient alpha of .95 (Jones et al., 1999).

Validity The five dimensions (supervisory support, accuracy, justification, bias suppression, and process control) were all positively correlated. Process control was correlated positively with judgments of job evaluation, pay raise, and performance appraisal fairness, pay satisfaction, supervisor satisfaction, and organizational commitment. All of the non-control dimensions and the non-control index were correlated positively with pay satisfaction, supervisor satisfaction, and organizational commitment (Jones et al., 1999).

Source Jones, F. F., Scarpello, V., & Bergmann, T. (1999). Pay procedures—What makes them fair? *Journal of Occupational and Organizational Psychology, 72*(2), 129-145. Items were taken from Table 1, pp. 134-135. Copyright © 1999. Reproduced with permission.

Items Responses are obtained on a 5-point Likert-type scale where 1 = *not at all accurate* and 5 = *very accurate*.

Supervisor support items:

These items are introduced with "In administrating the pay plan, my supervisor . . ."

1. Represents my pay interests to other management
2. Represents my pay interests with upper management
3. Is concerned about the amount of pay that I receive
4. Backs me up when he/she feels I have legitimate complaints about my pay
5. Is concerned that my work group gets its fair share of the pay budget
6. Is frank and candid with me about pay issues
7. Is honest and ethical in dealing with me about my pay
8. Is truthful and honest about pay issues that affect me
9. Applies the same standards to everyone when making pay decisions

Accuracy items:

These items are introduced with "In administrating the pay plan, my supervisor . . ."

10. Becomes familiar with my performance before evaluating it
11. Uses relevant information to appraise my performance
12. Obtains accurate information to appraise my performance
13. Uses consistent standards when evaluating my performance
14. Frequently observes my performance
15. Explains the reason for my performance appraisal
16. Considers my complaints about performance appraisals

Process control items:

These items are introduced with "The opportunity I had to express my opinion to [organization] administration about . . ."

17. The way pay is allocated within [the organization]
18. The pay for my job
19. My pay raises
20. My benefit package

These items are introduced with "In administrating the pay plan, my supervisor . . ."

21. Allows me to express opinions about pay decisions
22. Gets my input before making a recommendation about my pay raise

Justification items:

These items are introduced with "In administrating the pay plan, my supervisor . . ."

23. Answers questions about my pay and benefits
24. Answers my questions about my pay and benefit procedures
25. Lets me know about changes in pay procedures that may affect my pay
26. Explains the reason(s) for the size of my pay raise

Bias suppression items:

27. Allows personal motives or bias to influence performance appraisal ratings (R)
28. Is influenced by things that should not be considered in his/her pay decisions (R)
29. Shows a real interest in trying to be fair in his/her pay decisions
30. Does not show favoritism in his/her pay decisions

Items denoted with (R) are reverse scored.

Procedural Justice in Performance Appraisal

Description   This measure, developed by Dulebohn and Ferris (1999), uses six items to assess the fairness of the procedures and process used for performance evaluation. The measure focuses on the extent to which employees believe their supervisor used important and accurate information in appraising employee performance.

Reliability   In Dulebohn and Ferris (1999), coefficient alpha was .86.

Validity   Procedural justice evaluations correlated positively with decision control, quality of supervisor relationship, voice opportunity, employee performance ratings, and supervisor-influence tactics such as praising employees for accomplishments. Procedural justice evaluations correlated negatively with job-focused influence tactics, such as working harder (Dulebohn & Ferris, 1999). Confirmatory factor analysis showed that the six items loaded on the procedural justice factor as anticipated and that procedural justice evaluations were empirically distinct from assessments of the quality of the employee's supervisory relationship, opportunities for employees to question the basis for performance ratings (employee voice), and degree of control over performance rating decisions (Dulebohn & Ferris, 1999).

Source   Dulebohn, J. H., & Ferris, G. R. (1999). The role of influence tactics in perceptions of performance evaluations' fairness. *Academy of Management Journal, 42*(3), 288-303. © 1999 by Academy of Management. Items were taken from Table 3, p. 295. Reproduced with permission of Academy of Management in the format textbook via Copyright Clearance Center.

Items   Responses are obtained using a 4-point Likert-type scale where 1 = *strongly disagree* and 4 = *strongly agree*.

1. The supervisor considered the important aspects of your work when rating you
2. The supervisor rated you on how well you did your job, not on his/her personal opinion of you
3. The supervisor treated you with consideration when giving you your performance appraisal results
4. The supervisor that evaluated you showed concern for your rights as an employee

Responses to the following items are obtained with separate 4-point response scales where 1= *not at all* and 4 = *very much*.

5. Overall, how hard did the supervisor who rated your performance try to be fair to you?
6. Overall, how fairly were you treated by the supervisor who rated your performance?

Procedural Fairness in Restructuring and Layoffs

Description   This measure, developed by Mansour-Cole and Scott (1998), describes the fairness of the procedures used in an organization during company restructuring and associated layoffs. It also describes the respect and consideration shown to employees during the implementation of these procedures. The measure uses 14 items to assess employee perceptions of the way they are treated by management from both an interactive and a procedural standpoint. The items were originally selected in anticipation of two subscales, one for procedures and one for quality of interactions. An exploratory factor analysis showed that several items cross-loaded, and the two resulting subscales were highly correlated. Thus, the items were combined into a single measure.

Reliability   Coefficient alpha for the measure was .88 (Mansour-Cole & Scott, 1998).

Validity   Procedural fairness correlated positively with distributive fairness, employees having heard about a layoff from their manager (vs. other sources), leader-member exchange (LMX) with their manager, receiving personal benefit from the layoff, legitimacy of the account for the layoff, and organizational commitment. Procedural fairness correlated negatively with an employee having a closer relationship with layoff victims (Mansour-Cole & Scott, 1998).

Source   Mansour-Cole, D. M., &. Scott, S. G. (1998). Hearing it through the grapevine: The influence of source, leader-relations, and legitimacy on survivors' fairness perceptions. *Personnel Psychology, 51*(1), 25-54. Items were taken from the appendix, p. 54. Copyright © 1998. Reproduced with permission.

Items   Responses are obtained using a 5-point Likert-type scale where 1 = *strongly disagree* and 5 = *strongly agree.*

1. When decisions are made about job reductions and reassignments, management treated me with kindness and respect
2. Management made sure that all employee concerns were heard before job changes and elimination decisions were made
3. When making decisions about job changes and eliminations, management offered explanations that made sense to me
4. When decisions are made about my job, management was sensitive to my personal needs
5. To make this decision, management collected all the necessary information
6. Management explained very clearly all the decisions made about the restructuring
7. When decisions were made about job changes and eliminations, my manager and others in management treated me with respect and dignity

8. When decisions were made about the restructuring, management dealt with me in a truthful manner
9. Management clarified decisions and provided additional information when requested by employees
10. When decisions were made about job changes and eliminations, management showed concern for my rights as an employee
11. All job decisions were applied consistently across all affected employees
12. Employees were allowed to challenge or appeal job decisions made by management
13. People at my job level had adequate input in to the restructuring decision process
14. Procedures were put in place to provide the employees with timely information about the restructuring and its implementation

Perceived Fairness in Goal Setting

Description   This measure, developed by Roberson, Moye, and Locke (1999), uses three items to describe the extent to which employees believe that fair procedures are used to establish performance goals. Although procedural justice perceptions can cover both procedural fairness and opportunities for employees to discuss or influence the outcome of a goal-setting process, this measure focuses only on the procedural aspects of goal setting.

Reliability   Coefficient alpha was .94 (Roberson et al., 1999).

Validity   Perceived fairness of procedures correlated positively with perceived participation and task satisfaction (Roberson et al., 1999).

Source   Roberson, Q. M., Moye, N. A., & Locke, E. A. (1999). Identifying a missing link between participation and satisfaction: The mediating role of procedural justice perceptions. *Journal of Applied Psychology, 84*(4), 585-593. Items were taken from text, p. 588. Reprinted with permission.

Items   Responses are obtained using a 9-point Likert-type scale where 1 = *not at all* and 9 = *extremely.*

1. How fair were the procedures used to set your goals?
2. How fair were the procedures used to determine your goal?
3. To what extent do you consider the goal-setting process to be fair?

Fairness Perceptions of an Organizational Policy

Description   This measure, developed by Grover (1991), is an example of a measure of fairness directed to a specific policy area. The policy area is organizational policies that allow parents to take family-related leave immediately following the birth of a child. The measure uses nine items to assess employee perceptions of fairness (two items), parental deservingness (three items), and institutional responsibility (four items).

Reliability   Coefficient alpha for fairness perceptions was .95 (Grover, 1991). Factor analysis of the nine items produced a single factor.

Validity   Fairness perceptions correlated positively with positive attitudes toward male leave-takers, positive attitudes toward female leave-takers, being of childbearing age, being female, greater likelihood of having additional children, and greater likelihood of taking parental leave (Grover, 1991).

Source   Grover, S. L. (1991). Predicting the perceived fairness of parental leave policies. *Journal of Applied Psychology, 76*(2), 247-255. Items were taken from the appendix, p. 255. Copyright © 1991 by the American Psychological Association. Reprinted with permission.

Items   Responses are obtained using a 7-point Likert-type scale where 1 = *strongly disagree*, 2 = *disagree somewhat*, 3 = *disagree a little*, 4 = *neither agree nor disagree*, 5 = *agree a little*, 6 = *agree somewhat*, and 7 = *agree strongly.*

Fairness perception items:

1. Paying faculty members for having babies is not fair to non-childbearing faculty members (R)
2. Every parent deserves the right to paid leave when a child is born
3. It is everyone's, including non-parents, responsibility to provide for children, and a parental leave policy helps to accomplish this task
4. It is not [the organization's] responsibility to provide paid time off to new parents (R)
5. Having a child is a strain on parents, and they deserve the aid of parental leave
6. Children are a necessary part of society and it is the responsibility of large institutions like [organization] to help in the effort
7. Those who choose not to have children should subsidize those who choose to have children under a parental leave program
8. In the past, employees have borne children without the benefit of special leave, and therefore it is not fair to offer parental leave to new parents (R)
9. Having a baby is a personal choice and provisions for that event should be made by the family, rather than by the employer (R)

Items denoted with (R) are reverse scored.

7

Work-Family Conflict

The Construct

Balancing the demands of work and family roles has become a daily task for many employed adults (Williams & Alliger, 1994). On one hand, occupying multiple roles provides individuals with important psychological benefits, such as status, ego gratification, and increased self-esteem. On the other hand, there are potential costs associated with such role accumulation, including role strain, psychological distress, and somatic complaints (Frone, Russell, & Cooper, 1992). In general, the subjective quality of the experiences an individual has in both work and family roles is a critical determinant of psychological well-being (Frone et al., 1992). For example, work experienced as demanding or not rewarding may increase the chances of work-family strain, whereas work that is more rewarding may reduce the chances of strain. In addition, work and family experiences may have reciprocal effects so that perceptions and behavior in one role are affected to some degree by experiences in the other (Williams & Alliger, 1994).

Work-family conflict has been defined as a form of interrole conflict in which the role pressures from the work and family domains are mutually incompatible and the demands of participation in one role make participation in the other role more difficult (Aryee, Luk, & Stone, 1998; Bacharach, Bamberger, & Conley, 1991; Frone et al., 1992; Kossek & Ozeki, 1998; Thomas & Ganster, 1995). Generally, as people experience more conflict between these major roles, their level of job and life satisfaction falls. For example, increased burnout may be a direct consequence of work-home conflict (Carlson & Perrewé, 1999). Work-family conflict has been shown to affect not only the psychological well-being of employees, but also their work-related attitudes such as organizational commitment and their work-related behaviors such as absenteeism, tardiness, and turnover (Aryee et al., 1998). As a result, a growing number of organizations in industrialized countries have introduced organizational family-responsive policies or benefits. The overriding objective of these policies is to assist employed parents in managing their family responsibilities while also maintaining employment (Aryee et al., 1998). However, workplace programs and organizational policies designed to help employees better integrate work and family roles do not seem to have much effect on work-family conflict (Kossek & Ozeki, 1998).

The relationships among roles can be complicated. Some studies suggest that the relationship between work demands and family responsibilities is best described as correlational rather then causal, with minimal spillover from one domain to the other (Frone, Russell, & Cooper, 1994). In addition, Lambert (1990) has suggested that studies of work-family conflict should take into account differences in the tendency of employees to compensate for difficulties or disappointments in one area of life, such as work, by increasing their involvement in other areas, such as family. It is not surprising that studies have found varying degrees of strength in the relationship between work-family conflict and job and life satisfaction (Kossek & Ozeki, 1998). In addition, there is evidence suggesting that work and family conflicts should be measured separately for men and women, as gender differences in customary household or domestic responsibilities may result in different relationships of role conflict with other variables (Wiersma & Van den Berg, 1991). For example, Williams and Alliger (1994) found that spillovers of distress and fatigue from work to family and from family to work were stronger for women than for men.

The Measures

Early studies of work and family role strain tended to treat conflict between work and family roles as a single construct (Netemeyer, Boles, & McMurrian, 1996). More recent studies have found evidence that work-family conflict (work interfering with family) and family-work conflict (family interfering with work) are related but distinct constructs (Frone et al., 1992; Netemeyer et al., 1996). Measures that clearly specify the direction of the role conflict (work demands interfering with family responsibilities compared to family demands interfering with work responsibilities) seem to provide clearer results than measures that combine indicators of both types of role conflicts into one global measure. The two domains of conflict may be related through spillover, where attitudes carry over from one domain (work vs. family) to the other. It is also possible that work and family roles may be related in a counterbalancing fashion or segmented so that individuals compartmentalize potentially competing role demands. Aryee (1993) and Small and Riley (1990) also found differences among work-spouse, work-parent, and work-housework role conflicts. Thus, work-family conflict (and presumably family-work conflict) may differ depending on the focus of the conflict. Indeed, a meta-analysis by Kossek and Ozeki (1998) found that differences in the strength of the relationship between work-family conflict and satisfaction may reflect differences in the measures used and in the samples studied.

The measures included in this chapter provide alternatives that measure work-family and family-work conflict separately as well as others that measure only work-family conflict. The measures also cover more general work versus nonwork conflict, career-family conflict, and lack of control at work.

Work Interference With Family and Family Interference With Work

Description   This measure was developed by Gutek, Searle, and Klepa (1991). The original measure used eight items to describe the extent to which an employee's work demands interfere with family responsibilities (four items) and the extent to which family demands interfere with work responsibilities (four items). Two additional items were added to each of these subscales by Carlson and Perrewé (1999). The two subscales have also been combined into a composite measure of work and family interference (Carlson & Perrewé, 1999).

Reliability   Coefficient alpha values for the measure of work interference with family ranged from .71 to .87. For the measure of family interference with work, alpha values ranged from .74 to .83 (Aryee, Fields, & Luk, 1999; Gutek et al., 1991; Judge, Boudreau, & Bretz, 1994; Williams & Alliger, 1994). Coefficient alpha values for the composite measure of work and family interference ranged from .66 to .89 (Adams, King, & King, 1996; Carlson & Perrewé, 1999; Frone, Russell, & Cooper, 1996; Gutek et al., 1991).

Validity   Work interference with family correlated positively with family interference with work, hours spent in paid work, number of children at home, job conflict, family conflict, flextime, working a compressed work week, child care needs, and working at home. Work interference with family correlated negatively with job satisfaction, life satisfaction, family satisfaction, age of an employee's youngest child, control over hours worked, and tangible support from other family members (Aryee et al., 1999; Frone et al., 1996; Gutek et al., 1991; Judge et al., 1994).

    Family interference with work correlated positively with number of children at home, work interference with family, hours spent in family work, family involvement, job conflict, flextime, working a compressed work week, child care needs, working at home, and family conflict. Family interference with work correlated negatively with job satisfaction, life satisfaction, age of the youngest child, hours spent in paid work, and control over hours worked (Adams et al., 1996; Aryee et al., 1999; Frone et al., 1996; Gutek et al., 1991; Judge et al., 1994).

    Factor analyses conducted by Gutek et al. (1991) and Frone et al. (1996) showed that work interference with family was empirically distinct from family interference with work. Judge et al. (1994) examined confirmatory factor models that indicated that work-family conflict, family-work conflict, job satisfaction, life satisfaction, and job stress were empirically distinct. Structural equation models evaluated by Aryee et al. (1999) and Frone et al. (1992) also showed that work-family and family-work conflict covary, but were empirically distinct.

Sources   Original eight items: Gutek, B. A., Searle, S., & Klepa, L. (1991). Rational versus gender role explanations for work-family conflict. *Journal of Applied*

Psychology, 76(4), 560-568. Items were taken from Table 1, p. 563. Copyright © 1991 by the American Psychological Association. Reprinted with permission.

Additional two items: Carlson, D. S., & Perrewé, P. L. (1999). The role of social support in the stressor-strain relationship: An examination of work-family conflict. *Journal of Management, 25*(4), 513-533. Items were taken from the appendix, pp. 523-524. Copyright © 1999. Reprinted with permission from Elsevier Science.

Items

Responses are obtained using a 5-point Likert-type scale where 1 = *strongly agree* and 5 = *strongly disagree.*

Work interference with family items:

1. After work, I come home too tired to do some of the things I'd like to do
2. On the job I have so much work to do that it takes away from my personal interests
3. My family/friends dislike how often I am preoccupied with my work while I am at home
4. My work takes up time that I'd like to spend with family/friends

Family interference with work items:

1. I'm often too tired at work because of the things I have to do at home
2. My personal demands are so great that it takes away from my work
3. My superiors and peers dislike how often I am preoccupied with my personal life while at work
4. My personal life takes up time that I'd like to spend at work.

The additional items added to the measures by Carlson and Perrewé (1999) are the following.

Additional work interference with family items:

1. My job or career interferes with my responsibilities at home, such as yard work, cooking, cleaning, repairs, shopping, paying the bills, or child care
2. My job or career keeps me from spending the amount of time I would like to spend with my family

Additional family interference with work items:

1. My home life interferes with my responsibilities at work, such as getting to work on time, accomplishing daily tasks, or working overtime
2. My home life keeps me from spending the amount of time I would like to spend on job or career-related activities

Work-Family Conflict

Description This measure, developed by Kopelman, Greenhaus, and Connolly (1983), uses eight items to assess the extent of the interrole conflict that occurs between work and family roles (work-family conflict). Grandey and Cropanzano (1998) suggest that by reversing the wording of the items so that the stressor is family demands, the measure can also be used to describe the spillover of family responsibilities to work roles (family-work conflict).

Reliability Coefficient alpha values for the eight-item measure of work-family conflict ranged from .78 to .90 (Adams et al., 1996; Goff, 1990; Grandey & Cropanzano, 1998; Thomas & Ganster, 1995; Wallace, 1999).

Validity Work-family conflict correlated positively with job involvement, work role conflict, work role ambiguity, work time demands, family role conflict, and family time demands. It correlated negatively with social support from work and family, family satisfaction, job satisfaction, and life satisfaction (Adams et al., 1996; Carlson & Perrewé, 1999). When both the work-family conflict items and the items reworded to assess family-work conflict were examined in a factor analysis, two distinct factors were found with the items loading appropriately on the separate factors.

Source Thomas, L. T., & Ganster, D. C. (1995). Impact of family-supportive work variables on work-family conflict and strain: A control perspective. *Journal of Applied Psychology, 80*(1), 6-15. Items were taken from the appendix, p. 15. Copyright © 1995 by the American Psychological Association. Reprinted with permission.

Items Responses are obtained using a 5-point Likert-type scale where 1 = *strongly disagree* and 5 = *strongly agree*.

1. My work schedule often conflicts with my family life
2. After work, I come home too tired to do some of the things I'd like to do
3. On the job, I have so much work that it takes away from my other interests
4. My family dislikes how often I am preoccupied with my work while I'm at home
5. Because my work is demanding at times I am irritable at home
6. The demands of my job make it difficult to be relaxed all the time at home
7. My work takes up time that I'd like to spend with my family
8. My job makes it difficult to be the kind of spouse or parent that I'd like to be

Work-Family Conflict and Family-Work Conflict

Description   This measure was developed by Netemeyer et al. (1996). It uses separate subscales to assess the extent of both work-family conflict and family-work conflict. The subscales for work-family conflict and family-work conflict are parsimonious, using five items each. The measure was designed to eliminate items present in other measures of work-family and family-work conflict that may measure outcomes rather then the conflict itself.

Reliability   Coefficient alpha values for the subscales for both work-family conflict and family-work conflict ranged from .88 to .89. In addition, confirmatory factor analyses showed that the factor loadings and factor correlations were invariant across three samples (Netemeyer et al., 1996).

Validity   Work-family conflict and family-work conflict both correlated negatively with job satisfaction and life satisfaction across three samples. Work-family conflict and family-work conflict both correlated positively with job tension, intention to leave, and burnout. Work-family conflict correlated positively with number of hours worked. Family-work conflict correlated positively with number of children living at home. Confirmatory factor analysis showed that the subscales for work-family conflict and family-work conflict were empirically distinct (Netemeyer et al., 1996).

Source   Netemeyer, R. G., Boles, J. S., & McMurrian, R. (1996). Development and validation of work-family conflict and family-work conflict scales. *Journal of Applied Psychology, 81*(4), 400-410. Items were taken from the appendix, p. 410. Copyright © 1996 by the American Psychological Association. Reprinted with permission.

Items   Responses are obtained using a 7-point Likert-type scale where 1 = *strongly disagree* and 7 = *strongly agree*.

Work-family conflict items:

1. The demands of my work interfere with my home family life
2. The amount of time my job takes up makes it difficult to fulfill family responsibilities
3. Things I want to do at home do not get done because of the demands my job puts on me
4. My job produces strain that makes it difficult to make changes to my plans for family activities
5. Due to work-related duties, I have to make changes to my plans for family activities

Family-work conflict items:

1. The demands of my family or spouse/partner interfere with work-related activities
2. I have to put off doing things at work because of demands on my time at home
3. Things I want to do at work don't get done because of the demands of my family or spouse/partner
4. My home life interferes with my responsibilities at work such as getting to work on time, accomplishing daily tasks, and working overtime
5. Family-related strain interferes with my ability to perform job-related duties

Job-Family Role Strain Scale

Description   This measure, developed by Bohen and Viveros-Long (1981), describes the frequency with which respondents experience stress and strain related to combining work and parenting. The measure assesses multiple aspects of role strain including ambiguity about norms, lack of congruity between personality and social roles, insufficiency of resources for role fulfillment, low rewards for role conformity, conflict between norms, and role overload.

Reliability   Coefficient alpha values ranged from .88 to .91 (Duxbury & Higgins, 1991; Higgins, Duxbury, & Irving, 1992; Thomas & Ganster, 1995).

Validity   Duxbury and Higgins (1991) showed that work-family role strain was empirically distinct from work conflict, family conflict, work and family involvement, and work and family expectations. Work-family role strain correlated positively with work involvement, work expectations, depression, control at work, family expectations, and perceptions of family supportive policies at work. Work-family role strain correlated negatively with quality of work life, quality of family life, job satisfaction, and life satisfaction (Duxbury & Higgins, 1991; Higgins et al., 1992; Thomas & Ganster, 1995).

Source   Bohen, H., & Viveros-Long, A. (1981). *Balancing jobs and family life.* Philadelphia: Temple University Press. Items were taken from Appendix H, pp. 274, 278. Reprinted with permission.

Items   Responses are obtained on a 5-point Likert-type scale where 1 = *always*, 2 = *most of the time*, 3 = *some of the time*, 4 = *rarely*, and 5 = *never.*

1. My job keeps me away from my family too much
2. I feel I have more to do than I can handle comfortably
3. I have a good balance between my job and my family time
4. I wish I had more time to do things for my family
5. I feel physically drained when I get home from work
6. I feel emotionally drained when I get home from work
7. I feel I have to rush to get everything done each day
8. My time off from work does not match other family members' schedules well
9. I feel I don't have enough time for myself
10. I worry that other people at work think my family interferes with my job
11. I feel more respected than I would if I didn't have a job
12. I worry whether I should work less and spend more time with my children
13. I am a better parent because I am not with my children all day
14. I find enough time for the children

15. I worry about how my kids are when I am working
16. I have as much patience with my children as I would like
17. I am comfortable with the arrangements for my children while I am working
18. Making arrangements for my children while I work involves a lot of effort
19. I worry that other people feel I should spend more time with my children.

Career-Family Attitudes

Description   This measure was developed by Sanders, Lengnick-Hall, Lengnick-Hall, and Steele-Clapp (1998). It uses 50 items to assess employee attitudes toward managing their career and family interface. The measure was designed to be gender neutral and to assess not only what respondents expect for themselves but also what they expect from their spouse in the area of career-family conflict. The measure includes subscales that assess family-career interface from the standpoint of the extent to which the respondent defers career matters to take care of family matters as well as the extent to which a spouse defers his or her career. The measure covers possible conflicts in the areas of career, household, and child care responsibilities (family focus); the extent of equal balance in sharing home and career chores (balance); the extent to which a respondent may pay more attention to career than to marriage or children (career focus); the extent to which the respondent has decision power in the household and the spouse defers his or her career to raise children (dominance); the extent to which a spouse will support the respondent's career by giving in on issues, moving, and so on (spousal support); and the extent to which spouses socialize or vacation independent of the other.

Reliability   Coefficient alpha values for the subscales were .78 for family focus, .78 for balance, .84 for career focus, .75 for dominance, .67 for spousal support, and .66 for independence (Sanders et al., 1998).

Validity   Family focus correlated negatively with educational aspirations and an employee's grade point average. Balance correlated negatively with male gender of respondent and positively with educational aspirations and a respondent's grade point average. Career focus correlated positively with educational aspirations and an employee's grade point average. Dominance correlated positively with being a male respondent and living in a rural setting. Spousal support correlated positively with being male and correlated negatively with educational aspirations and grade point average. Independence correlated negatively with being a male respondent and positively with educational aspirations and grade point average (Sanders et al., 1998). Factor analysis of the scale items found six factors corresponding to family focus, balance career focus, dominance, spousal support, and independence. The family focus factor was subsequently separated into "I defer" and "someone defers" subscales (Sanders et al., 1998).

Source   Sanders, M. M., Lengnick-Hall, M. L., Lengnick-Hall, C. A., & Steele-Clapp, L. (1998). Love and work: Career-family attitudes of new entrants into the labor force. *Journal of Organizational Behavior, 19,* 603-619. Items were taken from Appendix A, pp. 617-619. Copyright © 1998. Reproduced by permission of John Wiley & Sons Limited.

Items
Responses are obtained using a 7-point Likert-type scale where 1 = *strongly disagree* and 7 = *strongly agree*.

Family focus items ("I defer" subscale):

1. I expect to go as far as I can in my career and expect encouragement from my spouse (R)
2. I would like for my spouse to make most of the financial decisions regardless of who makes the most money
3. I do not expect to have a career
4. I would like for my spouse to have more education than I do
5. It would bother me a lot if I make more money than my spouse does
6. If my spouse and I can't agree on something, I think I should most often give in to my spouse
7. I will be mostly responsible for raising our children, regardless of whether or not I work outside the home
8. If I do not work outside the home, I will do all the housework
9. I expect to stay home full-time with our children
10. My spouse's career is more important than mine

Family focus items ("Someone defers" subscale):

1. Professional child care providers (day care, sitter) will take care of our children while my spouse and I work (R)
2. I expect that either my spouse or I will be home during the day with our children
3. Marriage and two careers do not mix
4. Children and two careers do not mix

Balance items:

1. I expect my spouse to be mostly responsible for raising our children, regardless of whether or not my spouse is employed (R)
2. If my spouse works outside the home, I will help somewhat with the housework
3. My career and my spouse's career will be equally important
4. I expect my spouse and I to share responsibility for raising our children
5. I don't care whether my spouse or I make the most money
6. If I am employed, I expect my spouse to help with the housework
7. I intend to encourage my spouse to fully develop his or her career
8. I would like my spouse and me to make financial decisions together regardless of how much money we each make
9. If both my spouse and I are employed, I expect housework to be a jointly shared responsibility
10. I would like to take some vacations with my spouse but no children

Career focus items:

1. I expect that there will be times when my spouse will have to pay more attention to job problems than to our relationship
2. Sometimes I will have to pay more attention to my job than to my family
3. I do not expect to ever have to pay more attention to my job than to my relationship with my spouse (R)
4. I expect that sometimes my spouse will have to pay more attention to his or her job than to our family
5. I expect there will be times when I will have to pay more attention to my job than to my relationship with my spouse
6. I expect that neither my spouse nor I will pay more attention to our careers than to our family (R)

Dominance items:

1. I expect my spouse to stay home full-time with our children
2. My spouse should be able to go to school as long as he or she wishes whether or not we have children (R)
3. It would bother me a lot if my spouse makes more money than I do
4. Yard work and fix-it tasks will mainly be done by me
5. My career will be more important than my spouse's career
6. I would like my spouse and I to share yard work and fix-it tasks (R)
7. I do not expect my spouse to have a career
8. I would like to make most of the financial decisions regardless of how much money my spouse makes
9. I would like to have more education than my spouse

Spousal support items:

1. If my spouse and I can't agree on something, I think my spouse should give in to me
2. If my spouse is not employed, he or she should do all the housework
3. If I get an excellent job offer elsewhere, I will expect my spouse to move to the new place
4. Weekends will be time for me to relax, watch TV, etc., and I expect my spouse to keep distractions (i.e., visitors, children, chores) to a minimum
5. Weekends will be time for my spouse to relax, watch TV, etc., and I expect to keep distractions (i.e., visitors, children, chores) to a minimum
6. Yard work and fix-it tasks will mainly be done by my spouse
7. Both on the job and at home, some tasks are "men's work" and some tasks are "women's work"

Independence items:

1. I expect my spouse to take some vacations alone
2. I would like to occasionally go out in the evening without my spouse
3. I would like to take some vacations by myself
4. I expect my spouse to occasionally go out in the evening without me

Items denoted with (R) are reverse scored.

Job and Non-Work Conflict

Description   This measure, developed by Small and Riley (1990), assesses the extent of spillover of work demands into four nonwork roles. These are leisure, homemaker, parent, and spouse. The measure is based on the scarcity hypothesis, which contends that individuals have a finite amount of energy. When an individual is involved in multiple social roles, these roles tend to drain (stress) them resulting in the depletion of energy resources or burnout in their roles as worker, spouse, and parent.

Reliability   Coefficient alpha values for the job-spouse and job-parent conflict scales were .70 and .81, respectively (Aryee, 1993).

Validity   Job-parent conflict correlated positively with number of children under six years of age and job-spouse conflict for both husbands and wives. Job-parent conflict also correlated positively with hours spent on the job for wives, but not husbands. For husbands, job-parent conflict was correlated positively with burnout and negatively with quality of spousal experience. Job-spouse conflict was correlated positively with burnout for husbands, but not for wives. For wives, job-spouse conflict correlated positively with time at work, work role ambiguity, and lack of career progress (Aryee, 1993).

Source   Small, S., & Riley, D. (1990). Towards a multidimensional assessment of work spillover into family life. *Journal of Marriage and the Family, 52*, 51-61. Items were taken from Table 1, p. 53. Copyright © 1990 by the National Council on Family Relations, 3989 Central Ave. NE, Suite 550, Minneapolis, MN 55421. Reprinted by permission.

Items   Responses are obtained using a 5-point Likert-type scale where 1 = *strongly disagree* and 5 = *strongly agree*.

Job-marriage conflict items:

1. My job helps me have a better relationship with my spouse
2. My job keeps me from spending time with my spouse
3. Worrying about my job is interfering with my relationship with my spouse
4. After work I am too tired to do things with my spouse
5. My marriage suffers because of my work

Job-parent conflict items:

1. My job makes it hard for me to have a good relationship with my children
2. My working hours interfere with the amount of time I spend with my children

3. Because I am often irritable after work, I am not as good a parent as I like
4. When I get home from work, I often do not have the energy to be a good parent
5. I am a better parent because of my job

Job-leisure conflict items:

1. My job makes it difficult to enjoy my free time outside of work
2. The amount of time I spend working interferes with how much free time I have
3. Worry about my job makes it hard for me to enjoy myself outside of work
4. Because I am often tired after work, I don't see friends as much as I would like
5. My job doesn't affect whether I enjoy my free time outside of work

Job-home management conflict items:

1. My job makes it difficult to get household chores done
2. I spend so much time working that I am unable to get much done at home
3. Worrying about my job interferes with my ability to get things done around the house
4. When I get home from my job, I do not have the energy to do work around the house
5. Having a job makes it easier to get my household chores done

Work-Home Conflict

Description   This measure, developed by Bacharach et al. (1991), assesses the extent of conflict between work and home responsibilities. Work-home conflict is a form of interrole conflict in which the role pressures from the work and home domains are incompatible in some respects. The measure is designed to tap the degree to which a job disrupts and affects a person's life at home and attempts to incorporate a broad range of personal and social concerns for both married and unmarried employees.

Reliability   Coefficient alpha was .77 (Bacharach et al. 1991).

Validity   Work-home conflict correlated positively with role conflict and role overload. Work-home conflict correlated negatively with job satisfaction (Bacharach et al., 1991).

Source   Bacharach, S. B., Bamberger, P., & Conley, S. (1991). Work-home conflict among nurses and engineers: Mediating the impact of role stress on burnout and satisfaction at work. *Journal of Organizational Behavior, 12*(1), 39-53. Items were taken from text, p. 44. Copyright © 1991. Reproduced by permission of John Wiley & Sons Limited.

Items   Responses are obtained using a 4-point Likert-type scale where 1 = *never* and 4 = *almost always.*

1. Do the demands of work interfere with your home, family, or social life?
2. Does the time you spend at work detract from your family or social life?
3. Does your work have disadvantages for your family or social life?
4. Do you not seem to have enough time for your family or social life?

Work to Family Conflict Scale

Description   This measure, developed by Stephens and Sommer (1996), assesses work-family conflict. The measure uses 14 items to describe conflicts that originate in the workplace and may affect the family. The measure attempts to described these conflicts using three dimensions. These are time-based conflict resulting from the competition for an individual's time from multiple roles; strain-based conflict resulting from conditions where stressors in one domain induce physical or psychological strain in the individual, hampering role fulfillment in one or both domains; and behavior-based conflict that occurs when patterns of behavior appropriate to each domain are incompatible.

Reliability   The behavior-based dimension had a coefficient alpha of .80. The time-based dimension had a coefficient alpha of .74. The strain-based dimension had a coefficient alpha of .77 (Stephens & Sommer, 1996).

Validity   Stephens and Sommer (1996) examined the items with exploratory factor analysis and found three latent factors. Eight items covering both time-based and strain-based work-home conflict loaded on one factor, and the remaining six items loaded on two factors. One of these factors contained the positively worded items describing strain due to behavior-based conflict, and the other contained the negatively worded behavior-based conflict items. Because negatively worded items can create dimensions associated only with the direction of the item wording, the six behavior-related items seemed to represent a single conceptual dimension factor (Stephens & Sommer, 1996). Confirmatory factor analysis in a separate sample found three factors. One factor contained the behavior-related items, the second factor contained four time-based items, and the third factor contained four strain-based items.

Source   Stephens, G. K., & Sommer, S. M. (1996). The measurement of work to family conflict. *Educational and Psychological Measurement, 56*(3), 475-486. Copyright © 1996 by Sage Publications, Inc. Items were taken from Table 5, p. 484. Reprinted by permission of Sage Publications, Inc.

Items   Responses are obtained using a 7-point Likert-type scale where 1 = *strongly disagree* and 7 = *strongly agree.*

Time-based conflict items:

1. My work keeps me from my family more than I would like
2. My work takes up time that I feel I should spend with my family
3. The time I must devote to my job does not keep me from participating equally in household responsibilities and activities

4. I generally seem to have enough time to fulfill my potential both in my career and as a spouse and parent

Strain-based conflict items:

5. I often feel the strain of attempting to balance my responsibilities at work and home
6. Because my work is so demanding, I am often irritable at home
7. The demands of my job make it difficult for me to maintain the kind of relationship with my spouse and children that I would like
8. The tension of balancing my responsibilities at home and work often causes me to feel emotionally drained

Behavior-based conflict items:

9. The problem-solving approaches I use in my job are effective in resolving problems at home
10. The things I do that make me effective at work also help me to be a better parent and spouse
11. What works for me at home seems to be effective at work as well, and vice versa
12. I am not able to act the same way at home as at work
13. I act differently in responding to interpersonal problems at work than I do at home
14. Behavior that is effective and necessary for me at work would be counter-productive at home

Control Over Areas of Work and Family

Description   This measure, developed by Thomas and Ganster (1995), describes an employee's perceptions of control over aspects of work and family responsibilities and demands that have been shown to contribute to work-family conflict. The measure uses 14 items to assess the extent to which employees perceive they have control over such work and home areas as work scheduling and taking time off to attend to a sick parent.

Reliability   Coefficient alpha was .75 (Thomas & Ganster, 1995).

Validity   Control over work and family areas correlated positively with job satisfaction and perceived support. Control correlated negatively with perceived work-family conflict and depression (Thomas & Ganster, 1995).

Source   Thomas, L. T., & Ganster, D. C. (1995). Impact of family-supportive work variables on work-family conflict and strain: A control perspective. *Journal of Applied Psychology, 80*(1), 6-15. Items were taken from the appendix, p. 15. Copyright © 1995 by the American Psychological Association. Reprinted with permission.

Items   Responses are obtained on a 5-point Likert-type scale where 1 = *very little* and 5 = *very much.*

1. How much choice do you have over the amount and quality of day care available for your child/children?
2. How much choice do you have over the amount and quality of care available for a sick child?
3. How much choice do you have in obtaining adult supervision for your child/children before or after school?
4. How much choice do you have over the amount and quality of day care available for a dependent parent or other relative?
5. How much choice do you have over when you begin and end each workday or each workweek?
6. How much choice do you have in arranging part-time employment?
7. To what extent can you choose to do some of your work at home instead of your usual place of employment?
8. How much choice do you have over amount and timing of work that you must do at home in order to meet your employment demands?
9. How much choice do you have over the amount you pay for dependent care?
10. How much choice do you have over when you can take vacations or days off?
11. How much choice do you have over when you can take a few hours off?

12. To what extent are you expected to limit the number of times you make or receive personal phone calls while you work?
13. How much choice do you have in making unanticipated child care arrangements (e.g., during snow days or unexpected job delays)?
14. In general, how much control do you have over the way you balance working and parenting?

8

Person-Organization Fit

The Construct

Consideration of person-organization fit is based on the perspective that aspects of both an individual employee and a job situation combine to influence the individual's response to work (O'Reilly, Chatman, & Caldwell, 1991). That is, attitudes, behaviors, and other individual-level outcomes result not from the person or environment separately, but rather from the relationship between the two. The concept of fit is particularly prominent in studies of organizational stress where measures must recognize individual differences in the way situations are cognitively appraised (Edwards, 1996).

Person-organization fit refers to the degree of congruence or compatibility between the attributes of an organization member and those of the organization. For individuals, these attributes may include personality traits, beliefs, values, and interests. For the organization, these characteristics traditionally include the culture, climate, values, goals, and norms (Chan, 1996). Congruence may occur when a person supplements or matches with other individuals in an environment, when a person's characteristics add something to the environment that was missing, when an organization satisfies individual needs, and/or when an individual has the abilities required to meet organizational demands (Kristof, 1996).

Value congruence is an important form of fit because organizational values are fundamental components of organizational culture that affect employees' attitudes and behaviors (Chatman, 1989). Person-organization fit can be operationalized as an individual's goal congruence with organizational leaders and peers (Vancouver & Schmitt, 1991). An alternative approach defines fit as the match between individual preferences or needs and organizational systems and structures. In general, a person will be more satisfied with work if the environment fulfills his or her needs. Alternately, person-organization fit can be viewed as the match between the personality characteristics of an individual employee and organizational climate. For example, an organization's collectivist climate may be reflected by a team-based compensation system that may or may not meet an individual's need for achievement (Kristof, 1996).

There is some debate as to whether person-organization fit should be operationalized as the compatibility of employees with specific jobs. Edwards (1991) defined person-job fit as the agreement between the abilities of a person and the demands of a job or the desires of a person and the attributes of a job. Although it could be argued that jobs tend to offer a narrow view that may not be representative of an organization, there is substantial evidence that employees may form their views about an organization based on their experiences in their job (Hackman & Oldham, 1980). Person-organization fit does not generally include person-vocation fit, which often reflects the similarity between an individual's personality and that of a vocational environment, or person-group fit, which describes the compatibility between individuals and their work groups (Kristof, 1996).

The Measures

The validity of measurement of person-organization fit depends on the ability to assess relevant aspects of the person and the organization and then to determine the degree of match. One of the measurement problems in the field is the fact that not all characteristics will apply to all people. Thus, when trying to assess match with an organization, it is desirable to select only those characteristics that are pertinent for determining a person's fit (O'Reilly et al., 1991). Once the individual and organizational characteristics have been selected, researchers have a variety of techniques at their disposal for assessing the extent of fit. Some measures use direct assessment, which involves asking people explicitly whether they believe that a good fit exists. Using this approach, employees directly rate how compatible their values are with those of their organizations. Direct measures are beneficial if the construct under investigation is subjective or perceived fit, defined as the judgment that a person fits well in an organization (Kristof, 1996). A disadvantage of direct measures is that they may confound perceptions of the person and environment, thereby preventing estimation of the independent effects of each. Addi-

tionally, when the questions do not explicitly describe what values or other characteristics are to be considered in the respondents' answers, it is almost impossible to ensure that commensurate dimensions are being considered (Edwards, 1991; Kristof, 1996).

An alternative measurement approach is to rely on indirect measures to assess fit. Indirect measures involve an explicit comparison between individual and organizational characteristics rated separately. This type of measurement allows an assessment of similarity without asking for implicit judgments of fit by those involved in the situation being analyzed (Chatman, 1989; Kristof, 1996).

There are different techniques for indirect measurement of person-organization fit. The first is cross-level measurement. In this approach, each respondent describes himself or herself by answering questions such as "What do you value?" Measurement of the organizational level variable is more complicated. The organizational constructs of interest are variables such as values, goals, climate, or culture. Therefore, aggregations of individual perceptions must be used to compute organizational variables (Kristof, 1996). There is debate about whether a sufficient level of agreement should be shown before individual data can be aggregated to create an organizational-level variable (Kristof, 1996). On one hand, agreement among individuals about organizational attributes may be unnecessary because variance between individuals can be considered error surrounding the one true score of the organizational variable. Alternatively, when the organizational variable is perceptual in nature, one true organizational score may not exist. Variance in individual perceptions about the organization may be substantive and not be simply error. To use the mean of two individuals' ratings of an organization's values may mask the existence of different perceptions about organizational values in different parts of the organization (Kristof, 1996). Because organizational values are generally viewed as those that a group (the organization) possesses, a majority of active members should show some level of agreement about them to establish the organizational variable (Chatman, 1989; Kristof, 1996).

It is also possible to study person-organization fit based on individual employee perceptions of their preferences and their perceptions of organizational values. That is, each respondent answers parallel questions such as "What do you value?" and "What does your company value?" The similarity of the answers to these questions is then calculated, using either traditional difference scores or polynomial regression, resulting in an individual-level measure of person-organization fit. Regardless of the statistical approach used to estimate fit, all measurement occurs at the individual level of analysis (Edwards & Van Harrison, 1993; Kristof, 1996).

Whether cross-level or individual-level measurement is used, researchers must consider alternative methods for calculating a single index reflecting the degree of similarity between employees and their organization. In the case of multiple predictors, profile similarity indices can be calculated as the sum of algebraic differences, the sum of absolute differences, the sum of the squared differences, the Euclidean distance (square root of the sum of squared differences), or the correlation between two profiles (Kristof, 1996). Despite their widespread use in the fit literature, difference scores and profile similarity indices have been criticized for a variety of problems (Edwards & Van Harrison, 1993). An alternative procedure is polynomial regression. Using this technique, Edwards and Van Harrison (1993) revealed meaningful findings previously concealed by the use of difference scores and showed that nonlinear relationships may provide superior measures of person-environment fit.

Organizational Culture Profile

Description   The Organizational Culture Profile (OCP) was developed by O'Reilly et al. (1991). It uses a profile comparison approach to calculate person-organization fit. The OCP uses 54 value statements that describe individual and/or organizational values. Respondents Q-sort the items into nine categories based on their desirability to an employee or the accuracy with which they described an organization. The Q-sort method requires respondents to put a specified number of statements into each of nine categories. The required item-category pattern for the 54 items is 2-4-6-9-12-9-6-4-2. The two most desired or characteristic attributes are placed in Q-sort category 9, the next four in Q-sort category 8, and so on.

To develop a profile of an organization's culture, a group of key informants familiar with the organization is asked to sort the 54 value statements according to the extent to which the items are characteristic of the organization. The degree to which the organization's values are consistently shared can be investigated by the interrelation among raters using a variation of the Spearman-Brown general prophecy formula (O'Reilly et al., 1991). Employees are asked to sort the items according to their personal preferences for each value in their ideal organization. The person-organization fit score for each individual is calculated by correlating the individual preference profile with the profile of the organization for which the person works.

Analysis of the individual responses to the OCP found that 27 of the items describing organizational values loaded on seven dimensions (O'Reilly et al., 1991). Three dimensions relate to how work tasks are handled in an organization. These include detail, which is an emphasis on being highly analytical and oriented to accuracy; stability, which emphasizes predictability and organizational rules; and innovation, which is an organization's tendency to take risks and be responsive to new opportunities. Two dimensions, team orientation and respect for people, describe values or norms for interpersonal relationships. Two additional dimensions describe organizational norms for individual actions. These include outcome orientation, which describes an emphasis on high expectations for performance, and aggressiveness, which describes an emphasis on competition. Cable and Judge (1997) reduced the number of items used in the OCP to 40.

In Caldwell and O'Reilly (1990), the profile comparison approach was used to examine person-job fit. In this case, a panel of subject matter experts described jobs based on a pool of competency statements. Individuals then rated their skills and abilities using a Q-sort of the same competency statements.

Reliability   The reliability of the ratings of the organization's values obtained with OCP is assessed using the Spearman-Brown prophecy formula. The Spearman-Brown reliability ranged from .84 to .94 (Caldwell & O'Reilly, 1990; Chatman & Jehn, 1994; O'Reilly et al., 1991; Sheridan, 1992; Vandenberghe, 1999). Chatman and Jehn (1994) found that the correlations of the value ratings between all the pairs of raters within each of 15 organizations ranged from .26 to .66, with a median of .44. Cable and Judge (1997) found that assessments of organizational profiles 6 months apart showed test-retest reliability averaged .61. The mean test-retest reliability for those items rated as very characteristics of an organization (in categories 7, 8, or 9 in the Q-sort) and very uncharacteristic (in categories 1, 2, or 3 in the Q-sort) was .87.

Validity

In O'Reilly et al. (1991), factor analysis of the individual employee ratings of the 54 items describing what employees would like in their organization and the ratings of the same items for organizations produced seven factors: innovation, stability, respect for people, outcome orientation, attention to detail, team orientation, and aggressiveness.

Attention to detail correlated positively with stability and correlated negatively with both team orientation and having an outcome orientation in interpersonal relationships. Stability correlated negatively with innovation and outcome orientation. Innovation correlated positively with an outcome focus in interpersonal relations. Team orientation correlated positively with respect for people and correlated negatively with aggressiveness in interpersonal relations. Respect for people correlated negatively with aggressiveness in interpersonal relations (Sheridan, 1992). Chatman and Jehn (1994) found that the factor structure of the OCP was consistent across 15 firms.

Person-organization fit correlated positively with normative organizational commitment and job satisfaction. Person-organization fit correlated negatively with intention to leave and turnover (O'Reilly et al., 1991). Person-job fit correlated positively with employee performance ratings across five samples (Caldwell & O'Reilly, 1990). Cable and Judge (1996) found that perceived person-organization fit measured with the OCP correlated positively with a separate subjective assessment of person-organization fit, a subjective person-job fit measure, perception of an organization's rewards system, and general organizational image. Person-organization fit correlated negatively with work experience (Cable & Judge, 1996).

Source

O'Reilly, C. A., III, Chatman, J., & Caldwell, D. F. (1991). People and organizational culture: A profile comparison approach to assessing person-organization fit. *Academy of Management Journal, 34*(3), 487-516. © 1991 by Academy of Management. Items were taken from the appendix, p. 516. Reproduced with permission of Academy of Management in the format textbook via Copyright Clearance Center.

Items

Instructions for assessing organizational profiles:

To obtain profiles of the cultures of firms, informants with broad experience are asked to sort the 54 items in terms of how characteristic each is of their organization's culture. Respondents receive the following definition and instructions: "Important values may be expressed in the form of norms or shared expectations about what's important, how to behave, or what attitudes are appropriate. Please sort the 54 values into a row of nine categories, placing at one end of the row those cards that you consider to be the most characteristic aspects of the culture of your organization, and at the other end those cards that you believe to be the least characteristic." The Q-sort ratings from multiple key informants for an organization are then averaged to develop a single profile for the organization.

Assessing individual preferences:

To assess individual preferences for organizational cultures, respondents are asked to sort the 54-item deck into the nine categories by responding to the question "How important is it for this characteristic to be a part of the organization you work for?" The categories range from "most desirable" to "most undesirable."

Calculating the person-organization fit score:

The person-organization fit score for each individual is calculated by correlating the individual preference profile with the profile of the organization for which the person works. Additional descriptions of the approach to assessing fit appear in Chatman (1989) and in Caldwell and O'Reilly (1990).

Organizational Culture Profile items:

The original 54 OCP items are provided. The items retained in the 40-item version of the OCP used by Cable and Judge (1997) are indicated with (CJ).

1. Flexibility
2. Adaptability (CJ)
3. Stability (CJ)
4. Predictability
5. Being innovative (CJ)
6. Being quick to take advantage of opportunities (CJ)
7. A willingness to experiment
8. Risk taking (CJ)
9. Being careful
10. Autonomy (CJ)
11. Being rule oriented (CJ)
12. Being analytical (CJ)
13. Paying attention to detail (CJ)
14. Being precise
15. Being team oriented (CJ)
16. Sharing information freely (CJ)
17. Emphasizing a single culture throughout the organization
18. Being people oriented (CJ)
19. Fairness (CJ)
20. Respect for the individual's right
21. Tolerance (CJ)
22. Informality (CJ)
23. Being easygoing

24. Being calm (CJ)
25. Being supportive (CJ)
26. Being aggressive (CJ)
27. Decisiveness (CJ)
28. Action orientation
29. Taking initiative
30. Being reflective (CJ)
31. Achievement orientation (CJ)
32. Being demanding
33. Taking individual responsibility (CJ)
34. Having high expectations for performance (CJ)
35. Opportunities for professional growth (CJ)
36. High pay for good performance (CJ)
37. Security of employment (CJ)
38. Offers praise for good performance (CJ)
39. Low level of conflict
40. Confronting conflict directly (CJ)
41. Developing friends at work (CJ)
42. Fitting in
43. Working in collaboration with others
44. Enthusiasm for the job (CJ)
45. Working long hours (CJ)
46. Not being constrained by many rules (CJ)
47. An emphasis on quality (CJ)
48. Being distinctive or different from others (CJ)
49. Having a good reputation (CJ)
50. Being socially responsible (CJ)
51. Being results oriented (CJ)
52. Having a clear guiding philosophy (CJ)
53. Being competitive (CJ)
54. Being highly organized (CJ)

Goal Congruence

Description   This measure, developed by Vancouver and Schmitt (1991), uses 14 items to assess the degree of congruence between the goals of an individual employee and the goals of his or her supervisor or peers. The instrument was originally developed and used in an educational environment. After obtaining ratings of goals from an employee and a supervisor, the two profiles are compared by calculation of a measure of congruence called "D" (the Euclidean distance), which is the square root of the sum of the squared differences between the ratings of an employee and the supervisor. The larger the D measure, the lower the congruence level. To obtain congruence between an employee and his or her peers, the D scores are calculated for an employee and each member of a group of peers. The congruence measure for each employee is the average of the D scores across all peers in the group.

Reliability   Reliability was indirectly assessed by the intraclass correlations of the goal congruence measures within schools. These averaged .24 (Vancouver & Schmitt, 1991).

Validity   Supervisor-subordinate goal congruence and employee-peer goal congruence were both positively correlated with subordinate job satisfaction and organizational commitment, and negatively correlated with intention to quit (Vancouver & Schmitt, 1991).

Source   Vancouver, J. B., & Schmitt, N. W. (1991). An exploratory examination of person-organization fit: Organizational goal congruence. *Personnel Psychology, 44,* 333-352. Items were taken from Table 1, p. 343. Copyright © 1991. Reproduced with permission.

Items   Response are obtained on a 7-point Likert-type scale where 0 = *of no importance* and 6 = *of primary importance*. Respondents are asked to rate the importance of the following goals:

1. Increase students' basic skills
2. Increase breadth of courses
3. Enhance athletic programs
4. Enhance co-curricular activities
5. Upgrade staff development
6. Increase cost-effectiveness
7. Upgrade physical resources
8. Achieve full racial integration
9. Maximize instructional time through systemic changes
10. Upgrade special education programs
11. Upgrade discipline practices
12. Increase parent/community involvement
13. Upgrade academic programs
14. Upgrade vocational educational programs

Person-Organization Fit Scale

Description   This measure, developed by Bretz and Judge (1994), consists of two questionnaires containing 15 items each. One questionnaire asks employees to indicate how accurately each statement describes their current organization. The other questionnaire asks employees for their individual preferences for an organization to work in. A fit score for each individual is calculated as the sum of the differences between the responses to the two questionnaires. Thus, low scores indicate better person-organization fit. The questions used to assess person-organization fit were developed to reflect fit between an employee's knowledge, skills, and abilities and his or her job requirements; congruence between employee needs and organizational systems and structures; agreement between an employee's value orientations and the perceived values orientation of the organization; and perceived match between an employee's personality and the organization's personality or image (Bretz & Judge, 1994).

Reliability   Rather than coefficient alpha, Bretz and Judge (1994) assessed the internal reliability of the measures of employee preferences, organizational characteristics, and differences between the two using confirmatory factor analysis. A single factor was found for each of the three scales, indicating internal consistency reliability.

Validity   Person-organization fit correlated positively with job satisfaction, salary level, job level, hours worked per week, access to a mentor, and career interruption. Person-organization fit correlated negatively with being nonwhite and having a Ph.D. (Bretz & Judge, 1994).

Source   Bretz, R. D., Jr., & Judge, T. A. (1994). Person-organization fit and the theory of work adjustment: Implications for satisfaction, tenure, and career success. *Journal of Vocational Behavior, 44,* 32-54. Items were taken from Table 1, p. 39. Copyright © 1994 by Academic Press. Reproduced with permission.

Items   Responses are obtained using a 5-point Likert-type scale where 1 = *not true at all* and 5 = *definitely true.*

Instructions: Each employee is asked to complete the first questionnaire describing his or her perceptions about the organization. Then the employee is asked to complete the second questionnaire describing the type of organization he or she would prefer. Lack of fit is calculated as the sum of the differences between the corresponding items of the two questionnaires.

Job and organization perception items:

1. This organization pays on the basis of individual performance
2. This organization has a profit or gain-sharing plan

3. This organization makes promotions based mostly on individual performance
4. This organization encourages competition between employees
5. This organization encourages and rewards loyalty
6. Teamwork and cooperation are valued and rewarded here
7. When the organization has a good year it pays bonuses to the employees
8. People generally have to work in groups to get their work done
9. This organization offers long-term employment security
10. This organization has a "fast-track" program
11. This organization has/follows a promote-from-within policy
12. The typical employee here works very hard to fulfill work expectations
13. There is an emphasis on helping others
14. Fairness is an important consideration in organizational activities
15. When mistakes are made it is best to be honest and "take your lumps"

Perceived Person-Organization Fit

Description   This measure, developed by Cable and Judge (1996), uses three items to directly assess an employee's perception of his or her fit with an organization.

Reliability   Cable and Judge (1996) found that coefficient alpha was .87.

Validity   Perceived person-organization fit correlated positively with employee perceptions of their person-job fit, job satisfaction, organizational commitment, willingness to recommend the organization to others, and employee rating of the importance of person-job fit (Cable & Judge, 1996).

Source   Cable, D. M., & Judge, T. A. (1996). Person-organization fit, job choice decisions, and organizational entry. *Organizational Behavior and Human Decision Processes, 67*(3), 294-311. Items were taken from text, p. 299. Copyright © 1996 by Academic Press. Reproduced with permission.

Items   Responses are obtained on a 5-point Likert-type scale where 1 = *not at all* and 5 = *completely.*

1. To what degree do feel your values "match" or fit this organization and the current employees in this organization?
2. My values match those of the current employees in this organization.
3. Do you think the values and "personality" of this organization reflect your own values and personality?

Perceived Person-Organization Fit

Description   This measure was developed by Lovelace and Rosen (1996). It assesses perceived person-organization fit by directly asking respondents for the degree of fit between their own personal values, ethics, goals, and objectives and those of the organization for which they work.

Reliability   Coefficient alpha was .92. A factor analysis of the 14 items showed that they all loaded on a single factor (Lovelace & Rosen, 1996).

Validity   Person-organization fit correlated positively with job satisfaction, direct feedback, and age. Person-organization fit correlated negatively with perceived stress and intentions to leave (Lovelace & Rosen, 1996).

Source   Lovelace, K., & Rosen, B. (1996). Differences in achieving person-organization fit among diverse groups of managers. *Journal of Management, 22*(5), 703-722. Items were taken from text, p. 708. Copyright © 1996. Reprinted with permission from Elsevier Science.

Scale items   Responses are obtained on a 7-point Likert-type scale where 1 = *very poor fit* and 7 = *very good fit*.

Instructions: Employees are directed to "describe the fit between your values and the organization's values."

These assessments are made for the following 14 items:

1. Values
2. Ethics
3. Goals and objectives
4. Skills
5. Attitudes
6. Participation in extracurricular activities
7. Interactions with co-workers
8. Outside interests
9. Work-family balance
10. Politics
11. Religion
12. Definition of career success
13. Dress
14. Personal style

Person-Environment Fit

Description   This measure was developed by Caplan, Cobb, French, Van Harrison, and Pinneau (1980). It asks employees to provide responses to parallel sets of items covering four job dimensions. One set of items described the employee perceptions of what is offered by the work environment. The other set of responses described what the employee prefers. The four job dimensions are job complexity (six item pairs), role ambiguity (four item pairs), responsibility for persons (four item pairs), and quantitative workload (seven item pairs). The items are averaged for each job dimension to obtain a score for the environment (E) and a score for the person (P).

Person-environment fit can then be calculated by various methods, such as the absolute value of the difference in the E and P scores.

Reliability   Coefficient alpha values for job complexity were .72 for the environment (E) subscale and .71 for the person (P) subscale. Alpha values for role ambiguity were .84 for the E subscale and .86 for the P subscale. Alpha values for responsibility of persons were .89 for the E subscale and .87 for the P subscale. Alpha values for quantitative workload were .71 for the E subscale and .60 for the P subscale (Edwards & Van Harrison, 1993).

Validity   Edwards and Van Harrison (1993) found that lack of person-environment fit calculated as the absolute value of the difference between P and E values for job complexity correlated positively with job dissatisfaction, workload dissatisfaction, boredom, depression, anxiety, and somatic complaints. Lack of person-environment fit in responsibility for persons correlated positively with workload dissatisfaction, job dissatisfaction, and boredom. Lack of fit in quantitative workload correlated positively with workload dissatisfaction, boredom, depression, and irritation (Edwards & Van Harrison, 1993).

Source   Caplan, R. D., Cobb, S., French, J. R. P., Van Harrison, R., & Pinneau, S. R. (1980). *Job demands and worker health.* Ann Arbor: University of Michigan, Institute for Social Research. Items were taken from Appendix E, pp. 238, 241, 242-243, and 246. Copyright © 1980. Reproduced with permission.

Items   Quantitative workload items:

The wording shown for each item measures the E subscale. The rewording required for the P subscale is shown in parentheses. Responses are obtained for these items using a 5-point Likert-type scale where 1 = *hardly any*, 2 = *a little*, 3 = *some*, 4 = *a lot*, and 5 = *a great deal*.

1. How much slowdown in the workload do you experience? (would you prefer) (R)
2. How much time do you have to think and contemplate? (would you like) (R)

3. How much workload do you have? (would you like to have)
4. What quantity of work do others expect you to do? (would you prefer others to expect of you)
5. How much time do you have to do all your work? (would you like to have) (R)

Responses for the following items are obtained using a 5-point Likert-type scale where 1 = *hardly any*, 2 = *a few*, 3 = *some*, 4 = *a lot*, and 5 = *a great number.*

6. How many projects, assignments, or tasks do you have? (would you like to have)
7. How many lulls between heavy workload periods do you have? (would you like to have) (R)

Responsibility for persons items:

The wording shown for each item measures the E subscale. The rewording required for the P subscale is shown in parentheses. Responses are obtained for these items using a 5-point Likert-type scale where 1 = *very little*, 2 = *a little*, 3 = *some*, 4 = *a lot*, and 5 = *a great deal.*

1. How much responsibility do you have for the future of others? (would you like to have)
2. How much responsibility do you have for the job security of others? (would you like to have)
3. How much responsibility do you have for the morale of others? (would you like to have)
4. How much responsibility do you have for the welfare and lives of others? (would you like to have)

Job complexity items:

Job complexity provided by the work environment (E) responses are based on reference to " My job is. . . ." Job complexity preferred by the employee (P) responses are based on reference to "I would prefer a job. . . ." The responses are provided following each item pair.

1a. Van's job is defined and described in almost every detail. Nothing is left to chance. There is a procedure for every type of task.
1b. On Ed's job, a person has some idea of the purpose of the job—but no exact instructions are given on how to do the work. There is often no set procedure.

Responses to this item pair are obtained on a 7-point Likert-type scale where 1 = *exactly like Van's*, 2 = *a lot like Van's*, 3 = *somewhat like Van's*, 4 = *halfway between Van's /Ed's*, 5 = *somewhat like Ed's*, 6 = *a lot like Ed's*, and 7 = *exactly like Ed's.*

2a. Jack works on the same tasks every day. He uses the same procedures or equipment all of the time. Each task is like the one he just finished.

2b. Almost every day things change in Alan's job. Each task is rarely the same as the previous one. He is likely to use different procedures or equipment from case to case.

Responses to this item pair are obtained on a 7-point Likert-type scale where 1 = *exactly like Jack's*, 2 = *a lot like Jack's*, 3 = *somewhat like Jack's*, 4 = *halfway between Jack's /Alan's*, 5 = *somewhat like Alan's*, 6 = *a lot like Alan's*, and 7 = *exactly like Alan's*.

3a. Tom's job requires him to be around people constantly. He works or talks with people most of the time.

3b. Bob's job does not require him to work with anyone else. In his job, Bob works alone. He rarely deals with other people.

Responses to this item pair are obtained on a 7-point Likert-type scale where 1 = *exactly like Bob's*, 2 = *a lot like Bob's*, 3 = *somewhat like Bob's*, 4 = *halfway between Bob's / Tom's*, 5 = *somewhat like Tom's*, 6 = *a lot like Tom's*, and 7 = *exactly like Tom's*.

4a. In Rich's job, he works with people from several different groups. He has to handle each group differently because they have different needs and want to get different things done.

4b. Don's contact at work is strictly with the people in his own work group or department. He does not need to deal with different groups or departments or organizations.

Responses to this item pair are obtained on a 7-point Likert-type scale where 1 = *exactly like Don's*, 2 = *a lot like Don's*, 3 = *somewhat like Don's*, 4 = *halfway between Don's /Rich's*, 5 = *somewhat like Rich's*, 6 = *a lot like Rich's*, and 7 = *exactly like Rich's*.

5a. In Tom's job, he works on many different tasks which are all in different stages of completion. Some things are just getting started, while others are halfway finished, and others may be finished by someone else.

5b. Jim's job requires him to work on one job at a time. When that work unit is completed, he starts to work on another unit or task. Two or more units are never worked on at the same time. He always finishes one unit before starting another.

Responses are obtained on a 7-point Likert-type scale where 1 = *exactly like Jim's*, 2 = *a lot like Jim's*, 3 = *somewhat like Jim's*, 4 = *halfway between Jim's/Tom's*, 5 = *somewhat like Tom's*, 6 = *a lot like Tom's*, and 7 = *exactly like Tom's*.

6a. Don's job has changes in workload: Every once in a while Don has to work to his absolute maximum. When that happens, he has to concentrate as hard as he can and be as careful as he can.

6b. Dick's job goes along evenly from hour to hour and from day to day. The pace of the work stays about the same. He rarely, if ever, has to suddenly change the pace of his work and work even faster and harder.

Responses for this item pair are obtained on a 7-point Likert-type scale where 1 = *exactly like Dick's*, 2 = *a lot like Dick's*, 3 = *somewhat like Dick's*, 4 = *halfway between Dick's /Don's*, 5 = *somewhat like Don's*, 6 = *a lot like Don's*, and 7 = *exactly like Don's*.

Role ambiguity items:

The wording shown for each item measures the E subscale. The rewording required for the P subscale is shown in parentheses.

Responses to these items are obtained on a 5-point Likert-type scale where 1 = *rarely*, 2 = *occasionally*, 3 = *sometimes*, 4 = *fairly often*, and 5 = *very often*.

1. How often are you clear about what your job responsibilities are? (would you like to be)
2. How often can you predict what others will expect of you on the job? (would you like to be able to)
3. How much of the time are your work objectives well defined? (would you like)
4. How often are you clear about what others expect of you on the job? (would you like to be)

Items denoted with (R) are reverse scored.

Perceived Ability-Job Fit

Description   This measure, developed by Abdel-Halim (1981), uses five items to assess an employee's perceived ability-job fit. According to the person-environment fit model of stress, whether a given level of job demands is stressful to a jobholder is determined by his or her ability (or perceived ability) to perform the job (Xie, 1996). Xie and Johns (1995) found that employees with lower perceived ability-job fit are affected to a greater degree by job demands than those who have higher job-ability fit.

Reliability   Coefficient alpha values ranged from .73 to .74 (Xie, 1996; Xie & Johns, 1995).

Validity   Xie (1996) found through factor analysis that perceived ability-job fit, decision latitude, and job demands were empirically distinct. Perceived ability-job fit correlated positively with job demands, control, job satisfaction, life satisfaction, age, adequacy of income, and tenure. Ability-job fit correlated negatively with anxiety and depression (Xie, 1996).

Source   Xie, J. L. (1996). Karasek's model in the People's Republic of China: Effects of job demands, control, and individual differences. *Academy of Management Journal, 39*(6), 1594-1619. © 1996 by Academy of Management. Items were taken from text, p. 1603. Reproduced with permission of Academy of Management in the format textbook via Copyright Clearance Center.

Items   Responses are obtained on a 5-point Likert-type scale where 1 = *strongly disagree* and 5 = *strongly agree.*

1. I feel that my work utilizes my full abilities
2. I feel competent and fully able to handle my job
3. My job gives me a chance to do the things I feel I do best
4. I feel that my job and I are well matched
5. I feel I have adequate preparation for the job I now hold

9

Workplace Behaviors

Kathleen Patterson, Fellow in the Regent University Center for Leadership Studies, contributed to this chapter.

The Construct

The utility of job satisfaction and other measures of employee attitudes as a predictor of variables such as turnover and employee performance varies considerably across situations. As a result, Hodson (1991) advocates examination of the effects of the characteristics of jobs and work environments on employee work behaviors. Employee behavior at work generally can be characterized as either contributing to organizational goals or contributing to an employee's occupational control. Employee behaviors can be described as following patterns of "good soldiers," "smooth operators," and "saboteurs" (Hodson, 1991). Good soldiers take the organization's goals as their own, are highly committed, and don't question organizational decisions but strive to implement these decisions efficiently. Smooth operators give first priority to their own occupational goals and may inadvertently advance organizational goals. Saboteurs are employees who neither adopt organizational goals nor achieve their own occupational goals. There-fore, they undertake such behaviors as passively resisting authority, carelessly violating work rules, or intentionally destroying property to get even with their boss or organization. The distinctions among these categories may be subtle; for example, some good soldiers may work diligently at preventing their boss from understanding how quickly work actually could be completed (Hodson, 1991).

A good deal of attention has been devoted to work behavior that is beyond the reach of traditional measures of job performance because these organizational citizenship behaviors may contribute to organizational innovation, flexibility, and responsiveness to changing external conditions (Sagie, 1998). There have been two approaches to describing these behaviors. The first approach proposes that organizational citizenship behavior (OCB) and traditional conceptualizations of job performance are separate constructs. Thus, OCB is viewed as extrarole behavior that is separate from in-role job performance. This approach requires determining what is in-role and what is extrarole, a distinction that may vary across jobs, organizations, and circumstances.

Much of the theoretical and empirical work on OCB creates the impression that the boundary between in-role and extrarole behavior is agreed upon and clearly defined and that OCB is the same for all employees (Taber & Alliger, 1995). However, roles in organizations are rarely fixed, and role perceptions evolve as employees and supervisors negotiate the scope of work activities. Furthermore, psychological contracts perceived by employees may result in a different understanding of employment obligations from that of their employers. Social information processing theory predicts that jobs are cognitive constructions created when employees (and employers) make sense of social and behavioral cues. For example, an employee who comes to work earlier than required is defined as engaging in OCB regardless of how the employee sees this behavior. In terms of understanding OCB, it makes a difference whether an employee helps a co-worker because he or she wishes to engage in extra effort on behalf of the organization, or alternatively, because he or she simply sees the behavior as part of his or her job. For example, if an employee defines helping co-workers as an in-role behavior, he or she will conceptualize the behavior very differently than an extrarole behavior and will perceive a different set of incentives surrounding the helping behavior (Taber & Alliger, 1995).

A second approach to OCB is based on the theoretical heritage of civic citizenship. Civic citizenship is viewed as including all positive community-relevant behaviors of individual citizens. From this perspective, organizational citizenship can be conceptualized as a global concept that includes all positive organizationally relevant behaviors of employees including traditional in-role job performance behaviors, organizationally functional extrarole behaviors, and political behaviors, such as full and responsible organizational participation. (Sagie, 1998). There are three categories of civic citizen responsibilities that also apply within work organizations. First, organizational obedience reflects acceptance of the necessity and desirability of rational rules and regulations governing organizational structure, job descriptions, and personnel policies. Obedience can be demonstrated by respect for rules and instructions, punctuality in attendance and task completion, and stewardship of organizational resources. Second, organizational loyalty is identification with and allegiance to an organization's leaders and the organization as a whole, transcending the parochial interests of individuals, work groups, and departments. Representative behaviors include defending the organization against threats, contributing to its good reputation, and cooperating with others to serve the interests of the whole. Third, organizational participation is interest in organizational affairs guided by ideal standards of virtue, validated by an individual's keeping informed, and expressed through full and responsible involvement in organizational governance. Representative activities include attending nonrequired meetings, sharing informed opinions and new ideas with others, and being willing to deliver bad news or support an unpopular view to combat "groupthink" (Sagie, 1998).

The Measures

As expected from the discussion above, measurement of work behaviors requires consideration of the consistency with which certain activities are seen as required by the job or considered discretionary actions across different job roles. Intrarole behaviors might include actions such as adherence to policies and procedures or timely completion of tasks (Williams & Anderson, 1991). Extrarole behaviors might include voluntary actions behaviors, such as taking charge (Morrison & Phelps, 1999).

Morrison (1994) found a high level of agreement as to which behaviors fit into basic categories of work-related behaviors such as conscientiousness, altruism, civic virtue, and sportsmanship. There seems to be agreement that conscientiousness consists of behaviors that go well beyond minimum requirements in the areas of attendance, obeying rules, taking breaks, and so forth. Altruism consists of behaviors directed at helping other employees in the organization, such as taking a portion of a co-worker's overload. Civic virtue consists of behaviors reflecting responsible participation in, involvement with, and concern about the life of the employing organization. Sportsmanship is the willingness to tolerate less than ideal circumstances without complaining and refraining from activities such as having petty grievances (Taber & Alliger, 1995).

Morrison (1994) also examined the extent to which employees and supervisors differed in how broadly they define job responsibilities. There was considerable disagreement between supervisors and employees. Significant agreement between supervisors and employee was found for only 1 out of 20 work behaviors. Considerably more employees defined a given behavior as in-role than as extrarole. For 17 of 20 behaviors, employees who defined a behavior as in-role engaged in the behavior significantly more often that employees that defined the behavior as extrarole.

This chapter includes measures of OCB that focus on extrarole actions, some that contain separate descriptions of in-role behaviors, and others that the integrate both in-role and extrarole perspectives.

Workplace behaviors can also be measured by self-reports and descriptions provided by others, such as peers and supervisors. As might be expected from the leadership literature, the correlation of self- and other reports of behaviors is typically low. Some of the difference may be due to self-serving biases of modesty. Other differences may be due to lack of knowledge of others about the actual behaviors of a co-worker or subordinate (Organ & Ryan, 1995). The descriptions of an employee's behavior by others are typically averaged to derive a rating for the focal employee. Prior to using the mean, however, it is essential to examine the pattern of responses from others. This is done using within-group correlations (Morrison & Phelps, 1999; Van Dyne & LePine, 1998).

Organizational Citizenship Behavior

Description This measure, developed by Moorman and Blakely (1995), uses 19 items to describe four dimensions of organizational citizenship behavior. These dimensions are interpersonal helping, individual initiative, personal industry, and loyal boosterism. Interpersonal helping (five items) consists of altruistic behaviors, such as responding to the personal needs of co-workers in dealing with job-related problems. Personal industry (four items) describes adherence to rules and instructions, unusual attention to quality, and the performance of tasks above and beyond the call of duty. Individual initiative (five items) refers to employee efforts to improve individual and team performance, challenge groupthink, and encourage participation. Loyal boosterism (five items) consists of an uncritical faithfulness to the organization, defense of organizational interests, and contributions to the organizations good reputation and general welfare.

Reliability Coefficient alpha values ranged from .67 to .78 for the interpersonal helping subscale, .76 to .80 for the individual initiative subscale, .61 to .83 for the personal industry subscale, and .76 to .86 for the loyal boosterism subscale (Moorman & Blakely, 1995; Moorman, Blakely, & Niehoff, 1998; Thompson & Werner, 1997).

Validity The four organizational citizenship behavior subscales correlated positively with one another. All four subscales also correlated positively with procedural justice, organizational commitment, and job satisfaction (Moorman & Blakely, 1995; Moorman et al., 1998). Interpersonal helping, individual initiative, and personal industry all correlated positively with the acceptance of collective norms and in-role behavior (Moorman & Blakely, 1995; Moorman et al., 1998; Thompson & Werner, 1997). Interpersonal helping and loyal boosterism correlated positively with working values (Moorman & Blakely, 1995). Interpersonal helping, personal industry, and loyal boosterism correlated positively with perceived organizational support (Moorman et al., 1998). Confirmatory factor analysis showed that the 19 items related to the four dimensions as expected and that the organizational citizenship behavior dimensions were empirically distinct (Moorman & Blakely, 1995).

Source Moorman, R. H., & Blakely, G. L. (1995). Individualism-collectivism as an individual difference predictor of organizational citizenship behavior. *Journal of Organizational Behavior, 16,* 127-142. Items were taken from Table 1, p. 132. Copyright © 1995. Reproduced by permission of John Wiley & Sons Limited.

Items Responses are obtained using a 7-point Likert-type scale where 1 = *strongly disagree* and 7 = *strongly agree*.

The items provided are worded for describing another organizational member. For self-descriptions, the items are modified to refer to the respondent.

Interpersonal helping items:

1. Goes out of his/her way to help co-workers with work-related problems
2. Voluntarily helps new employees settle into the job
3. Frequently adjusts his/her work schedule to accommodate other employees' requests for time off
4. Always goes out of the way to make newer employees feel welcome in the work group
5. Shows genuine concern and courtesy toward co-workers, even under the most trying business or personal situation

Individual initiative items:

6. For issues that may have serious consequences, expresses opinions honestly even when others may disagree
7. Often motivates others to express their ideas and opinions
8. Encourages others to try new and more effective ways of doing their job
9. Encourages hesitant or quiet co-workers to voice their opinions when they otherwise might not speak up
10. Frequently communicates to co-workers suggestions on how the group can improve

Personal industry items:

11. Rarely misses work even when he/she has a legitimate reason for doing so
12. Performs his/her duties with unusually few errors
13. Performs his/her job duties with extra-special care
14. Always meets or beats deadlines for completing work

Loyal boosterism items:

15. Defends the organization when other employees criticize it
16. Encourages friends and family to utilize the organization's products
17. Defends the organization when outsiders criticize it
18. Shows pride when representing the organization in public
19. Actively promotes the organization's products and services to potential users

Organizational Citizenship Behaviors

Description   This measure was developed by Williams and Anderson (1991). It uses 21 items to describe three types of organizational citizenship behaviors. These are behaviors directed at specific individuals (OCBI), behaviors directed at an organization (OCBO), and employee in-role behaviors (IRB). Organizational citizenship behaviors directed at an individual are those of immediate benefit to a specific person and that indirectly contribute to the organization, such as helping those who are absent or taking a personal interest in another employee. Organizational citizenship behaviors that focus primarily on benefiting the organization include providing advance notice of inability to come to work and the adherence to informal rules. In-role behaviors are those that are recognized by the formal reward systems and that are part of the job requirements. These include performance of duties and undertaking activities that are expected.

Reliability   Coefficient alpha values ranged from .61 to .88 for organizational citizenship behaviors directed at individuals, .70 to .75 for organizational citizenship behaviors directed at the organization, and .80 to .94 for in-role behaviors (Funderburg & Levy, 1997; Morrison & Phelps, 1999; Randall, Cropanzano, Bormann, & Birjulin, 1999; Thompson & Werner, 1997; Williams & Anderson, 1991; Van Dyne & LePine, 1998). Exploratory factor analysis showed that the items loaded on the three hypothesized dimensions as expected (Williams & Anderson, 1991).

Validity   Organizational citizenship behaviors benefiting specific individuals correlated positively with higher employee ratings of intrinsic and extrinsic job characteristics, perceived organizational support, employee self-esteem, employee internal locus of control, affective organizational commitment, and working for a supervisor who encourages participation. OCBI correlated negatively with turnover intentions (Funderburg & Levy, 1997; Randall et al., 1999; Thompson & Werner, 1997; Williams & Anderson, 1991). Peer ratings of OCBI correlated negatively with employee internal locus of control and working for a supervisor with participatory style (Funderburg & Levy, 1997). Organizational citizenship behaviors benefiting the organization correlated positively with higher employee ratings of intrinsic and extrinsic job characteristics and perceived organizational support. The OCBO subscale also correlated negatively with turnover intentions (Funderburg & Levy, 1997; Randall, 1999; Thompson & Werner, 1997; Williams & Anderson, 1991). In-role behaviors correlated positively with perceived organizational support, job satisfaction, affective organizational commitment, interpersonal helping, personal industry, individual initiative, and loyal boosterism (Funderburg & Levy, 1997; Randall et al., 1999; Thompson & Werner, 1997; Van Dyne & LePine, 1998; Williams & Anderson, 1991).

Funderburg and Levy (1997) found that self-ratings and peer ratings of OCBI had opposite-sign correlations (self-ratings positive; peer ratings negative) with internal locus of control and participatory supervisory style. Van Dyne and LePine (1998) found that self-ratings of in-role behaviors correlated positively with peer ratings of in-role behaviors.

Source   Williams, L. J., & Anderson, S. E. (1991). Job satisfaction and organizational commitment as predictors of organizational citizenship and in-role behaviors. *Journal of Management, 17*(3), 601-617. Items were taken from Table 1, p. 606. Copyright © 1991. Reproduced with permission.

Items   Responses are obtained using a 5-point Likert-type scale where 1 = *strongly disagree* and 5 = *strongly agree*. The measure can be used for peer, supervisor, or self-reports.

Items for OCBI:

1. Helps others who have been absent
2. Helps others who have heavy work loads
3. Assists supervisor with his/her work (when not asked)
4. Takes time to listen to co-workers' problems and worries
5. Goes out of way to help new employees
6. Takes a personal interest in other employees
7. Passes along information to co-workers

Items for OCBO:

1. Attendance at work is above the norm
2. Gives advance notice when unable to come to work
3. Takes undeserved work breaks (R)
4. Great deal of time spent with personal phone conversations (R)
5. Complains about insignificant things at work (R)
6. Conserves and protects organizational property
7. Adheres to informal rules devised to maintain order

Items for IRB:

1. Adequately completes assigned duties
2. Fulfills responsibilities specified in job description
3. Performs tasks that are expected of him/her
4. Meets formal performance requirements of the job
5. Engages in activities that will directly affect his/her performance
6. Neglects aspects of the job he/she is obligated to perform (R)
7. Fails to perform essential duties (R)

Items denoted with (R) are reverse scored.

Organizational Citizenship Behavior

Description This organizational citizenship behavior measure was developed by Podsakoff, MacKenzie, Moorman, and Fetter (1990). The measure uses 24 items to describe five dimensions of organizational citizenship behavior. These dimensions are altruism, conscientiousness, sportsmanship, courtesy, and civic virtue. Altruism (five items) is discretionary behavior directed at helping other people with an organizationally relevant task or problem, such as taking some of the workload of other employees who have been absent. Conscientiousness (five items) is discretionary behavior that goes beyond the minimum role requirements of the organization, such as not taking extra breaks and adhering to company rules at all times. Sportsmanship (five items) is discretionary behavior that indicates the willingness of an employee to tolerate less than ideal circumstances without excessive complaining. Courtesy (five items) is behavior that is aimed at preventing the occurrence of work-related problems, such as considering the impact of actions on other employees. Civic virtue (four items) is discretionary behavior that indicates that the employee participates responsibly in, or is concerned about, the political life of the organization, such as keeping up with company developments (Podsakoff et al., 1990). The items can also be combined to form a single measure of organizational citizenship behavior (Pillai, Schriesheim, & Williams, 1999).

Reliability Coefficient alpha values ranged from .67 to .91 for altruism, .76 to .89 for sportsmanship, .69 to .86 for courtesy, and .66 to .90 for civic virtue. Alpha for conscientiousness was .79. Coefficient alpha for the single Organizational Citizenship Behavior scale was .94 (Klein & Verbeke, 1999; Lam, Hui, & Law, 1999; Moorman, 1993; Pillai et al., 1999; VanYerpen, Van Den Berg, & Willering, 1999). Exploratory factor analysis showed that the items loaded on the five dimensions as expected (Moorman, 1993). Confirmatory factor analysis also found that the structure of the dimensions was the same across samples from Hong Kong, Japan, Australia, and the United States (Lam et al., 1999).

Validity Altruism, conscientiousness, courtesy, sportsmanship, and civic virtue correlated positively with one another (Lam et al., 1999; Moorman, 1993; Podsakoff et al., 1990; VanYerpen et al., 1999). The organizational citizenship behavior dimensions all correlated negatively with role ambiguity, emotional exhaustion, reduced accomplishment, and depersonalization (Klein & Verbeke 1999). Organizational citizenship behavior described by all the items combined into a single measure correlated positively with distributive justice, procedural justice, trust, and organizational commitment (Pillai et al., 1999). Altruism, civic virtue, sportsmanship, and courtesy correlated all positively with the in-role behaviors of controlling expenses, providing information to others, and keeping up with technical developments as well as job satisfaction and organizational commitment. Altruism also correlated positively with managerial support, perceived organizational support, participation in decision making, contingent rewards, and trust. Civic virtue also correlated positively with perceived organizational support and participation in decision making. Sportsmanship also correlated positively with perceived organizational support, participation in decision making, individualized support, contingent rewards, and trust. Courtesy also correlated positively with managerial support, individualized support, contingent rewards, and trust. Conscientiousness correlated positively with perceived organizational support, participation in decision making, individualized support, individualized stimulation, contingent rewards, and trust. Civic virtue correlated negatively with employee positive affect. Sportsmanship and courtesy correlated negatively with turnover intentions (Klein & Verbeke 1999; Lam et al., 1999; Moorman, 1993; VanYerpen et al., 1999).

Source   Podsakoff, P. M., MacKenzie, S. B., Moorman, R. H., & Fetter, R. (1990). Transformational leader behaviors and their effects on followers' trust in leader, satisfaction, and organizational citizenship behaviors. *Leadership Quarterly, 1*(2), 107-142. Items were taken from Table 5, p. 121. Copyright © 1990. Reprinted with permission from Elsevier Science.

Items   Responses are obtained using a 7-point Likert-type scale where 1 = *strongly disagree* and 7 = *strongly agree*. The item wording provided is for supervisor or peer description of a focal employee. The item wording can be modified for self-reporting.

Altruism items:

1. Helps others who have heavy workloads
2. Is always ready to lend a helping hand to those around him/her
3. Helps others who have been absent
4. Willingly helps others who have work-related problems
5. Helps orient new people even though it is not required

Conscientiousness items:

1. Is one of my most conscientious employees
2. Believes in giving an honest day's work for an honest day's pay
3. Attendance at work is above the norm
4. Does not take extra breaks
5. Obeys company rules and regulations even when no one is watching

Sportsmanship items:

1. Is the classic "squeaky wheel" that always needs greasing (R)
2. Consumes a lot of time complaining about trivial matters (R)
3. Tends to make "mountains out of molehills" (R)
4. Always focuses on what's wrong, rather than the positive side (R)
5. Always finds fault with what the organization is doing (R)

Courtesy items:

1. Tries to avoid creating problems for co-workers
2. Considers the impact of his/her actions on co-workers
3. Does not abuse the rights of others
4. Takes steps to try to prevent problems with other employees
5. Is mindful of how his/her behavior affects other people's jobs

Civic virtue items:

1. Keeps abreast of changes in the organization
2. Attends meetings that are not mandatory, but are considered important
3. Attends functions that are not required, but help the company image
4. Reads and keeps up with organization announcements, memos, and so on

Items denoted with (R) are reverse scored.

Organizational Citizenship Behavior

Description   This measure was developed by Smith, Organ, and Near (1983). The measure uses 16 items to describe two dimensions of organizational behavior. The two dimensions are altruism and generalized compliance. Altruism is defined as helping co-workers personally, such as assisting a co-worker lift a heavy load. Generalized compliance is impersonal helpful behavior, such as punctuality and not wasting time on the job.

Reliability   Coefficient alpha values for altruism ranged from .86 to .91. Alpha for generalized compliance was .91 (Cropanzano, Howes, Grandey, & Toth, 1997; Wayne, Shore, & Liden, 1997).

Validity   Altruism correlated positively with generalized compliance, developmental experiences, promotions, supervisor's liking for an employee, perceived organizational support, leader-member exchange (LMX), affective commitment, and employee performance ratings. Altruism correlated negatively with intentions to quit (Cropanzano et al., 1997; Wayne, Shore, & Liden, 1997). Wayne, Shore, and Liden (1997) found through factor analysis that altruism was empirically distinct from employee performance ratings and supervisor's liking for an employee.

Source   Smith, C. A., Organ, D. W., & Near, J. P. (1983). Organizational citizenship behavior: Its nature and antecedents. *Journal of Applied Psychology, 68,* 653-663. Items were taken from Table 1, p. 657. Copyright © 1983 by the American Psychological Association. Reprinted with permission.

Items   Responses are obtained using a 7-point Likert-type scale where 1 = *never* and 7 = *always*. The respondent is asked to think about someone who works or has worked for or with the respondent.

Altruism items:

1. Helps others who have been absent
2. Volunteers for things that are not required
3. Orients new people even though it is not required
4. Helps others who have heavy workloads
5. Assists supervisor with his or her work
6. Makes innovative suggestions to improve department
7. Attends functions not required but that help the company image

Generalized compliance items:

8. Punctuality
9. Takes undeserved breaks (R)

10. Attendance at work is above the norm
11. Coasts toward the end of the day (R)
12. Gives advance notice if unable to come to work
13. Great deal of time spent with personal phone conversations (R)
14. Does not take unnecessary time off work
15. Does not take extra breaks
16. Does not spend time in idle conversation

Items denoted with (R) are reverse scored.

Chinese Organizational Citizenship Scale

Description   This measure was developed by Farh, Earley, and Lin (1997). It uses 20 items to describe five dimensions of organizational citizenship behavior in the context of Chinese society. The dimensions are identification with the company, altruism to colleagues, conscientiousness, interpersonal harmony, and protecting company resources. Identification with the company describes an employee's willingness to protect the reputation of the company and make suggestions for improving operations. Altruism toward colleagues describes employee willingness to help other employees solve problems and cover work assignments. Conscientiousness includes employee willingness to go beyond organizational expectations in such areas as attendance, obeying rules, and hard work. Interpersonal harmony describes employee willingness to avoid the pursuit of personal power and gain. Protecting company resources covers employee willingness to avoid and discourage negative behaviors such as abusing company policies and resources for personal use.

Reliability   Coefficient alpha values were .87 for identification with the company, .87 for altruism, .82 for conscientiousness, .86 for interpersonal harmony, and .81 for protecting company resources (Farh et al., 1997).

Validity   Altruism, conscientiousness, interpersonal harmony, and protecting company resources correlated positively with one another. These dimensions also all correlated positively with interactive justice and organizational commitment (Farh et al., 1997). In addition, identification with the company correlated positively with employee participation and the presence of appeal mechanisms. Altruism also correlated positively with pay satisfaction and employee education level. Conscientiousness also correlated positively with distributive justice. Interpersonal harmony and protecting company resources also correlated positively with employee participation, distributive justice, presence of appeal mechanisms, and pay satisfaction. Confirmatory factor analysis showed that the five dimensions were empirically distinct with the items loading as expected (Farh et al., 1997).

Source   Farh, J. L., Earley, P. C., & Lin, S. C. (1997). Impetus for action: A cultural analysis of justice and organizational citizenship behavior in Chinese society. *Administrative Science Quarterly, 42*(3), 421-444. Items were taken from Table 1, p. 428. Copyright © 1997. Reproduced with permission.

Items   Responses are obtained using a 7-point Likert-type scale where 1 = *strongly disagree* and 7 = *strongly agree*. This measure can be used to describe another focal employee or for self-reporting.

Identification with the company items:

1. Willing to stand up to protect the reputation of the company
2. Eager to tell outsiders good news about the company and clarify their misunderstandings
3. Makes constructive suggestions that can improve the operation of the company
4. Actively attends company meetings

Altruism items:

1. Willing to assist new colleagues to adjust to the work environment
2. Willing to help colleagues solve work-related problems
3. Willing to cover work assignments for colleagues when needed
4. Willing to coordinate and communicate with colleagues

Conscientiousness items:

1. Complies with company rules and procedures even when nobody watches and no evidence can be traced
2. Takes one's job seriously and rarely makes mistakes
3. Does not mind taking on new or challenging assignments
4. Tries to self-study to increase the quality of work outputs
5. Often arrives early and starts to work immediately

Interpersonal harmony items:

1. Uses illicit tactics to seek personal influence and gain with harmful effect on interpersonal harmony in the organization (R)
2. Uses position power to pursue selfish personal gain (R)
3. Takes credits, avoids blame, and fights fiercely for personal gain (R)
4. Often speaks ill of the supervisor or colleagues behind their backs (R)

Protecting company resources items:

1. Conducts personal business on company time (e.g., trading stocks, shopping, going to barber shops) (R)
2. Uses company resources to do personal business (e.g., company phones, copy machines, computers, and cars) (R)
3. Views sick leave as benefit and makes excuse for taking sick leave (R)

Items denoted with (R) are reverse scored.

Measuring Ingratiatory Behaviors in Organizational Settings

Description   Measuring Ingratiatory Behaviors in Organizational Settings (MIBOS), developed by Kumar and Beyerlein (1991), uses 24 items to assess the frequency with which employees use four types of ingratiatory behaviors in superior-subordinate relationships. The types of ingratiatory behaviors are opinion conformity, other enhancement, favor rendering, and self-presentation. Opinion conformity covers behaviors such as agreeing with the supervisor's opinions and judgments and mimicking a supervisor's behaviors. Other enhancement covers finding ways to communicate that emphasize the supervisor's strengths, virtues, and qualities while ignoring negative attributes. Favor rendering covers actions such as doing favors for a supervisor to create the obligation to reciprocate. Self-presentation covers making explicit verbal statements of one's own attributes. The items can also be combined into a single measure of ingratiatory behaviors in an organization (Kumar & Beyerlein, 1991).

Reliability   Coefficient alpha values ranged from .56 to .79 for opinion conformity, .74 to .84 for other enhancement, .72 to .86 for favor rendering, and .73 to .77 for self-presentation (Harrison, Hochwarter, Perrewé, & Ralston, 1998; Kacmar & Valle, 1997). Coefficient alpha values for the single combined measure of ingratiatory behaviors single measure ranged from .86 to .93 (Harrison et al., 1998; Kacmar & Valle, 1997; Kumar & Beyerlein, 1991).

Validity   The four dimensions (other enhancement, favor rendering, self preservation, and opinion conformity) were all positively intercorrelated. Favor rendering behavior correlated positively with influential reasoning, bargaining skills, assertiveness, higher authority, interpersonal skills, liking, and perceived similarity with manager (Harrison et al., 1998). Self-presentation behavior correlated positively with influential reasoning, bargaining skills, and assertiveness (Wayne, Liden, Graf, & Ferris, 1997). The combined MIBOS correlated positively with self-monitoring, need for power, internal locus of control, and alternative measures of the use of upward influence in organizations (Harrison et al., 1998; Kumar & Beyerlein, 1991). Kumar and Beyerlein (1991) found that the MIBOS based on combining the items into a single measure had small positive correlations with the use of rational persuasuion tactics, suggesting the concepts are empirically distinct.

   Kacmar and Valle (1997) tried but could not replicate the factor structure using either exploratory or confirmatory analysis. Harrison et al. (1998) also could not obtain acceptable fit with either one-dimension or four-dimension confirmatory factor analysis models.

Source   Kumar, K., & Beyerlein, M. (1991). Construction and validation of an instrument for measuring ingratiatory behaviors in organizational settings. *Journal of Applied Psychology, 76,* 619-627. Items were taken from Table 2,

p. 623. Copyright © 1991 by the American Psychological Association. Reprinted with permission.

Items

Responses are obtained using a 5-point Likert-type scale where 1 = *never do it*, 2 = *seldom do it*, 3 = *occasionally do it*, 4 = *often do it*, and 5 = *almost always do it*.

Opinion conformity items:

1. Show him/her that you share his/her enthusiasm about his/her new idea even when you may not actually like it
2. Give frequent smiles to express enthusiasm/interest about something he/she is interested in even if you do not like it
3. Express work attitudes that are similar to your supervisor's as a way of letting him/her know that the two of you are alike
4. Disagree on trivial or unimportant issues but agree on those issues in which he/she expects support from you
5. Try to imitate such work behaviors of your supervisor as working late or occasionally working on weekends
6. Let your supervisor know the attitudes you share with him/her
7. Laugh heartily at your supervisor's jokes even when they are not really funny

Other enhancement items:

1. Impress upon your supervisor that only he/she can help you in a given situation mainly to make him/her to feel good about himself/herself
2. Highlight the achievements made under his/her leadership in a meeting not being attended by him/her
3. Tell him/her that you can learn a lot from his/her experience
4. Exaggerate his/her admirable qualities to convey the impression that you think highly of him/her
5. Ask your supervisor for advice in areas in which he/she thinks he/she is smart to let him/her feel that you admire his/her talent
6. Look out for opportunities to admire your supervisor
7. Compliment your supervisor on his/her achievement however trivial it may actually be to you personally

Favor rendering items:

1. Try to do things for your supervisor that show your selfless generosity
2. Go out of your way to run an errand for your supervisor
3. Offer to help your supervisor by offering to use your personal contacts
4. Volunteer to be of help to your supervisor in matters like locating a good apartment, finding a good insurance agent, and so on

5. Spend time listening to your supervisor's personal problems even if you have no interest in them
6. Volunteer to help your supervisor in his/her work even if it means extra work for you

Self-preservation items:

1. Try to let him/her know that you have a reputation for being liked
2. Try to make sure that he/she is aware of your successes
3. Look for opportunities to let the supervisor know your virtues/ strengths
4. Try to persuasively present your own qualities when attempting to convince your supervisor about your abilities

Taking Charge

Description
This measure, developed by Morrison and Phelps (1999), uses 10 items to describe the behavior of "taking charge." Taking charge entails voluntary constructive efforts to bring about functional changes in an organization. These may include changes in how work is performed. It is discretionary behavior that is inherently change oriented, aimed at improvement in the organization. The items in this measure are generally completed by co-workers to describe a focal employee.

Reliability
Coefficient alpha values ranged from .93 to .95. Exploratory factor analysis showed that the 10 items loaded on a single factor. In the cases where there were multiple co-workers' ratings of an employee, the median intraclass correlation of these ratings was .36 (Morrison & Phelps, 1999).

Validity
Taking charge correlated positively with top management openness, general self-efficacy, felt responsibility, expert power, and organizational level. Exploratory factor analysis showed that taking charge was empirically distinct from in-role behaviors, civic virtue, and altruism (Morrison & Phelps, 1999).

Source
Morrison, E. W., & Phelps, C. C. (1999). Taking charge at work: Extra-role efforts to initiate workplace change. *Academy of Management Journal, 42,* 403-419. © 1999 by Academy of Management. Items were taken from Table 1, p. 410. Reproduced with permission of Academy of Management in the format textbook via Copyright Clearance Center.

Items
Responses are obtained using a 5-point Likert-type scale where 1 = *very infrequently* and 5 = *very frequently.*

1. This person often tries to adopt improved procedures for doing his or her job
2. This person often tries to change how his or her job is executed in order to be more effective
3. This person often tries to bring about improved procedures for the work unit or department
4. This person often tries to institute new work methods that are more effective for the company
5. This person often tries to change organizational rules or policies that are nonproductive or counterproductive
6. This person often makes constructive suggestions for improving how things operate within the organization
7. This person often tries to correct a faulty procedure or practice
8. This person often tries to eliminate redundant or unnecessary procedures
9. This person often tries to implement solutions to pressing organizational problems
10. This person often tries to introduce new structures, technologies, or approaches to improve efficiency

Helping and Voice Behaviors

Description   This measure, developed by Van Dyne and LePine (1998), uses 13 items to describe two job behaviors called helping and voice. These two work behaviors are viewed as extrarole behaviors in that they are actions that employees may undertake at their own discretion and are not part of their formal job role. Helping is defined as proactive behavior that emphasizes small acts of consideration. It can be characterized as cooperative behavior that emphasizes harmony and builds working relationships. Voice is defined as proactive behavior that emphasizes expressions of challenge to the status quo in order to improve organizational performance. Employees exercising voice will tend to make innovative suggestions for change even when others disagree (Van Dyne & LePine, 1998).

Reliability   Coefficient alpha values for helping behaviors rated by self, peers, and supervisors ranged from .85 to .95. Alpha values for voice rated by self, peers, and supervisors ranged from .82 to .96. Test-retest reliability was .81 for helping behaviors and .78 for voice behaviors. Where there were multiple peer ratings of the same employee, within-group correlation of the ratings averaged .85 and ranged from .77 to .89 (Van Dyne & LePine, 1998).

Validity   Self, peer, and supervisor ratings of helping behaviors and voice behaviors were all positively correlated. Self-rated helping correlated positively with performance. Self-rated voice correlated positively with education level and job level. Peer-rated helping and voice both correlated positively with education level, being male, and job level; both also correlated negatively with employee age. Supervisor-rated helping and voice correlated positively with job level; both correlated negatively with age and tenure in the work group. Supervisor-rated voice also correlated positively with employee education level (Van Dyne & LePine, 1998). Confirmatory factor analysis showed that helping, voice, and in-role behaviors were empirically distinct and that the factor structure of these dimensions was the same across time periods and across ratings by employees, their peers, and their supervisors (Van Dyne & LePine, 1998).

Source   Van Dyne, L., & LePine, J. A. (1998). Helping and voice extra-role behaviors: Evidence of construct and predictive validity. *Academy of Management Journal, 41*(1), 108-119. © 1998 by Academy of Management. Items were taken from Table 1, p. 112. Reproduced with permission of Academy of Management in the format textbook via Copyright Clearance Center.

Items   Responses are obtained using a 7-point Likert-type scale where 1 = *strongly disagree* and 7 = *strongly agree*. The items provided are worded for peer reporting. For supervisor reports, the items are reworded to replace *coworker* with *subordinate*. For self-reporting, each item begins with *I*.

Helping items:

1. This particular co-worker volunteers to do things for this work group
2. This particular co-worker helps orient new employees in this group
3. This particular co-worker attends functions that help the work group
4. This particular co-worker assists others in this group with their work for the benefit of the work group
5. This particular co-worker gets involved to benefit this work group
6. This particular co-worker helps others in this group learn about the work
7. This particular co-worker helps others in this group with their work responsibilities

Voice items:

1. This particular co-worker develops and makes recommendations concerning issues that affect this work group
2. This particular co-worker speaks up and encourages others in this group to get involved in issues that affect this group
3. This particular co-worker communicates his/her opinions about work issues to others in this group even if his/her opinion is different and others in this group disagree with him/her
4. This particular co-worker keeps well informed about issues where his/her opinion might be useful to this work group
5. This particular co-worker gets involved with issues that affect the quality of life here in this group
6. This particular co-worker speaks up in this group with ideas for new projects or changes in procedures

On-the-Job Behaviors

Description   This measure was developed by Lehman and Simpson (1992). It uses 22 items to describe on-the-job behaviors falling into four categories. The categories are positive work behaviors, psychological withdrawal behaviors, physical withdrawal behaviors, and antagonistic work behaviors. Positive work behaviors (five items) include such things as volunteering for additional work, working overtime, and attempting to change one's job for the better. Psychological withdrawal behaviors (eight items) include thinking of being absent, daydreaming, excessive chatting, and concentrating on personal tasks. Physical withdrawal behaviors (four items) include leaving early, taking long breaks, and sleeping at work. Antagonistic work behaviors include arguing with co-workers, disobedience of supervisors, and gossiping.

Reliability   Coefficient alpha values ranged from .68 to .70 for positive work behaviors, .70 to .84 for psychological withdrawal behaviors, and .60 to .62 for antagonistic behaviors. Coefficient alpha was .58 for the physical withdrawal behavior subscale (Cropanzano et al., 1997).

Validity   Positive work behaviors correlated positively with job satisfaction, organizational commitment, job involvement, job tension, and general fatigue. Antagonistic behaviors correlated positively with psychological withdrawal behaviors, organizational politics, job tension, general fatigue, and burnout. Psychological withdrawal behaviors also correlated positively with organizational politics, turnover intentions, general fatigue, and burnout. Psychological withdrawal behavior correlated negatively with perceived organizational support, job satisfaction, organizational commitment, and job involvement (Cropanzano et al., 1997).

Source   Lehman, W. E. K., & Simpson, D. D. (1992). Employee substance use and on-the-job behaviors. *Journal of Applied Psychology, 77,* 309-321. Items were taken from Table 1, p. 313. Copyright © 1992 by the American Psychological Association. Reprinted with permission.

Items   Responses are obtained using a 7-point Likert-type scale where 1 = *never* and 7 = *very often*. Items are introduced with the statement "In the past twelve months, how often have you. . . .?"

Positive work behaviors:

1. Done more work than required
2. Volunteered to work overtime
3. Made attempts to change work conditions
4. Negotiated with supervisors to improve job
5. Tried to think of ways to do the job better

Psychological withdrawal behaviors:

1. Thought of being absent
2. Chatted with co-workers about nonwork topics
3. Left work situation for unnecessary reasons
4. Daydreamed
5. Spent work time on personal matters
6. Put less effort into the job than should have
7. Thought of leaving current job
8. Let others do your work

Physical withdrawal behaviors:

1. Left work early without permission
2. Taken longer lunch or rest break than allowed
3. Taken supplies or equipment without permission
4. Fallen asleep at work

Antagonistic work behaviors:

1. Reported others for breaking rules or policies
2. Filed formal complaints
3. Argued with co-workers
4. Disobeyed supervisor's instructions
5. Spread rumors or gossip about co-workers

Antisocial Behaviors

Description   This measure was developed by Robinson and O'Leary-Kelly (1998). It describes negative behaviors by employees that have the potential to harm individuals and/or the organization. Antisocial behaviors include breaking rules, damaging company property, hurting other workers, starting arguments with co-workers, and saying rude things about a supervisor or the organization.

Reliability   Coefficient alpha values ranged from .68 to .81 (Robinson & O'Leary-Kelly, 1998).

Validity   Employee antisocial behaviors correlated positively with group antisocial behavior and correlated negatively with general satisfaction. Group antisocial behaviors correlated positively with an individual's tenure in the group and correlated negatively with gender, age, job tenure, and the intention to leave. Antisocial behaviors correlated positively with similar measures such as antagonistic behaviors. Antisocial behaviors correlated negatively with organizational citizenship behaviors (Robinson & O'Leary-Kelly, 1998).

Source   Robinson, S. L., & O'Leary-Kelly, A. M. (1998). Monkey see, monkey do: The influence of work groups on the antisocial behavior of employees. *Academy of Management Journal, 41,* 658-672. © 1998 by Academy of Management. Items were taken from text, p. 663. Reproduced with permission of Academy of Management in the format textbook via Copyright Clearance Center.

Items   Responses are obtained using a 5-point Likert-type scale where 1 = *very infrequently* and 5 = *very frequently*. Respondents are instructed to report how frequently a focal person had engaged in each behavior within the year prior.

1. Damaged property belonging to my employer
2. Said or did something to purposely hurt someone at work
3. Did work badly, incorrectly, or slowly on purpose
4. Griped with co-workers
5. Deliberately bent or broke a rule(s)
6. Criticized people at work
7. Did something that harmed my employer or boss
8. Started an argument with someone at work
9. Said rude things about my supervisor or organization

Victimization Behavior in the Workplace

Description   This measure, developed by Aquino, Grover, Bradfield, and Allen (1999), uses eight items to describe victimization resulting from another's aggressive behavior. The measure contains two dimensions: indirect victimization and direct victimization. Indirect victimization includes behaviors that inflict harm without being detected, such as someone sabotaging an employee's work. Direct victimization includes behaviors that are overt and visibly aggressive, such as being cursed at by another employee.

Reliability   Coefficient alpha value for indirect victimization was .81. Alpha for direct victimization was .76. Exploratory factor analysis showed the items loaded on the two dimensions (Aquino, Grover, et al., 1999).

Validity   Direct victimization correlated positively with indirect victimization and negative affectivity. Direct victimization correlated negatively with greater employee self-determination (Aquino, Grover, et al., 1999). Indirect victimization also correlated positively with negative affectivity and negatively with employee self-determination. Confirmatory factor analysis showed the two factors were empirically distinct (Aquino, Grover, et al., 1999).

Source   Aquino, K., Grover, S. L., Bradfield, M., & Allen, D. G. (1999). The effects of negative affectivity, hierarchal status, and self-determination on workplace victimization. *Academy of Management Journal, 42*(3), 260-272. © 1999 by Academy of Management. Items were taken from Table 1, p. 265. Reproduced with permission of Academy of Management in the format textbook via Copyright Clearance Center.

Items   Responses are obtained using a 5-point Likert-type scale where 1 = *never*, 2 = *one to three times*, 3 = *four to six times*, 4 = *seven to nine times*, and 5 = *more than ten times*. Respondents are instructed to answer based on the number of times they personally have witnessed a co-worker directing the described behaviors toward themselves within the last year.

Indirect victimization behaviors:

1. Said bad things about you to your co-workers
2. Sabotaged your work
3. Did something to make you look bad
4. Lied to get you in trouble

Direct victimization behaviors:

1. Made an ethnic, racial, religious, or offensive slur toward you
2. Made an obscene comment or gesture in front of you
3. Threatened you with physical harm
4. Cursed at you

Deviant Behaviors

Description   This measure, developed by Aquino, Lewis, and Bradfield (1999), uses 14 items to describe two categories of deviant employee behaviors. The two categories are interpersonal deviance and organizational deviance. Interpersonal deviant behaviors inflict harm upon other individuals and include such actions as making an ethnic or racial slur against a co-worker or making an obscene gesture at a co-worker. Organizational deviance includes behaviors that are directed at the organization itself or its systems, such as calling in sick when not really ill, lying about the number of hours worked, or purposely ignoring a supervisor's instructions.

Reliability   Coefficient alpha value for interpersonal deviance was .73. Alpha for organizational deviance was .76 (Aquino, Lewis, & Bradfield, 1999).

Validity   Interpersonal deviance correlated positively with organizational deviance and employee negative affect. Interpersonal deviance correlated negatively with distributive justice, procedural justice, and interactive justice. Organizational deviance also correlated positively with employee negative affect. Organizational deviance correlated negatively with interactive justice (Aquino, Lewis, & Bradfield, 1999). Confirmatory factor analysis indicated that the two dimensions were empirically distinct from one another and distinct from distributive, interactive, and procedural justice (Aquino, Lewis, & Bradfield, 1999).

Source   Aquino, K., Lewis, M. U., & Bradfield, M. (1999). Justice constructs, negative affectivity, and employee deviance: A proposed model and empirical test. *Journal of Organizational Behavior, 20,* 1073-1091. Items were taken from Table 1, p. 1082. Copyright © 1999. Reproduced by permission of John Wiley & Sons Limited.

Items   Responses are obtained using a 5-point Likert-type scale where 1 = *never,* 2 = *one to three times,* 3 = *four to ten times,* 4 = *eleven to twenty times,* and 5 = *more than twenty times.*

Interpersonal deviance items:

1.   Made an ethnic, racial, or religious slur against a co-worker
2.   Swore at a co-worker
3.   Refused to talk to a co-worker
4.   Gossiped about my supervisor
5.   Made an obscene comment or gesture at a co-worker
6.   Teased a co-worker in front of other employees

Organizational deviance items:

1. Intentionally arrived late for work
2. Called in sick when I was not really ill
3. Took undeserved breaks to avoid work
4. Made unauthorized use of organizational property
5. Left work early without permission
6. Lied about the number of hours I worked
7. Worked on a personal matter on the job instead of working for my employer
8. Purposely ignored my supervisor's instructions

Influence Tactics

Description   This measure, developed by Schriesheim and Hinkin (1991), resulted from a refinement of the measure of influence tactics originally developed by Kipnis, Schmidt, and Wilkinson (1980). The measure uses 18 items to describe six types of behaviors used by subordinates to influence their supervisors. The categories of tactics are ingratiation, such as making a supervisor feel important; exchange of benefits, such as offering to make a personal sacrifice if the supervisor would do a request; rationality, such as using logical arguments to convince a supervisor; assertiveness, such as repeatedly reminding the supervisor of what the subordinate wanted; upward appeal, such as making a formal appeal about a supervisor to higher levels in the organization; and coalition, such as obtaining the support of co-workers to back up a request.

Reliability   Coefficient alpha values ranged from .73 to .84 for ingratiation, .74 to .76 for exchange of benefits, .78 to .80 for rationality, .73 to .76 for assertiveness, .79 to .82 for upward appeal, and .83 to .87 for coalition (Schriesheim & Hinkin, 1990).

Validity   Exploratory and confirmatory factor analysis of the 18-item measure in two independent samples showed that items loaded on the dimensions as expected and that the six dimensions were empirically distinct (Schriesheim & Hinkin, 1990).

Source   Schriesheim, C. A., & Hinkin, T. R. (1990). Influence tactics used by subordinates: A theoretical and empirical analysis and refinement of the Kipnis, Schmidt and Wilkinson subscales. *Journal of Applied Psychology, 75*(3), 246-257. Items were taken from Table 1, p. 250, and Table 4, p. 255. Copyright © 1990 by the American Psychological Association. Reprinted with permission.

Items   Respondents are asked to describe how frequently in the last 6 months they had used each influence tactic on their boss. Responses are obtained using a 5-point Likert-type scale where 1 = *never use this tactic to influence him/her* and 5 = *usually use this tactic to influence him/her*.

Ingratiation items:

1.   Acted very humbly to him or her while making my request
2.   Acted in a friendly manner prior to asking for what I wanted
3.   Made him or her feel good about me before making my request

Exchange of benefits items:

1. Reminded him or her of past favors that I did for him or her
2. Offered an exchange (e.g., if you do this for me, I will do something for you)
3. Offered to make a personal sacrifice if he or she would do what I wanted (e.g., work late, work harder, do his or her share of the work, etc.)

Rationality items:

1. Used logic to convince him or her
2. Explained the reasons for my request
3. Presented him or her with information in support of my point of view

Assertiveness items:

1. Had a showdown in which I confronted him or her face-to-face
2. Expressed my anger verbally
3. Used a forceful manner; I tried things such as demands, the setting of deadlines, and the expression of strong emotion

Upward appeal items:

1. Obtained the informal support of higher-ups
2. Made a formal appeal to higher levels to back up my request
3. Relied on the chain of command—on people higher up in the organization who have power over him or her

Coalition items:

1. Obtained the support of co-workers to back up my request
2. Obtained the support of my subordinates to back up my request
3. Mobilized other people in the organization to help me in influencing him or her

10

Workplace Values

Kathleen Patterson, Fellow in the Regent University Center for Leadership Studies, contributed to this chapter.

The Construct

The values of members of organizations have received increased attention as the source of both what is wrong and what is right about companies. For example, performance differences between Japanese and American firms in the same industry have been attributed to differences in the values of the workers. In addition, the values of higher-ranking members of an organization probably affect the types of decisions the organization considers and makes (Ravlin & Meglino, 1987). An underlying assumption is that the values individuals have directly affect their behaviors. However, the specific behaviors exhibited by an employee at a selected point in time may be influenced by numerous situational variables, such as incentives, orders from a boss, and peer pressures. Thus, it may be difficult to detect the behavioral effects of values that have been internalized to form a central part of the individual's identity and view of the world (Ravlin & Meglino, 1987).

Despite being studied in a variety of contexts, values, especially as applied within the workplace, have been construed to mean different things. Values have been described as beliefs, needs, goals, criteria for choosing goals, criteria for choosing behaviors, and preferences (Dose, 1997; Froelich & Kottke, 1991). There does seem to be consensus that values are standards or criteria for choosing goals or actions and that they are relatively stable over time. In general, values are believed to develop through the influences of culture, society, and personality. Compared with attitudes, values are thought to occupy a more central place in a person's cognitive system and may be more closely linked to motivation (Dose, 1997). In the context of work, studies of work values have tended to focus on the following:

- Vocational work values, which are essentially goals that a worker seeks to achieve. Examples are material success, altruism, work conditions and co-workers, and independence.
- The importance of various aspects of a job or organization. These may include safety, autonomy, comfort, altruism, and achievement.
- Preferences for the characteristics of a job. These may include security, self-development, altruism, lifestyle, prestige, and creativity.

■ The extent to which individuals adhere to aspects of the Protestant work ethic. These aspects may include industriousness, self-discipline, and individualism (Dose, 1997).

Values may be comprised of cognitive, affective, and behavioral components (Rokeach, 1973). An example of the cognitive component is an individual's knowledge regarding how to behave correctly. Examples of the affective component are those behaviors or preferences that a person feels emotional about. Examples of the behavioral component are those things that a person would feel compelled to act on (Rokeach, 1973). Rokeach (1973) also has suggested that values are both terminal and instrumental. Terminal values are end states of existence, either self-centered or society centered, for which a person may attach different levels of importance. Instrumental values are those that concern desirable modes of conduct, either having a moral focus or a competence focus. Moral-focused instrumental values are those referring to behavior without thought of the end state, such as honesty. Competence-focused instrumental values are those referring to self-actualization, without concern for morality (Rokeach, 1973).

Dose (1997) has suggested that work values should be considered the work-related standards by which employees discern what is right or establish preferences. This perspective also suggests that work values may have a moral element or they may simply be preferences without a moral focus (Dose, 1997). Work values are moral focused to the extent that they follow standards of right and wrong such as laws or Biblical teachings. Preferences do not include an objective standard for right or wrong, but simply follow the standard that the employee will be better off because he or she has exercised a preference (Dose, 1997). However, if values are studied in an effort to understand their effects on current employee behavior or to predict future behaviors, we should be most concerned with those values that are beliefs in how people should behave (Ravlin & Meglino, 1987).

Because an individual's work-related values tend to reflect his or her socialization experiences and the behavioral norms within a culture, differences in the experiences of individuals within a culture and differences between cultures might systemically affect values. For example, women and men often have different experiences growing up and living as adults within a culture. Traditionally, two broad approaches have been used to explain gender differences in work values: the gender socialization model and the social structural model (Rowe & Snizek, 1995). The gender socialization model argues that observed differences in work values (e.g., men's greater emphasis on pay and career advancement and women's greater concern for social aspects of their work) reflect traditional patterns of gender socialization. The social structural model argues that observed differences in work values reflect men's and women's differential positions in the workplace hierarchy and their differential access to the system of workplace rewards (Rowe & Snizek, 1995). However, Rowe and Snizek (1995) studied the work preferences of a sample of more than 7,000 employees and found no substantial differences in the preference patterns of men and women employees.

In general, business ideology and country culture are primary forces that may shape employee's work-related values. One view, termed convergence theory, is that as nations embrace capitalism, their value systems will evolve toward the value systems of the established Western capitalistic economies. An alternative view, termed divergence theory, suggests that country culture drives values. Therefore, even if a country adopts capitalism, the value system of the workforce will remain largely unchanged. A third alternative, termed "cross-vergence," suggests that work ideology and country culture interact to create a new and unique value system that is based on the melding of both cultural and ideological influences (Ralston, Holt, Terpstra, & Kai-cheng, 1995). Ralston and colleagues (1995) found considerable support for the cross-vergence perspective in a study of managers from the United States, Russia, Japan, and China.

The Measures

A first concern in measuring work-related values of employees is the extent to which responses to questions or statements about values may reflect the desire of an employee to appear as much like a socially desirable model as possible. For example, if a question asks employees in most situations if they should be proactive, achievement oriented, customer conscious, and concerned for other employees, most would strongly agree (Ravlin & Meglino, 1987). The results would be a convergence of responses inflated in degree of their intercorrelation by social desirability bias. One approach to minimizing the effects of possible social desirability response bias is to obtain responses that force a rank ordering of alternative values. That is, respondents cannot "strongly agree" with several items but must differentiate the importance of one value from another. The result of using this approach to obtaining

employee responses is an ipsative measure, which is difficult to analyze using parametric statistical techniques, such as correlation (Ravlin & Meglino, 1987). Ipsative measures may also introduce other measurement error because they force respondents to choose between items that may in reality have equal importance. In a study involving the use of four alternative method for measuring values (rank ordering of a set of values, assignment of a fixed number of points to a set of values, Likert-type ratings of incidents linked to the set of values, and forced choice of values related to the incidents), Ravlin and Meglino (1987) found that values measured with rank ordering, point assignment, and forced choice all had larger correlations with a simulated decision task involving the use of the values. On the other hand, the Likert-type measure had a larger correlation with a measure assessing agreement with the Protestant work ethic. Schwartz (1994) has examined the consistency of response to a values survey that uses a Likert-type response scale and found the groupings of values to be consistent across samples in 44 different countries.

The measures included in this chapter include some that ask for ranking within a values set and others that use a Likert-type response scale. Indeed, one of the oldest and most frequently used values measures developed by Rokeach (1973) has been used with both rank order and Likert-type responses.

Value Attainment

Description   This measure was originally developed by Rokeach (1973). The original measure was designed to assess the importance ranking that a person assigned to 18 terminal values and 18 instrumental values. Terminal values describe desirable end states such as a comfortable life and can be categorized as self-centered or society centered. Instrumental values refer to modes of behavior and can be categorized as moral focused or competence focused. Moral-focused instrumental values include such modes of behavior as honesty or responsibility. Competence-focused instrumental values refer to modes of behavior such as logical or self-controlled. Studies of organizations have tended to use terminal values to assess the extent to which an employee's job or work situation has helped the employee attain desired end states (George & Jones, 1996; Hochwarter, Perrewé, Ferris, & Brymer, 1999). Agle, Mitchell, and Sonnenfeld (1999) used an eight-item subset of the terminal values to describe the extent to which CEOs were self-focused or other focused. Although originally developed as a rank-ordering (ipsative) measure, the response options have also been changed to a Likert-type scale in some applications in the 1990s (Agle et al., 1999; George & Jones, 1996; Hochwarter, Perrewé, Ferris, & Brymer, 1999).

Reliability   Coefficient alpha values for terminal values using a Likert-type response scale ranged from .85 to .93 (George & Jones, 1996; Hochwarter, Perrewé, Ferris, & Brymer, 1999).

Validity   Attainment of terminal values correlated positively with job satisfaction, job performance, and employee positive affectivity Attainment of terminal values correlated negatively with turnover intentions and employee negative affectivity (George & Jones, 1996; Hochwarter, Perrewé, Ferris, & Brymer, 1999).

Source   Rokeach, M. (1973). *The nature of human values*. New York: Free Press. Items were taken from Table 2.1, p. 28, or Appendix A, pp. 359-361. Reprinted and adapted with the permission of The Free Press, a Division of Simon & Schuster, Inc. Copyright © 1973 by The Free Press.

Items   For the Likert-type measure of attainment of terminal values, responses are obtained on a 7-point Likert-type scale where 1 = *least important* and 7 = *most important*. Responses may also be obtained by requesting respondents to rank the values in order of importance (Brief, Dukerich, & Doran, 1991).

Terminal values items:

1. A comfortable life (a prosperous life)
2. An exciting life (a stimulating, active life)
3. A sense of accomplishment (lasting contribution)

4. A world at peace (free of war and conflict)
5. A world of beauty (beauty of nature and the arts)
6. Equality (brotherhood, equal opportunity for all)
7. Family security (taking care of loved ones)
8. Freedom (independence, free choice)
9. Happiness (contentedness)
10. Inner harmony (freedom from inner conflict)
11. Mature love (sexual and spiritual intimacy)
12. National security (protection from attack)
13. Pleasure (an enjoyable, leisurely life)
14. Saved (eternal life)
15. Self-respect (self-esteem)
16. Social recognition (respect, admiration)
17. True friendship (close companionship)
18. Wisdom (a mature understanding of life)

Instrumental values items:

1. Ambitious (hard-working, aspiring)
2. Broadminded (open-minded)
3. Capable (competent, effective)
4. Cheerful (lighthearted, joyful)
5. Clean (neat, tidy)
6. Courageous (standing up for your beliefs)
7. Forgiving (willing to pardon others)
8. Helpful (working for the welfare of others)
9. Honest (sincere, truthful)
10. Imaginative (daring, creative)
11. Independent (self-reliant, self-sufficient)
12. Intellectual (intelligent, reflective)
13. Logical (consistent, rational)
14. Loving (affectionate, tender)
15. Obedient (dutiful, respectful)
16. Polite (courteous, well-mannered)
17. Responsible (dependable, reliable)
18. Self-controlled (restrained, self-disciplined)

Work Values Inventory

Description   This measure, developed by Manhardt (1972), assesses the importance of 25 different job characteristics. Manhardt found that 21 of these characteristics grouped into three dimensions. These dimensions are comfort and security, competence and growth, and status and independence. Comfort and security includes job characteristics such as having comfortable working conditions, job security, and a regular routine. Competence and growth includes job characteristics such as intellectual stimulation, continued development of skills, and a feeling of accomplishment. Status and independence includes job characteristics such as opportunities to earn a high income, supervision of other employees, and working on problems of importance to the organization (Manhardt, 1972). The measure has also been modified to assess the extent to which these characteristics are present in a current job (Meyer, Irving, & Allen, 1998).

Reliability   Coefficient alpha values ranged from .63 to .72 for comfort and security; .65 to .80 for competence and growth; and .62 to .68 for status and independence (Meyer et al., 1998).

Validity   The value placed on comfort and security correlated positively with the value placed on status and independence and continuance commitment after 6 and 12 months in a job. The value placed on competence and growth correlated positively with the value placed on status and independence, normative commitment after 6 months in a job, and affective commitment after 12 months in a job (Meyer et al., 1998).

Source   Meyer, J. P., Irving, P. G., & Allen, N. J. (1998). Examination of the combined effects of work values and early work experiences on organizational commitment. *Journal of Organizational Behavior, 19*, 29-52. Items were taken from Table 1, p. 36. Copyright © 1998. Reproduced by permission of John Wiley & Sons Limited.

Items   Responses are obtained using a 5-point Likert-type scale where 1 = *unimportant* and 5 = *very important*.

Comfort and security items:

1. Permits a regular routine in time and place of work
2. Provides job security
3. Has clear-cut rules and procedures to follow
4. Provides ample leisure time off the job
5. Provides comfortable working conditions

Competence and growth items:

1. Requires meeting and speaking with many other people
2. Is intellectually stimulating
3. Requires originality and creativity
4. Make a social contribution by the work you do
5. Satisfies your cultural and aesthetic interests
6. Encourages continued development of knowledge and skills
7. Permits you to develop your own methods of doing the work
8. Provides a feeling of accomplishment
9. Provides change and variety in duties and activities

Status and independence items:

1. Permits advancement to high administrative responsibility
2. Provides the opportunity to earn a high income
3. Requires supervising others
4. Is respected by other people
5. Requires working on problems of central importance to the organization
6. Permits working independently
7. Gives you the responsibility for taking risks

Protestant Work Ethic

Description   This measure was developed by Mirels and Garrett (1971). It uses 19 items to describe the extent to which a respondent agrees with the Protestant work ethic. The Protestant work ethic includes regard for diligence about business affairs, not being idle, punctual repayment of credit, being frugal in consumption, and not letting money lie idle. The Protestant work ethic typically also has been characterized as including emphasis on occupational success, asceticism, and rationality (Furnham, 1990). Mudrack, Mason, and Stepanski (1999) found that the 19 items factored into the three dimensions emphasizing work, asceticism, and anti-leisure.

Reliability   Coefficient alpha values ranged from .69 to .79 (Cohen, 1995; Furnham, 1990; Mudrack et al., 1999).

Validity   The Protestant work ethic correlated positively with organizational and occupational commitment, job and work involvement, and the unacceptability of taking self-benefits from ethically dubious activities at work (Cohen, 1995; Mudrack et al., 1999). The Protestant work ethic correlated negatively with age, education level, a positive view of leisure, and the unacceptability of an organization gaining benefits for ethically dubious activities (Cohen, 1995; Furnham, 1990; Mudrack et al., 1999).

Source   Mirels, H. L., & Garrett, J. B. (1971). The Protestant ethic as a personality variable. *Journal of Consulting and Clinical Psychology, 36,* 40-44. Items were taken from Table 1, p. 41. Copyright © 1971 by the American Psychological Association. Reprinted with permission.

Items   Responses are obtained using a 7-point Likert-type scale where 1 = *strongly disagree* and 7 = *strongly agree.*

1. Most people spend too much time in unprofitable amusement
2. Our society would have fewer problems if people had less leisure time
3. Money acquired easily, e.g., through gambling or speculation, is usually spent unwisely
4. There are few satisfactions equal to the realization that one has done his [her] best at a job
5. The most difficult college courses usually turn out to be the most rewarding
6. Most people who do not succeed in life are just plain lazy
7. The self-made man is likely to be more ethical than the man born to wealth
8. I often feel I would be more successful if I sacrificed certain pleasures
9. People should have more leisure time to spend in relaxation

10. Any man who is able and willing to work hard has a good chance of succeeding

11. People who fail at a job have usually not tried hard enough

12. Life would have very little meaning if we never had to suffer

13. Hard work offers little guarantee of success

14. The credit card is a ticket to careless spending

15. Life would be more meaningful if we had more leisure time

16. The person who can approach an unpleasant task with enthusiasm is the person who gets ahead

17. If one works hard enough he is likely to make a good life for himself

18. I feel uneasy when there is little work for me to do

19. A distaste for hard work usually reflects a weakness of character

Chinese Values Survey

Description   This measure was developed by the Chinese Culture Connection (1987), an international network of organizational researchers headed by Michael H. Bond. It was originally developed in Chinese, subsequently translated to English, then back-translated to Chinese, and the two versions compared for consistency. The measure assesses four categories of values related to work. These are integration, Confucian work dynamism, human-heartedness, and moral discipline. Integration focuses on the importance placed on social stability and a sense of harmony with self, family, and associates. It includes values such as noncompetitiveness and tolerance of others. Confucian work dynamism focuses on the importance of preservation of the social hierarchy, protecting the status quo, having a sense of shame, and reciprocation of favors and gifts. Human-heartedness focuses on the importance of social awareness and needing to be kind and courteous to others, including values such as patience and sense of righteousness. Moral discipline focuses on the importance of personal control, especially in a group setting, and includes values such as moderation, carefulness, and having few desires. The measure has been used to compare values in different cultures (Ralston, Gustafson, Elsass, Cheung, & Terpstra, 1992).

Reliability   Coefficient alpha values were .80 for integration, .77 for Confucian work dynamism, .81 for human-heartedness, and .55 for moral discipline (Pearson & Chong, 1997).

Validity   The dimensions of the Chinese Values Survey differentiated Chinese managers from the People's Republic of China (PRC) from Chinese managers from Hong Kong. Hong Kong managers scored significantly higher on the importance of integration, which is consistent with Hong Kong's history of relative social stability, compared with the PRC where citizens have experienced disruptions of social stability, such as the Cultural Revolution. Similarly, Confucian work dynamism (CWD) differentiated PRC Chinese managers (high importance on CWD) from Hong Kong Chinese managers (medium importance on CWD) and American managers (low importance on CWD). Human-heartedness differentiated American managers (high importance) from both PRC and Hong Kong Chinese managers (Ralston et al., 1992). Pearson and Chong (1997) found that job characteristics had less effect on the satisfaction of employees who placed greater importance on the collective aspects of the Chinese Values Survey, such as work group harmony and preservation of the status quo.

Source   Ralston, D. A., Gustafson, D. J., Elsass, P. M., Cheung, F., & Terpstra, R. H. (1992). Eastern values: A comparison of managers in the United States, Hong Kong, and the People's Republic of China. *Journal of Applied Psychology*, 77, 664-671. Items were taken from Table 2, p. 667. Copyright © 1992 by the American Psychological Association. Reprinted with permission.

Items   Responses are obtained using a 9-point Likert-type scale where 1 = *no impor-tance* and 9 = *extreme importance.*

Integration items:

1. Tolerance of others
2. Harmony with others
3. Solidarity with others
4. Noncompetitiveness
5. Trustworthiness
6. Contentedness
7. Being conservative
8. A close, intimate friend
9. Filial piety
10. Patriotism
11. Chastity in women

Confucian work dynamism items:

1. Ordering relationships by status and observing order
2. Thrift
3. Persistence (perseverance)
4. Having a sense of shame
5. Reciprocation of greetings, favors, and gifts
6. Personal steadiness
7. Protecting your face
8. Respect for tradition

Human-heartedness items:

1. Kindness (forgiveness, compassion)
2. Sense of righteousness
3. Patience
4. Courtesy

Moral discipline items:

1. Moderation, following the middle way
2. Keeping oneself disinterested and pure
3. Adaptability
4. Prudence (carefulness)
5. Having few desires

Remaining items that did not load on the four factors:

1. Industry (working hard)
2. Humbleness
3. Loyalty to superior

4. Observation of rites and social rituals
5. Knowledge (education)
6. Self-cultivation
7. Benevolent authority
8. Resistance to corruption
9. Sincerity
10. Repayment of both the good or the evil that another person has caused you
11. A sense of cultural superiority
12. Wealth

Work Value Survey

Description   This measure, developed by Schwartz (1994), rates the importance of 56 outcomes and modes of behavior. The value items can be grouped into 10 categories:

- Power, which includes values such as social status, prestige, and control over resources or people
- Achievement, which includes values such as personal success attained by demonstrated competence
- Hedonism, which includes values such as pleasure and sensuous self-gratification
- Stimulation, which includes values such as excitement, novelty, and challenge
- Self-direction, which includes values such as independence in thought and action, as well as exploring
- Universalism, which includes values such as understanding, tolerance, and protection of the welfare of people or nature
- Benevolence, which includes values such as preservation and enhancement of the well-being of family, friends, and close associates
- Tradition, which includes values such as respect for acceptance of traditional culture and religion
- Conformity, which includes values such as restraint in actions and impulses that could upset or harm others or violate norms
- Security, which includes values such as safety, harmony, and stability of society (Schwartz, 1994)

Brett and Okumura (1998) used seven of the items to construct a measure of individualism/collectivism and six of the items to construct a measure of hierarchy/egalitarianism.

Reliability   Coefficient alpha values were .71 for power, .76 for achievement, .67 for hedonism, .77 for stimulation, .69 for self-direction, .80 for universalism, .76 for benevolence, .61 for tradition, .72 for conformity, and .56 for security (Feather, Norman, & Worsley, 1998). Coefficient alpha for individualism/collectivism was .80 and .77 for hierarchy/egalitarianism (Brett & Okumura, 1998).

Validity   In an examination of the extent to which the categories of values were replicated in 97 samples from 44 countries, Schwartz (1994) found that all 10 value categories were either distinct or overlapped with an adjacent value category in 84% of the cases. Eight categories were distinct in 98% of the studies. Schwartz also found that 47 of the 56 items demonstrated consistent meaning in at least 83% of the studies. The value items that showed the least consistency were healthy, self-respect, and detachment (Schwartz, 1994).

Brett and Okumura (1998) found that individualism correlated positively with the importance of hierarchy and the importance self-interest. Individualism correlated negatively with distributive tactics in negotiation and focusing on role power in negotiation. Importance attached to hierarchy correlated positively with the use of distributive tactics in negotiations and with planning the use of power in negotiation.

Source   Schwartz, S. H. (1994). Are there universal aspects in the structure and contents of human values? *Journal of Social Issues, 50*, 19-45. Items were taken from Table 3, p. 33. © Blackwell Science. Reprinted with permission.

Items   Responses are obtained using a 9-point Likert-type scale where −1 = *opposed to my values*, 0 = *not important*, 3 = *important*, 6 = *very important*, and 7 = *of supreme importance*.

Power items:

1. Social power
2. Authority
3. Wealth
4. Preserving my public image
5. Social recognition

Achievement items:

1. Successful
2. Capable
3. Ambitious
4. Influential
5. Intelligent
6. Self-respect

Hedonism items:

1. Pleasure
2. Enjoying life

Stimulation items:

1. Daring
2. A varied life
3. An exciting life

Self-direction items:

1. Creativity
2. Curious
3. Freedom
4. Choosing own goals
5. Independent

Universalism items:

1. Protecting the environment
2. A world of beauty
3. Unity with nature
4. Broad-minded
5. Social justice
6. Wisdom
7. Equality
8. A world at peace
9. Inner harmony

Benevolence items:

1. Helpful
2. Honest
3. Forgiving
4. Loyal
5. Responsible
6. True friendship
7. A spiritual life
8. Mature love
9. Meaning in life

Tradition items:

1. Devout
2. Accepting portion in life
3. Humble
4. Moderate
5. Respect for tradition
6. Detachment

Conformity items:

1. Politeness
2. Honoring parents and elders
3. Obedient
4. Self-discipline

Security items:

1. Clean
2. National security
3. Social order
4. Family security
5. Reciprocation of favors
6. Healthy
7. Sense of belonging

Measure of Ethical Viewpoints

Description   The Measure of Ethical Viewpoints (MEV) was developed by Brady and Wheeler (1996). It describes an employee's focus in making ethical judgments as either utilitarian or formal. People using a utilitarian approach are outcome oriented and tend to assess actions in terms of their consequences for people. A utilitarian approach defines ethical nature of actions in terms of the extent to which the actions create the greatest net social good. People using a formal approach tend to assess situations in light of their conformity with established rules or norms. A formal approach defines the ethical nature of actions in terms of the extent to which the action is consistent with rules or laws (Brady & Wheeler, 1996).

The measure uses two approaches to assess the extent of utilitarianism and formalism in a respondent's ethical viewpoint. The first approach is based on the responses to 28 items associated with seven vignettes. For each vignette, two choices represent a utilitarian solution and rationale and two choices represent a formal solution and rationale. Respondents are asked to rate each of the 28 items in terms of the degree of similarity to their way of thinking. The second approach to measuring utilitarianism and formalism requires respondents to rate the importance of 13 character traits.

Reliability   Test-retest reliability for the responses to the vignette items averaged .70 across seven vignettes. Test-retest reliability of the trait ratings was .77 (Brady & Wheeler, 1996). Coefficient alpha values for utilitarianism based on both vignette and trait ratings ranged from .85 to .86. Coefficient alpha values for formalism ranged from .74 to .75 (Brady & Wheeler, 1996; Schminke, Ambrose, & Noel, 1997).

Validity   Utilitarianism based on trait ratings correlated positively with formalism and correlated negatively with perceived procedural and distributive justice. Formalism correlated positively with utilitarianism and correlated negatively with perceived procedural and distributive justice (Schminke et al., 1997).

Source   Brady, F. N., & Wheeler, G. E. (1996). An empirical study of ethical predispositions. *Journal of Business Ethics, 15,* 927-940. Items were taken from Appendix A, pp. 938-939. © Kluwer Academic Publishers. Reprinted with permission.

Items   Responses are obtained using a 7-point Likert-type scale where 1 = *not at all like my way of thinking* and 7 = *very much like my way of thinking.*

Part 1: Vignettes

Below are several vignettes representing common ethical dilemmas or issues. Following each vignette is a set of four statements, each of which represents a different way of thinking about the situation. Please rate each statement on a scale of 1 to 7 indicating the extent to which it would fit your way of thinking about the situation.

1. In front of the cafeteria on a major university campus is a busy two-lane road with a cross walk and a traffic light. There is no intersection, but the light can be controlled by a pedestrian button an each sidewalk. When there is little traffic, a person could either press the button and wait for the light or just walk across without the light . . .

   a. No harm is done just go ahead; it's inconvenient to wait when there is little or no traffic
   b. In these matters one ought to be reasonable, not extreme; one ought to obey the spirit rather than the letter of the law
   c. It's better to be safe than sorry
   d. One should obey all traffic laws

2. You are the instructor of an evening class which meets every Wednesday night. One part of the course is a library tour, in which you acquaint the students with various materials and sources for study. Unfortunately, you have just received a memo from the library director notifying you that the tour must be conducted on the following Thursday night. When you take the proposed change to the students, all are still very interested in going on the new date except for two students who are unable to attend. Both have previous commitments, but it would be valuable for all to attend. The tour has always been part of the course . . .

   a. The class would be better off if a majority went on the tour than if none did
   b. The tour is in the course syllabus; you should do all you can to fulfill listed course assignments
   c. You can probably find other ways to help the students learn about the library
   d. Not even one student should be treated unfairly

3. Many people think that abortions should be allowed; others think they should be largely be prohibited . . .

   a. Thousands of children are born into homes where they are unwanted and where they add to existing financial and emotional problems
   b. It's the right of a woman to choose what she will do with her own body

    c. Often, women who have abortions feel guilt and remorse; it's better to bear the child and allow for its adoption

    d. Aborting a fetus is equivalent to (or very close to) the taking of a human life

4.   You are a sales representative for an electronics manufacturing firm. You have scheduled a dinner with a very important client for tomorrow and would very much like to impress him. A good friend of yours is a member of an exclusive country club near town. You could really impress your client if you took him to dinner at the club. You consider asking your friend to loan you his membership card . . .

    a. The product you are selling is good, and everyone would win if the deal goes through

    b. Friends ought to help each other

    c. You might be discovered and lose the client

    d. People should never ask friends to be dishonest

5.   One of your employees has accidentally come across a copy of your chief competitor's product price changes for next month. The booklet is on your desk in a manila envelope . . .

    a. The price will give you a temporary advantage over your competitor

    b. You owe it to your company and employees to use all legally obtained information to its best advantage

    c. You may need your competitor's cooperation on a couple of joint projects in the future. You should not jeopardize that relationship now

    d. Using the information would be basically unfair and dishonest

6.   You are middle-aged and have been out of work for nearly two months. You need a job to support your family, and you have just been notified that you have a promising interview in three days with a company for which you would very much like to work. Unfortunately, you are well aware that youth is favored in today's job market and you are afraid that your age might work against you. So, you are thinking of dying your hair to get rid of some of the gray and temporarily reporting your age as several years younger than your true age. After all, you are vigorous, healthy, and highly competent, and you have often been told you look young for your age . . .

    a. You need the job to support your family, and you would be good for the company

    b. Employers should be concerned only with how well an employee can do the job

     c. Deception is risky; you can get into serious trouble if it is discovered

     d. One should always be honest

7. You work for a state auditor's office which has a policy against accepting gifts from anyone with whom the state may have business. Your birthday is in one week, and a very good friend of your father's has just dropped by with a pair of fine leather gloves and a birthday card. This person also works for a construction company firm which has built city facilities in the past . . .

     a. Both the person and your father might be upset if you do not accept the gift

     b. One should respect another's good intentions

     c. The general welfare of the public is best served if you and other state employees remain independent of outside influences

     d. Employees have an obligation to follow state policy

Part 2: Traits

Responses are obtained on a 7-point Likert-type scale where 1 = *not important to me* and 7 = *very important to me.*

Utilitarian traits:

1. Innovative
2. Resourceful
3. Effective
4. Influential
5. Results oriented
6. Productive
7. A winner

Formal traits:

1. Principled
2. Dependable
3. Trustworthy
4. Honest
5. Noted for integrity
6. Law-abiding

Individual Beliefs About Organizational Ethics

Description   This measure, developed by Froelich and Kottke (1991), uses 10 items to describe the extent to which employees accept and support behaviors within an organization that may conflict with ethical norms. The measure contains two dimensions. The first is called support for the company, and it assesses the extent to which an employee disagrees with actions such as companies sometimes engaging in shady business practices due to competition or asking employees to falsify a document. The second dimension is called protect the company, and it assesses the extent to which it is unacceptable for an employee to lie to a customer, supervisor, or co-worker to protect the company. The measure has also been used as a single composite indicator of employee lack of acceptance of ethically dubious behaviors that benefit the company (Mudrack et al., 1999).

Reliability   Coefficient alpha for support for the company was .84. Alpha for protecting the company was .82 (Froelich & Kottke, 1991). Coefficient alpha for the 10-item composite measure was .82 (Mudrack et al., 1999).

Validity   Both dimensions of support for the company and protecting the company correlated positively with tenure and organizational commitment. Froelich and Kottke (1991) found that supporting the company and protecting the company were empirically distinct from organizational commitment and job satisfaction. The composite measure of lack of acceptance of ethically dubious actions correlated positively with equity sensitivity, unacceptability of gaining self-benefits at the expense of the company, and age. It correlated negatively with internal locus of control, social responsibility, and the Protestant work ethic (Mudrack et al., 1999).

Source   Froelich, K. S., & Kottke, J. L. (1991). Measuring individual beliefs about organizational ethics. *Educational and Psychological Measurement, 51,* 377-383. Copyright © 1991 by Sage Publications, Inc. Items were taken from Table 1, p. 380. Reprinted by permission of Sage Publications, Inc.

Items   Responses are obtained using a 7-point Likert-type scale where 1 = *strongly agree* and 7 = *strongly disagree*.

Support for the company items:

1. It is okay for a supervisor to ask an employee to support someone else's incorrect viewpoint
2. It is sometimes necessary for the company to engage in shady practices because the competition is doing so
3. An employee should overlook someone else's wrongdoings if it is in the best interest of the company

4. A supervisor should not care how results are achieved as long as the desired outcome occurs
5. There is nothing wrong with a supervisor asking an employee to falsify a document
6. Profits should be given a higher priority than the safety of a product

Protecting the company items:

1. An employee may need to lie to a co-worker to protect the company
2. An employee may need to lie to a supervisor/manager to protect the company
3. An employee may need to lie to another company's representative to protect the company
4. An employee may need to lie to a customer/client to protect the company

Perceived Importance of Workplace Values

Description   This measure was developed by Van Dyne, Graham, and Dienesch (1994). It uses 12 items to describe the extent to which employees believe their organization places importance on such areas as quality, innovation, cooperation, and wide participation in decision making.

Reliability   Coefficient alpha was .89 (Van Dyne et al., 1994).

Validity   The perceived importance of workplace values correlated positively with organizational loyalty, social participation, having a covenantal relationship with the organization, job satisfaction, tenure, and job level. Perceived importance of workplace values correlated negatively with cynicism (Van Dyne et al., 1994).

Source   Van Dyne, L., Graham, J. W., & Dienesch, R. M. (1994). Organizational citizenship behavior: Construct redefinition, measurement, and validation. *Academy of Management Journal, 37,* 765-802. © 1994 by Academy of Management. Items were taken from the appendix, p. 801. Reproduced with permission of Academy of Management in the format textbook via Copyright Clearance Center.

Items   Responses are obtained on a 7-point Likert-type scale where 1 = *not important at all* and 7 = *extremely important.*

1. High-quality products and services of central importance
2. Individual employees recognized and rewarded for superior performance
3. Reputation for quality surpasses major competitors
4. Innovative products and services of central importance
5. Individual employees recognized and rewarded for innovative work
6. Reputation for innovation surpasses major competitors
7. Widespread participation in decision making highly valued
8. Employees are encouraged to express minority points of view
9. Procedures facilitate widespread participation in decision making
10. Cooperation among employees highly valued
11. Individual employees recognized and rewarded for helping others
12. Reputation as very friendly place to work compared with other firms

References

Abdel-Halim, A. A. (1981). A reexamination of ability as a moderator of role perception-satisfaction relationship. *Personnel Psychology, 34*, 549-561.

Abraham, J. D., & Hansson, R. O. (1996). Gender differences in the usefulness of goal-directed coping for middle-aged and older workers. *Journal of Applied Social Psychology, 26*(8), 657-669.

Adams, G. A., King, L. A., & King, D. W. (1996). Relationships of job and family involvement, family social support, and work-family conflict with job and life satisfaction. *Journal of Applied Psychology, 81*(4), 411-420.

Adkins, C. L. (1995). Previous work experience and organizational socialization: A longitudinal examination. *Academy of Management Journal, 38*(3), 839-863.

Agho, A. O, Mueller, C. W., & Price, J. L. (1993). Determinants of employee job satisfaction: An empirical test of a causal model. *Human Relations, 46*(8), 1007-1020.

Agho, A. O., Price, J. L., & Mueller, C. W. (1992). Discriminant validity of measures of job satisfaction, positive affectivity and negative affectivity. *Journal of Occupational and Organizational Psychology, 65*, 185-196.

Agle, B. R., Mitchell, R. K., & Sonnenfeld, J. A. (1999). Who matters to CEOs? An investigation of stakeholder attributes and salience, corporate performance, and CEO values. *Academy of Management Journal, 42*(5), 507-525.

Allen, N. J., & Meyer, J. P. (1990a). The measurement and antecedents of affective, continuance, and normative commitment to the organization. *Journal of Occupational and Organizational Psychology, 63*, 1-18.

Allen, N. J., & Meyer, J. P. (1990b). Organizational socialization tactics: A longitudinal analysis of links to newcomers' commitment and role orientation. *Academy of Management Journal, 33*(4), 847-858.

Anderson, S. E., & Williams, L. J. (1996). Interpersonal, job, and individual factors related to helping processes at work. *Journal of Applied Psychology, 81*(3), 282-296.

Andrews, F. M., & Withey, S. B. (1976). *Social indicators of well-being: American's perception of life quality.* New York: Plenum.

Aquino, K., Grover, S. L., Bradfield, M., & Allen, D. G. (1999). The effects of negative affectivity, hierarchal status, and self-determination on workplace victimization. *Academy of Management Journal, 42*(3), 260-272.

Aquino, K., Lewis, M. U., & Bradfield, M. (1999). Justice constructs, negative affectivity, and employee deviance: a proposed model and empirical test. *Journal of Organizational Behavior, 20,* 1073-1091.

Arvey, R. D., Carter, G. W., & Buerkley, D. K. (1991). Job satisfaction: Dispositional and situational influences. In C. L. Cooper & I. T. Robertson (Eds.), *International Review of Industrial and Organizational Psychology* (Vol. 6, pp. 359-383). New York: John Wiley.

Aryee, S. (1993). Dual-earner couples in Singapore: An examination of work and non-work sources of their experienced burnout. *Human Relations, 46*(12), 1441-1469.

Aryee, S., Chay, Y. W., & Chew, J. (1996). The motivation to mentor among managerial employees. *Group & Organization Management, 21*(3), 261-278.

Aryee, S., Chay, Y. W., & Tan, H. H. (1994). An examination of the antecedents of subjective career success among a managerial sample in Singapore. *Human Relations, 47*(5), 487-510.

Aryee, S., Fields, D., Luk, V. (1999). A cross-cultural test of a model of the work-family interface. *Journal of Management, 25*(4), 491-511.

Aryee, S., Luk, V., & Stone, R. (1998). Family responsive variables and retention-relevant outcomes among employed parents. *Human Relations, 51*(1), 73-89.

Ashforth, B. E., & Saks, A. M. (1996). Socialization tactics: Longitudinal effects on newcomer adjustment, *Academy of Management Journal, 39*(1), 149-179.

Bacharach, S. B., & Bamberger, P. (1995). Contested control: Systems of control and their implications for ambiguity in elementary and secondary schools. *Work and Occupations, 22*(4), 439-467.

Bacharach, S. B., & Bamberger, P. R., & Conley, S. C. (1990). Work processes, role conflict, and role overload: The case of nurses and engineers in the public sector. *Work and Occupations, 17*(2), 199-229.

Bacharach, S. B., Bamberger, P., & Conley, S. (1991). Work-home conflict among nurses and engineers: Mediating the impact of role stress on burnout and satisfaction at work. *Journal of Organizational Behavior, 12*(1), 39-53.

Balfour, D., & Wechsler, B. (1996). Organizational commitment: Antecedents and outcomes in public organizations. *Public Productivity and Management Review, 29,* 256-277.

Ball, G., Trevino, L. K., & Sims, H. (1994). Just and unjust punishment: Influences on subordinate performance and citizenship. *Academy of Management Journal, 37*(2), 299-322.

Bauer, T. N., & Green, S. G. (1994). Effect of newcomer involvement in work-related activities: A longitudinal study of socialization. *Journal of Applied Psychology, 79*(2), 211-224.

Bearden, W. O., & Netemeyer, R. G. (1999). *Handbook of marketing scales: Multi-item measures for marketing and consumer behavior research* (2nd ed.). Thousand Oaks, CA: Sage..

Becker, T. E. (1992). Foci and bases of commitment: Are they distinctions worth making? *Academy of Management Journal, 35*(1), 232-250.

Becker, T. E., Billings, R. S., Eveleth, D. M., & Gilbert, N. L. (1996). Foci and bases of employee commitment: Implications for job performance. *Academy of Management Journal, 39*(2), 464-482.

Bedeian, A. G., Mossholder, K. W., Kemery, E. R., & Armenakis, A. A. (1990). Replication requisites: A second look at Klenke-Hamel and Mathieu. *Human Relations, 45*(10), 1093-1106.

Begley, T. M., & Czajka, J. M. (1993). Panel analysis of the moderating effects of commitment on job satisfaction, intent to quit, and health following organizational change. *Journal of Applied Psychology, 78,* 552-556.

Bennett, J., Lehman, W., & Forst, J. (1999). Change, transfer climate, and customer orientation: A contextual model and analysis of change-driven training. *Group & Organization Management, 24*(2), 188-217.

Birnbaum, D., & Somers, M. J. (1993). Fitting job performance into a turnover model: An examination of the form of the job performance-turnover relationship and path model. *Journal of Management, 19*(1), 1-11.

Blau, G. (1989). Testing generalizability of a career commitment measure and its impact on employee turnover. *Journal of Vocational Behavior, 35,* 88-103.

Blau, G. (1994). Testing the effect of level and importance of pay referents on pay level satisfaction. *Human Relations, 47* (10), 1251-1268.

Blau, G. (1999). Early-career job factors influencing the professional commitment of medical technologies. *Academy of Management Journal, 42*(6), 687-695.

Bluen, S. D., & Barling, J. (1987). Stress and the industrial relations process: Development of the Industrial Relations Event Scale. *South African Journal of Psychology, 17,* 150-159.

Bohen, H., & Viveros-Long, A. (1981). *Balancing jobs and family life.* Philadelphia: Temple University Press.

Brady, F. N., & Wheeler, G. E. (1996). An empirical study of ethical predisposition. *Journal of Business Ethics, 15,* 927-940.

Brayfield, A. H., & Rothe, H. F. (1951). An index of job satisfaction. *Journal of Applied Psychology, 35,* 307-311.

Breaugh, J. A., & Colihan, J. P. (1994). Measuring facets of job ambiguity: Construct validity evidence. *Journal of Applied Psychology, 79*(2), 191-202.

Breeden, S. A. (1993). Job and occupational change as a function of occupational correspondence and job satisfaction. *Journal of Vocational Behavior, 43,* 30-45.

Brett, J., Cron, W., & Slocum, J. (1995). Economic dependency on work: A moderator of the relationship between organizational commitment and performance. *Academy of Management Journal, 38*(1), 261-271.

Brett, J. M., & Okumura, T. (1998). Inter- and intracultural negotiation: U.S. and Japanese negotiators. *Academy of Management Journal, 41*(5), 495-510.

Bretz, R. D., Jr., & Judge, T. A. (1994). Person-organization fit and the theory of work adjustment: Implications for satisfaction, tenure, and career success. *Journal of Vocational Behavior, 44,* 32-54.

Brief, A. (1998). *Attitudes in and around organizations.* Thousand Oaks, CA: Sage.

Brief, A. P., Dukerich, J. M., & Doran, L. I. (1991). Resolving ethical dilemmas in management: Experimental investigations of values, accountability, and choice. *Journal of Applied Social Psychology, 21,* 380-396.

Brief, A. P., & Roberson, L. (1989). Job attitude organization: An exploratory study. *Journal of Applied Social Psychology, 19,* 717-727.

Brooke, P. P., Russell, D., & Price, J. L. (1988). Discriminant validation of measures of job satisfaction, job involvement, and organizational commitment. *Journal of Applied Psychology, 73,* 139-145.

Buchko, A. A. (1992). Effects of employee ownership on employee attitudes: A test of three theoretical perspectives. *Work and Occupations, 19*(1), 59-78.

Buckley, M. R., Carraher, S. M., & Cote, J. A. (1992). Measurement issues concerning the use of inventories of job satisfaction. *Educational and Psychological Measurement, 52,* 529-543.

Bussing, A., Bissels, T., Fuchs, V., & Perrar, K. M. (1999). A dynamic model of work satisfaction: Qualitative approaches. *Human Relations, 52*(8), 999-1028.

Cable, D. M., & Judge, T. A. (1996). Person-organization fit, job choice decisions, and organizational entry. *Organizational*

Behavior and Human Decision Processes, 67(3), 294-311.

Cable, D. M., & Judge, T. A. (1997). Interviewers' perceptions of person-organization fit and organizational selection decisions. *Journal of Applied Psychology, 82*, 546-561.

Caldwell, D. F., Chatman, J. A., & O'Reilly, C. A., III. (1990). Building organizational commitment: A multi-firm study. *Journal of Occupational and Organizational Psychology, 63*, 245-261.

Caldwell, D. F., & O'Reilly, C. A., III. (1990). Measuring person-job fit with a profile-comparison process. *Journal of Applied Psychology, 75*(6), 648-657.

Callen, V. J. (1993). Subordinate-manager communication in different sex dyads: Consequences for job satisfaction. *Journal of Occupational and Organizational Psychology, 66*,13-27.

Cammann, C., Fichman, M., Jenkins, D., & Klesh, J. (1983). Assessing the attitudes and perceptions of organizational members. In S. Seashore, E. Lawler, P. Mirvis, & C. Cammann (Eds.), *Assessing organizational change: A guide to methods, measures and practices* (pp. 71-138). New York: John Wiley.

Campion, M. A. (1988). Interdisciplinary approaches to job design: A constructive replication with extensions. *Journal of Applied Psychology, 73*, 467-481.

Campion, M. A., & McClelland, C. L. (1991). Interdisciplinary examination of the costs and benefits of enlarged jobs: A job design quasi-experiment. *Journal of Applied Psychology, 76*(2), 186-198.

Caplan, R. D., Cobb, S., French, J. R. P., Van Harrison, R., & Pinneau, S. R. (1980). *Job demands and worker health*. Ann Arbor: University of Michigan, Institute for Social Research.

Carlson, D. S., & Perrewé, P. L. (1999). The role of social support in the stressor-strain relationship: An examination of work-family conflict. *Journal of Management, 25*(4), 513-533.

Carraher, S. M., & Buckley, M. R. (1996). Cognitive complexity and the perceived dimensionality of pay satisfaction. *Journal of Applied Psychology, 81*(1), 102-109.

Chan, D. (1996). Cognitive misfit of problem-solving style at work: A facet of person-organization fit. *Organizational Behavior and Human Decision Processes, 68*(3), 194-207.

Chatman, J., & Jehn, K. (1994). Assessing the relationship between industry characteristics and organizational culture: How different can you be? *Academy of Management Journal, 37*(3), 522-553.

Chatman, J. A. (1989). Improving interactional organizational research: A model of person-organization fit. *Academy of Management Review, 14*(3), 333-349.

Chay, Y. W. (1993). Social support, individual differences, and well-being: A study of small business entrepreneurs and employees. *Journal of Occupational and Organizational Psychology, 66*(4), 285-303.

Chinese Culture Connection. (1987). Chinese values and the search for culture-free dimensions of culture. *Journal of Cross-Cultural Psychology, 18*(2), 143-164.

Cohen, A. (1993). Organizational commitment and turnover: A meta-analysis. *Academy of Management Journal, 36*(5), 1140-1157.

Cohen, A. (1995). An examination of the relationships between work commitment and non-work domains. *Human Relations, 48*(3), 239-263.

Cohen, A. (1996). On the discriminant validity of the Meyer and Allen measure of organizational commitment: How does it fit with the work commitment construct? *Educational and Psychological Measurement, 56*(3), 494-503.

Cohen, A. (1997). Non-work influences on withdrawal cognitions: An empirical examination of an overlooked issue. *Human Relations, 50*(12), 1511-1537.

Cohen, A. (1999). Relationships among five forms of commitment: An empirical assessment. *Journal of Organizational Behavior, 20,* 285-308.

Cohen, A., & Hudecek, N. (1993). Organizational commitment-turnover relationship across occupational groups: A meta-analysis. *Group & Organization Management, 18*(2), 188-213.

Cohen, A., & Kirchmeyer, C. (1995). A multidimensional approach to the relation between organizational commitment and non-work participation. *Journal of Vocational Behavior, 46,* 189-202.

Coleman, D. F., Irving, G. P., & Cooper, C. L. (1999). Another look at the locus of control-organizational commitment relationship: It depends on the form of commitment. *Journal of Organizational Behavior, 20,* 995-1001.

Cook, J., & Wall, T. D. (1980). New work attitude measures of trust, organizational commitment and personal need for non-fulfillment. *Journal of Organizational and Occupational Psychology, 53,* 39-52.

Cook, J. D., Hepworth, S. J., Wall, T. D., & Warr, P. B. (1981). *The experience of work: A compendium of 249 measures and their use.* London: Academic Press.

Cordery, J., Vevastos, P., Mueller, W., & Parker, S. (1993). Correlates of employee attitudes toward functional flexibility. *Human Relations, 46*(6), 705-723.

Cortina, J. M. (1993). What is coefficient alpha? An examination of theory and applications. *Journal of Applied Psychology, 78*(1), 98-104.

Cranny, C. J., Smith, C. P., & Stone, E. F. (1992). *Job satisfaction: How people feel about their jobs and how it affects their performance.* New York: Lexington Books.

Cropanzano, R., Howes, J. C., Grandey, A. A., & Toth, P. (1997). The relationship of organizational politics and support to work behaviors, attitudes, and stress. *Journal of Organizational Behavior, 18,* 159-180.

Cropanzano, R., James, K., & Konovsky, M. A. (1993). Dispositional affectivity as a predictor or work attitudes and job performance. *Journal of Organizational Behavior, 14,* 595-606.

Daly, J. P., & Geyer, P. D. (1994). The role of fairness in implementing large-scale change: Employee evaluations of process and outcome in seven facility relocations. *Journal of Organizational Behavior, 15* (7), 623-638.

Daniels, K., & Guppy, A. (1994). Occupational stress, social support, job control, and psychological well-being. *Human Relations, 47*(12), 1523-1545.

Davy, J. A., Kinicki, A. J., & Scheck, C. L. (1997). A test of job security's direct and mediated effects on withdrawal cognitions. *Journal of Organizational Behavior, 18,* 323-349.

Dean, J. W., & Snell, S. A. (1991). Integrated manufacturing and job design: Moderating effects of organizational inertia. *Academy of Management Journal, 34*(4), 776-804.

DeConinck, J. B., Stilwell, C. D., & Brock, B. A. (1996). A construct validity analysis of scores on measures of distributive justice and pay satisfaction. *Educational and Psychological Measurement, 56*(6), 1026-1036.

Deci, E. L., Connell, J. P., & Ryan, T. (1989). Self determination in an organization. *Journal of Applied Psychology, 74*(4), 580-591.

Deluga, R. J. (1991). The relationship of subordinate upward-influencing behavior, health care manager interpersonal stress, and performance. *Journal of Applied Social Psychology, 21*(1), 78-88.

Dewe, P. J. (1992). Applying the concept of appraisal to work stressors: Some exploratory analysis. *Human Relations, 45*(2), 143-165.

Dobbins, G. H., Cardy, R. L., & Platz-Vieno, S. J. (1990). A contingency approach to appraisal satisfaction: An initial investigation of the joint effects of organizational variables and appraisal characteristics. *Journal of Management, 16*(3), 619-633.

Dodd, N. G., & Ganster, D. C. (1996). The interactive effects of variety, autonomy, and feedback on attitudes and performance. *Journal of Organizational Behavior, 17,* 329-347.

Dose, J. J. (1997). Work values: An integrative framework and illustrative application to organizational socialization. *Journal of Occupational and Organizational Psychology, 70,* 219-240.

Duckworth, D. (1986). Managing without stress. *Personnel Management, 18(4)*, 40-44.

Duffy, M. K., Ganster, D. C., & Shaw, J. D. (1998). Positive affectivity and negative outcomes: The role of tenure and job satisfaction. *Journal of Applied Psychology, 83*(6), 950-959.

Dulebohn, J. H., & Ferris, G. R. (1999). The role of influence tactics in perceptions of performance evaluations' fairness. *Academy of Management Journal, 42*(3), 288-303.

Dulebohn, J. H., & Martocchio, J. J. (1998). Employee perceptions of the fairness of work group incentive pay plans. *Journal of Management, 24*(4), 469-488.

Dunham, R. B., Grube, J. A., & Castaneda, M. (1994). Organizational commitment: The utility of an integrative definition. *Journal of Applied Psychology, 79,* 370-380.

Dunham, R. B., & Smith, F. J. (1979). *Organizational surveys.* Glenview, IL: Scott, Foresman.

Duxbury, L. E., & Higgins, C. A. (1991). Gender differences in work-family conflict. *Journal of Applied Psychology, 76*(1), 60-74.

Dwyer, D. J., & Ganster, D. C. (1991). The effects of job demands and control on employee attendance and satisfaction. *Journal of Organizational Behavior, 12,* 595-608.

Edwards, J. R. (1991). Person-job fit: A conceptual integration, literature review, and methodological critique. In C. L. Cooper & I. T. Robertson (Eds.), *International review of industrial and organizational psychology,* New York: John Wiley.

Edwards, J. R. (1996). An examination of competing versions of the person-environment fit approach to stress. *Academy of Management Journal, 39*(2), 292-340.

Edwards, J. R., & Van Harrison, R. (1993). Job demands and worker health: Three-dimensional reexamination of the relationship between person-environment fit and strain. *Journal of Applied Psychology, 78*(4), 628-648.

Eisenberger, R., Cummings, J., Armeli, S., & Lynch, P. (1997). Perceived organizational support, discretionary treatment, and job satisfaction. *Journal of Applied Psychology, 82*(5), 812-820.

Eisenberger, R., Fasolo, P., & Davis-LaMastro, V. (1990). Perceived organizational support and employee diligence, commitment, and innovation. *Journal of Applied Psychology, 75*(1), 51-59.

Eisenberger, R., Huntington, R., Hutchinson, S., & Sowa, D. (1986). Perceived organizational support. *Journal of Applied Psychology, 71,* 500-507.

Erera-Weatherley, P. I. (1996). Coping with stress: Public welfare supervisors doing their best. *Human Relations, 49*(2), 157-171.

Etzion, D., Eden, D., & Lapidot, Y. (1998). Relief from job stressors and burnout: Reserve service as a respite. *Journal of Applied Psychology, 83,* 577-585.

Farh, J. L., Earley, P. C., & Lin, S. C. (1997). Impetus for action: A cultural analysis of justice and organizational citizenship behavior in Chinese society. *Administrative Science Quarterly, 42*(3), 421-444.

Feather, N. T., Norman, M. A., & Worsley, A. (1998). Values and valences: Variables relating to the attractiveness and choice of food in different contexts. *Journal of Applied Social Psychology, 28,* 639-656.

Feldman, J. M., & Lynch, J. G. (1988). Self-generated validity and other effects of measurement on belief, attitude, intention, and behavior. *Journal of Applied Psychology, 73*(3), 421-435.

Fields, D. L., & Blum, T. C. (1997). Employee satisfaction in work groups with different gender composition. *Journal of Organizational Behavior, 18,* 181-196.

Fisher, C. D., & Shaw, J. B. (1994). Relocation attitudes and adjustment: A longitudinal study. *Journal of Organizational Behavior, 15*(3), 209-224.

Folger, R., & Konovsky, M. A. (1989). Effects of procedural and distributive justice on reactions to pay raise decisions. *Academy of Management Journal, 32*(1), 115-130.

Fortunato, V. J., Jex, S., & Heinish, D. (1999). An examination of the discriminant validity of the strain-free negative affectivity scale. *Journal of Occupational and Organizational Psychology, 72,* 503-523.

Fox, M. L., & Dwyer, D. J. (1995). Stressful job demands and worker health: An investigation of the effects of self-monitoring. *Journal of Applied Social Psychology, 25,* 1973-1995.

Fox, M. L., Dwyer, D. J., & Ganster, D. C. (1993). Effects of stressful job demands and control on physiological outcomes. *Academy of Management Journal, 36*(2), 289-309.

Fried, Y., Ben David, H. A., Tiegs, R. B., Avital, N., & Yeverechyahu, U. (1998). The interactive effect of role conflict and role ambiguity on job performance. *Journal of Occupational and Organizational Psychology, 71(1),* 19-27.

Frese, M., Kring, W., Soose, A., & Zempel, J. (1996). Personal initiative at work: Differences between East and West Germany. *Academy of Management Journal, 39*(1), 37-64.

Frese, M., Teng, E., & Wijnin, C. J. (1999). Helping to improve suggestion systems: Predictors of making suggestions in companies. *Journal of Organizational Behavior, 20*(7), 1139-1155.

Fried, Y. (1998). The interactive effect of role conflict and role ambiguity on job performance. *Journal of Occupational and Organizational Psychology, 71,* 19-28.

Fried, Y., & Tiegs, R. B. (1995). Supervisors' role conflict and role ambiguity differential relations with performance ratings of subordinates and the moderating effect of screening ability. *Journal of Applied Psychology, 80*(2), 282-292.

Froelich, K. S., & Kottke, J. L. (1991). Measuring individual beliefs about organizational ethics. *Educational and Psychological Measurement, 51,* 377-383.

Frone, M. R., Russell, M., & Cooper, M. L. (1992). Antecedents and outcomes of work-family conflict: Testing a model of the work-family interface. *Journal of Applied Psychology, 77,* 65-78.

Frone, M. R., Russell, M., & Cooper, M. L. (1994). Relationship between job and family satisfaction: causal or non-causal co-variation? *Journal of Management, 20*(3), 565-580.

Frone, M. R., Russell, M., & Cooper, M. L. (1996). Workplace family-supportive programs: Predictors of employed parents' importance ratings. *Journal of Occupational and Organizational Psychology, 69,* 351-366.

Funderburg, S. A., & Levy, P. E. (1997). The influence of individual and contextual variables on 360-degree feedback system attitudes. *Group & Organization Management, 22,* 210-235.

Furnham, A. (1990). A content, correlational, and factor analytic study of seven questionnaire measures of the Protestant work ethic. *Human Relations, 43,* 383-399.

Furnham, A., Brewin, C. R., & O'Kelly, H. (1994). Cognitive style and attitudes to work. *Human Relations, 47*(12), 1509-1521.

Gagne, M., Senecal, C. B., & Koestner, R. (1997). Proximal job characteristics, feelings of empowerment, and intrinsic motivation: A multidimensional model. *Journal of Applied Social Psychology, 27*(14), 1222-1240.

Ganster, D. C., & Schaubroeck, J. (1991). Work stress and employee health. *Journal of Management, 17*(2), 235-271.

Ganzach, Y. (1998). Intelligence and job satisfaction. *Academy of Management Journal, 41*(5), 526-540.

George, J. M. (1995). Leader positive mood and group performance: The case of customer service. *Journal of Applied Social Psychology, 25*(9), 778-794.

George, J. M., & Jones, G. R. (1996). The experience of work and turnover intentions: Interactive effects of value attainment, job satisfaction, and positive mood. *Journal of Applied Psychology, 81*, 318-325.

George, J. M., & Jones, G. R. (1997). Experiencing work: Values, attitudes, and moods. *Human Relations, 50*(4), 393-416.

Gilliland, S. W. (1994). Effects of procedural and distributive justice on reactions to a selection system. *Journal of Applied Psychology, 79*(5), 691-701.

Goff, S. J. (1990). Employer supported child care, work/family conflict, and absenteeism: A field study. *Personnel Psychology, 43*(4), 793-810.

Grandey, A. A., & Cropanzano, R. (1998). The conservation of resources model applied to work-family conflict and strain. *Journal of Vocational Behavior, 54*, 350-370.

Greenhaus, J. H., Parasuraman, A., & Wormley, W. M. (1990). Effects of race on organizational experiences, job performance evaluations, and career outcomes. *Academy of Management Journal, 33*(1), 64-86.

Gregersen, H. B., & Black, J. S. (1992). Antecedents to commitment to a parent company and a foreign operation. *Academy of Management Journal, 35*(1), 65-71.

Gregersen, H. B., & Stroh, L. (1997). Coming home to the arctic cold: Antecedents to Finnish expatriate and spouse repatriation adjustment. *Personnel Psychology, 50*(3), 635-655.

Gregson, T. (1990). The separate constructs of communication satisfaction and job satisfaction. *Educational and Psychological Measurement, 50*, 39-48.

Grover, S. L. (1991). Predicting the perceived fairness of parental leave policies. *Journal of Applied Psychology, 76*(2), 247-255.

Gunz, H. P., & Gunz, S. P. (1994). Professional/organizational commitment and job satisfaction for employed lawyers. *Human Relations, 47*(7), 801-828.

Gutek, B. A., Searle, S., & Klepa, L. (1991). Rational versus gender role explanations for work-family conflict. *Journal of Applied Psychology, 76*(4), 560-568.

Hackett, R. D., Bycio, P., & Hausdorf, P. A. (1994). Further assessments of Meyer and Allen's three-component model of organizational commitment. *Journal of Applied Psychology, 79*(1), 15-23.

Hackman, J. R., & Oldham, G. R. (1974). *The Job Diagnostic Survey: An instrument for the diagnosis of jobs and the evaluation of job redesign projects* (Tech. Rep. No. 4). New Haven, CT: Yale University, Department of Administrative Sciences.

Hackman, J. R., & Oldham, G. R. (1980). *Work redesign.* Reading, MA: Addison-Wesley.

Harris, M. M. (1991). Role conflict and role ambiguity as substance versus artifact: A confirmatory factor analysis of House, Schuler, and Levanoni's (1983) scales. *Journal of Applied Psychology, 76*(1), 122-126.

Harris, M. M., & Bladen, A. (1994). Wording effects in the measurement of role conflict and role ambiguity: A multitrait-multimethod analysis. *Journal of Management, 20*(4), 887-902.

Harris, S. G., Hirschfeld, R. R., Field, H., & Mossholder, K. W. (1993). Psychological attachment: Relationships with job characteristics. *Group & Organization Management, 18*(4), 459-482.

Harrison, A. W., Hochwarter, W. A., Perrewé, P. L., & Ralston, D. A. (1998). The integration construct: An assessment of the validity of the Measure of Ingratiatory Behaviors in Organizational Settings (MIBOS). *Journal of Applied Psychology, 83*(6), 932-943.

Hart, P. M. (1999). Predicting employee life satisfaction: A coherent model of personality, work and non-work experiences and domain satisfactions. *Journal of Applied Psychology, 84*(4), 564-584.

Hatfield, J., Robinson, R. B., & Huseman, R. C. (1985). An empirical evaluation of a test for assessing job satisfaction. *Psychological Reports, 56*, 39-45.

Hemingway, M. A. (1999). Organizational climate and occupational stressors as predictors of withdrawal behaviours and injuries in nurses. *Journal of Occupational and Organizational Psychology, 72*, 285-300.

Heneman, H. G., & Schwab, D. P. (1985). Pay satisfaction: Its multidimensional nature and measurement. *Journal of Psychology, 20*, 129-141.

Higgins, C. A., Duxbury, L. E., & Irving, R. H. (1992). Work-family conflict in the dual-career family. *Organizational Behavior and Human Decision Processes, 51*, 51-75.

Hochwarter, W. A., Perrewé, P. L., Ferris, G. R., & Brymer, R. A. (1999). Job satisfaction and performance: The moderating effects of value attainment and affective disposition. *Journal of Vocational Behavior, 54*, 296-313.

Hochwarter, W. A., Perrewé, P. L., Ferris, G. R., & Gercio, R. (1999). Commitment as an antidote to the tension and turnover consequences of organizational politics. *Journal of Vocational Behavior, 55*(3), 277-297.

Hochwarter, W. A., Zellars, K. L., Perrewé, P. L., & Harrison, A. W. (1999). The interactive role of negative affectivity and job characteristics: Are high-NA employees destined to be unhappy at work? *Journal of Applied Social Psychology, 29*(10), 2203-2218.

Hodson, R. (1991). Workplace behaviors. *Work and Occupations, 18(3)*, 271-290.

Hodson, R., Creighton, S., Jamison, C. S., Rieble, S., & Welsh, S. (1994). Loyalty to whom? Workplace participation and the development of consent. *Human Relations, 47*(8), 895-909.

Holder, J. C., & Vaux, A. (1998). African American professionals: Coping with occupational stress in predominantly white work environments. *Journal of Vocational Behavior, (53)*, 315-333.

Hom, P. W., & Griffeth, R. W. (1991). Structural equations modeling test of a turnover theory: cross-sectional and longitudinal analyses. *Journal of Applied Psychology, 76*(3), 350-366.

House, J. S., McMichael, A. J., Wells, J. A., Kaplan, B. H., & Landerman, L. R. (1979). Occupational stress and health among factory workers. *Journal of Health and Social Behavior, 20*, 139-160.

House, R. J., & Rizzo, J. R. (1972). Role conflict and ambiguity as critical variables in a model of organizational behavior. *Organizational Behavior and Human Decision Processes, 7*, 467-505.

House, R. J., Schuler, R. S., & Levanoni, E. (1983). Role conflict and ambiguity scales: Reality or artifacts? *Journal of Applied Psychology, 68*(2), 334-337.

Howard, J. I., & Frink, D. D. (1996). The effects of organizational restructure on employee satisfaction. *Group & Organization Management, 21*(3), 278.

Huber, V, L., Seybolt, P. M., & Venemon, K. (1992). The relationship between individual inputs, perceptions, and multidimensional pay satisfaction. *Journal of Applied Social Psychology, 22*(17), 1369-1373.

Hunter, J. E. (1980). *Test validation for 12,000 jobs: An application of synthetic validity and validity generalization to the General Aptitude Test Battery (BATB).*

Washington, DC: U.S. Employment Service.

Hunter, J. E., Schmidt, E. L., & Judiesch, M. K. (1990). Individual differences in output variability as a function of job complexity. *Journal of Applied Psychology, 75*, 28-42.

Huselid, M. A., & Day, N. E. (1991). Organizational commitment, job involvement, and turnover: A substantive and methodological analysis. *Journal of Applied Psychology, 76*(3), 380-391.

Hutchinson, S., Valentino, K. E., & Kirkner, S. L. (1998). What works for the gander does not work as well for the goose: The effects of leader behavior. *Journal of Applied Social Psychology, 28*(2), 171-182.

Idaszak, J. R., & Drasgow, F. (1987). A revision of the Job Diagnostic Survey: Elimination of a measurement artifact. *Journal of Applied Psychology, 72*, 69-74.

Igalens, J., & Roussel, P. (1999). A study of the relationships between compensation package, work motivation and job satisfaction. *Journal of Organizational Behavior, 20*, 1003-1025.

Ironson, G., Smith, P., Brannick, M., Gibson, M., & Paul, K. (1989). Construction of a Job in General Scale: A comparison of global, composite and specific measures. *Journal of Applied Psychology, 74*, 193-200.

Ivancevich, J., & Matteson, M. (1980). *Stress and work: A managerial perspective.* Glenview, IL: Scott, Foresman.

Iverson, R. D. (1997). Predicting occupational injury: The role of affectivity. *Journal of Occupational and Organizational Psychology, 70*, 113-129.

Jackson, S. E., & Schuler, R. S. (1985). A meta-analysis and conceptual critique of research on role ambiguity and role conflict in work settings. *Organizational Behavior and Human Decision Processes, 36*, 16-78.

Jackson, P. R., Wall, T. D., Martin, R., & Davids, K. (1993). New measures of job control, cognitive demand, and produc-

tion responsibility. *Journal of Applied Psychology, 78*(5), 753-762.

Jalajas, D. S. (1994). The role of self-esteem in the stress process: Empirical results from job hunting. *Journal of Applied Social Psychology, 24*(22), 1984-2001.

Jamal, M. (1990). Relationship of job stress and Type-A behavior to employees' job satisfaction, organizational commitment, psychosomatic health problems, and turnover motivation. *Human Relations, 43*(8), 727-738.

Jamal, M., & Baba, V. V. (1992). Shiftwork and department-type related to job stress, work attitudes and behavioral intentions: A study of nurses. *Journal of Organizational Behavior, 13*, 449-464.

Jaros, S. J., Jermier, J. M., Koehler, J. W., & Sincich, T. (1993). Effects of continuance, affective, and moral commitment on the withdrawal process: An evaluation of eight structural equation models. *Academy of Management Journal, 36*(5), 951-996.

Jex, S. M. (1999). Self-esteem as a moderator: A comparison of global and organization-based measures. *Journal of Occupational and Organizational Psychology, 72*, 71-82.

Jex, S. M., Beehr, T. A., & Roberts, C. K. (1992). The meaning of occupational stress items to survey respondents. *Journal of Applied Psychology, 77*(5), 623-628.

Jex, S. M., & Gudanowski, D. M. (1992). Efficacy beliefs and work stress: An exploratory study. *Journal of Organizational Behavior, 13*, 509-517.

Johnston, G. P., & Snizek, W. E. (1991). Combining head and heart in complex organizations: A test of Etzioni's dual compliance structure hypothesis. *Human Relations, 44*(12), 1255-1272.

Jones, F. F., Scarpello, V., & Bergmann, T. (1999). Pay procedures—What makes them fair? *Journal of Occupational & Organizational Psychology, 72*(2), 129-145.

Joy, V. L., & Witt, L. A. (1992). Delay of gratification as a moderator of the procedural justice-distributive justice relationship. *Group & Organization Management, 17*(3), 297-308.

Judge, T. A. (1993a). Does affective disposition moderate the relationship between job satisfaction and voluntary turnover? *Journal of Applied Psychology, 78*(3), 395-401.

Judge, T. A. (1993b). Validity of the dimensions of the pay satisfaction questionnaire: Evidence of differential prediction. *Personnel Psychology, 46*(2), 331.

Judge, T. A., Boudreau, J. W., & Bretz, R. D., Jr. (1994). Job and life attitudes of male executives. *Journal of Applied Psychology, 79*(5), 767-782.

Judge, T. A., & Hulin, C. L. (1993). Job satisfaction as a reflection of disposition: A multiple source causal analysis. *Organizational Behavior and Human Decision Processes, 56,* 388-421.

Judge, T. A., Locke, E. A., Durham, C. C., & Kluger, A. N. (1998). Dispositional effects on job and life satisfaction: The role of core evaluations. *Journal of Applied Psychology, 83*(1), 17-34.

Judge, T. A., Thoresen, C. J., Pucik, V., & Welbourne, T. M. (1999). Managerial coping with organizational change: A dispositional perspective. *Journal of Applied Psychology, 84*(1), 107-122.

Judge, T. A., & Watanabe, S. (1993). Another look at the job satisfaction-life satisfaction relationship. *Journal of Applied Psychology, 78*(6), 939-948.

Kacmar, K. M. (1999). An examination of the perceptions of organizational politics model: Replication and extension. *Human Relations, 52*(3), 383-417.

Kacmar, K. M., Carlson, D. S., & Brymer, R. A. (1999). Antecedents and consequences of organizational commitment: A comparison of two scales. *Educational and Psychological Measurement, 59*(6), 976-994.

Kacmar, K. M., & Ferris, G. R. (1991). Perceptions of Organizational Politics Scale (POPS): Development and construct validation. *Educational and Psychological Measurement, 51,* 193-205.

Kacmar, K. M., & Valle, M. (1997). Dimensionality of the Measure of Ingratiatory Behaviors in Organizational Settings (MIBOS) scale. *Educational and Psychological Measurement, 57*(2), 314-330.

Kahn, R. L., Wolfe, D. M., Quinn, R. P., & Snoek, J. D. (with Rosenthal, R. A.). (1964). *Organizational stress: Studies in role conflict and ambiguity.* New York: John Wiley.

Kanner, A., Kafry, D., & Pines, A. (1978). Conspicuous in its absence: The lack of positive conditions as a source of stress. *Journal of Human Stress, 4,* 33-39.

Karasek, R. A. (1979). Job demands, job decision latitude, and mental strain: Implications for job redesign. *Administrative Science Quarterly, 24,* 285-308.

Kelloway, E. K., Barling, J., & Shah, A. (1993). Industrial relations stress and job satisfaction: Concurrent effects and mediation. *Journal of Organizational Behavior, 14,* 447-457.

King, L. A., & King, D. W. (1990). Role conflict and role ambiguity: A critical assessment of construct validity. *Psychological Bulletin, 107*(1), 48-57.

Kipnis, D., Schmidt, S. M., & Wilkinson, I. (1980). Intraorganizational influence tactics: Explorations in getting one's way. *Journal of Applied Psychology, 65*(4), 440-447.

Kirchmeyer, C. (1992). Non-work participation and work attitudes: A test of scarcity vs. expansion models of personal resources, *Human Relations, 45*(8), 775-795.

Klein, D. J., & Verbeke, W. (1999). Autonomic feedback in stressful environments: How do individual differences in autonomic feedback relate to burnout, job performance, and job attitudes in salespeople? *Journal of Applied Psychology, 84*(6), 911-924.

Klenke-Hamel, K. E., & Mathieu, J. E. (1990). Role strains, tension, and job satisfaction influences on employees' propensity to leave: A multi-sample replication and extension. *Human Relations, 43*(8), 791-807.

Kluger, A. N. (1998). Commute variability and strain. *Journal of Organizational Behavior, 19,* 147-165.

Konovsky, M. A., & Cropanzano, R. (1991). Perceived fairness of employee drug testing as a predictor of employee attitudes and job performance. *Journal of Applied Psychology, 76*(5), 698-707.

Kopelman, R. E., Greenhaus, J. H., & Connolly, T. F. (1983). A model of work, family, and inter-role conflict: A construct validation study. *Organizational Behavior and Human Performance, 32,* 198-215.

Kossek, E. E., & Ozeki, C. (1998). Work-family conflict, policies, and the job-life satisfaction relationship: A review and directions for organizational behavior-human resources research. *Journal of Applied Psychology, 83*(2), 139-149.

Kraimer, M. L., Seibert, S. E., & Liden, R. C. (1999). Psychological empowerment as a multidimensional construct: A test of construct validity. *Educational and Psychological Measurement, 59*(1), 127-142.

Kristof, A. L. (1996). Person-organization fit: An integrative review of its conceptualizations, measurement and implications. *Personnel Psychology, 49*(1), 1-30.

Kumar, K., & Beyerlein, M. (1991). Construction and validation of an instrument for measuring ingratiatory behaviors in organizational settings. *Journal of Applied Psychology, 76,* 619-627.

Kunin, C. (1955). The construction of a new type of attitude measure. *Personnel Psychology, 8*(1), 65-77.

Kushnir, T., & Melamed, S. (1991), Workload, perceived control and psychological distress in Type A/B industrial workers.

Journal of Organizational Behavior, 12, 155-168.

Lam, S. S. K., Hui, C., & Law, K. S. (1999). Organizational citizenship behavior: Comparing perspectives of supervisors and subordinates across four international samples. *Journal of Applied Psychology, 84*(4), 594-601.

Lambert, S. J. (1990). Processes linking work and family: A critical review and research agenda. *Human Relations, 43*(3), 239-257.

Larwood, L., Wright, T. A., Desrochers, S., & Dahir, V. (1998). Extending latent role and psychological contract theories to predict intent to turnover and politics in business organizations. *Group & Organization Management, 23*(2), 100-123.

Lee, C., & Farh, J. (1999). The effects of gender in organizational justice perception. *Journal of Organizational Behavior, 20,* 133-142.

Lee, C., Law, K. S., & Bobko, P. (1998). The importance of justice perceptions on pay effectiveness: A two-year study of a skill-based pay plan. *Journal of Management, 25*(6), 851-873.

Lee, R. T., & Ashforth, B. E. (1993). A further examination of managerial burnout: Toward an integrated model. *Journal of Organizational Behavior, 14,* 3-20.

Lee, T. W., & Johnson, D. R. (1991). The effects of work schedule and employment status on the organizational commitment and job satisfaction of full versus part time employees. *Journal of Vocational Behavior, 38,* 208-224.

Lee, T. W., Mitchell, T. R., Holtom, B. C., McDaniel, L. S., & Hill, J. W. (1999). The unfolding model of voluntary turnover: A replication and extension. *Academy of Management Journal, 42*(4), 450-462.

Lefkowitz, J. (1994). Sex-related differences in job attitudes and dispositional variables. *Academy of Management Journal, 37*(2), 323-354.

Lehman, W. E. K., & Simpson, D. D. (1992). Employee substance use and on-the-job behaviors. *Journal of Applied Psychology, 77,* 309-321.

Levy, P. E., & Williams, J. R. (1998). The role of perceived system knowledge in predicting appraisal reactions, job satisfaction, and organizational commitment. *Journal of Organizational Behavior, 19,* 53-65.

Lim, V. K. G. (1996). Job insecurity and its outcomes: Moderating effects of work-based and non-work-based social support. *Human Relations, 49*(2), 171.

Long, B. C. (1993). Coping strategies of male managers: A prospective analysis of predictors of psychosomatic symptoms and job satisfaction. *Journal of Vocational Behavior, 42,* 184-199.

Lovelace, K., & Rosen, B. (1996). Differences in achieving person-organization fit among diverse groups of managers. *Journal of Management, 22*(5), 703-722.

Lynch, P. D., Eisenberger, R., & Armeli, S. (1999). Perceived organizational support: Inferior versus superior performance by wary employees. *Journal of Applied Psychology, 84,* 467-483.

Major, D. A., Kozlowski, S. W. J., Chao, G. T., & Gardner, P. D. (1995). A longitudinal investigation of newcomer expectations, early socialization outcomes, and the moderating effects of role development factors. *Journal of Applied Psychology, 80*(3), 418-431.

Manhardt, P. J. (1972). Job orientation of male and female college graduates in business. *Personnel Psychology, 25,* 361-368.

Mannheim, B., Baruch, Y., & Tal, J. (1997). Alternative models for antecedents and outcomes of work centrality and job satisfaction of high-tech personnel. *Human Relations, 50*(12), 1537-1562.

Manning, M. R., Jackson, C. N., & Fusilier, M. R. (1996). Occupational stress, social support, and the costs of health care. *Academy of Management Journal, 39*(3), 738-751.

Mansour-Cole, D. M., & Scott, S. G. (1998). Hearing it through the grapevine: The influence of source, leader-relations, and legitimacy on survivors' fairness perceptions. *Personnel Psychology, 51*(1), 25-54.

Markel, K. S., & Frone, M. R. (1998). Job characteristics, work-school conflict, and school outcomes among adolescents: Testing a structural model. *Journal of Applied Psychology, 83*(2), 277-287.

Marsden, P. V., Kalleberg, A. L., & Cook, C. R. (1993). Gender differences in organizational commitment: Influences of work positions and family roles. *Work and Occupations, 20*(3), 368-390.

Martin, C. L., & Bennett, N. (1996). The role of justice judgments in explaining the relationship between job satisfaction and organizational commitment. *Group & Organization Management, 21*(1), 84-104.

Martin, J. K., & Roman, P. M. (1996). Job satisfaction, job reward characteristics, and employees' problem drinking behaviors. *Work and Occupations, 23*(1), 4-21.

Mathieu, J. E. (1991). A cross-level nonrecursive model of the antecedents of organizational commitment and satisfaction, *Journal of Applied Psychology, 76*(3), 607-618.

Mathieu, J. E., & Farr, J. L. (1991). Further evidence for the discriminant validity of measures of organizational commitment, job involvement and job satisfaction. *Journal of Applied Psychology, 76*(1), 127-133.

Mathieu, J. E., Hofmann, D. A., & Farr, J. L. (1993). Job perception-job satisfaction relations: An empirical comparison of three competing theories. *Organizational Behavior and Human Decision Processes, 56,* 370-387.

McFarlin, D. B., & Rice, R. W. (1992). The role of facet importance as a moderator in job satisfaction processes. *Journal of Organizational Behavior, 13,* 41-54.

McFarlin, D. B., & Sweeney, P. D. (1992). Distributive and procedural justice as predictors of satisfaction with personal and organizational outcomes. *Academy of Management Journal, 35*(3), 626-637.

McLain, D. L. (1995). Responses to health and safety risk in the work environment. *Academy of Management Journal, 38*(6), 1726-1746.

Medcof, J. W. (1996). The job characteristics of computing and non-computing work activities. *Journal of Occupational and Organizational Psychology, 69,* 199-212.

Melamed, S., Ben-Avi, I., Luz, J., & Green, M. S. (1995). Objective and subjective work monotony: Effects on job satisfaction, psychological distress, and absenteeism in blue-collar workers. *Journal of Applied Psychology, 80*(1), 29-42.

Melamed, S., Kushnir, T., & Meir, E. I. (1991). Attenuating the impact of job demands: Additive and interactive effects of perceived control and social support. *Journal of Vocational Behavior, 39,* 40-53.

Meyer, J., & Allen, N. (1984). Testing the side-bet theory of organizational commitment: Some methodological considerations. *Journal of Applied Psychology, 69,* 372-378.

Meyer, J. P., & Allen, N. J. (1997). *Commitment in the workplace.* Thousand Oaks, CA: Sage.

Meyer, J. P., Allen, N. J., & Smith, C. A. (1993). Commitment to organizations and occupations: Extension and test of a three-component conceptualization. *Journal of Applied Psychology, 78*(4), 538-551.

Meyer, J. P., Irving, P. G., & Allen, N. J. (1998). Examination of the combined effects of work values and early work experiences on organizational commitment. *Journal of Organizational Behavior, 19,* 29-52.

Miles, E. W., Patrick, S. L., & King, W. C., Jr. (1996). Job level as a systemic variable in predicting the relationship between supervisory communication and job satisfaction. *Journal of Occupational and Organizational Psychology, 69*(3), 277-297.

Millward, L. J., & Hopkins, L. J. (1998). Psychological contracts and job commitment. *Journal of Applied Social Psychology, 28*(16), 1530-1556.

Mirels, H. L., & Garrett, J. B. (1971). The Protestant ethic as a personality variable. *Journal of Consulting and Clinical Psychology, 36,* 40-44.

Moorman, R. H. (1991). Relationship between organizational justice and organizational citizenship behaviors: Do fairness perceptions influence employee citizenship? *Journal of Applied Psychology, 76*(6), 845-855.

Moorman, R. H. (1993). The influence of cognitive and affective based job satisfaction measures on the relationship between satisfaction and organizational citizenship behavior. *Human Relations 46*(6), 759-778.

Moorman, R. H., & Blakely, G. L. (1995). Individualism-collectivism as an individual difference predictor of organizational citizenship behavior. *Journal of Organizational Behavior, 16,* 127-142.

Moorman, R. H., Blakely, G. L., & Niehoff, B. P. (1998). Does perceived organizational support mediate the relationship between procedural justice and organizational citizenship behavior? *Academy of Management Journal, 41*(3), 351-357.

Morrison, (1994). **[AUTHOR: REFERENCE NEEDED]**

Morrison, D. L. (1997). The effect of one partner's job characteristics on the other partner's distress: A serendipitous, but naturalistic, experiment. *Journal of Occupational and Organizational Psychology, 70*(4), 307-325.

Morrison, E. W., & Phelps, C. C. (1999). Taking charge at work: Extra-role efforts to initiate workplace change. *Academy of Management Journal, 42,* 403-419.

Mossholder, K. W., Bedeian, A. G., Niebuhr, R. E., & Wesolowski, M. A. (1994). Dyadic duration and the performance-satisfaction relationship: A contextual perspective. *Journal of Applied Social Psychology, 24*(14), 1251-1269.

Mossholder, K. W., Bennett, N., Kemery, E. R., & Wesolowski, M. A. (1998). Relationships between bases of power and work reactions: The mediational role of procedural justice. *Journal of Management, 24*(4), 533-552.

Mossholder, K. W., Bennett, N., & Martin, C. L. (1998). A multilevel analysis of procedural justice context. *Journal of Organizational Behavior, 19*(2), 131-141.

Motowidlo, S. J., Packard, J. S., & Manning, M. R. (1986). Occupational stress: Its causes and consequences for job performance. *Journal of Applied Psychology, 71,* 618-629.

Mowday, R. T., Porter, L. W., & Steers, R. M. (1982). *Employee-organization linkages: The psychology of commitment, absenteeism, and turnover.* New York: Academic Press.

Mowday, R. T., Steers, R. M., & Porter, L. W. (1979). The measurement of organizational commitment. *Journal of Vocational Behavior, 14,* 224-247.

Moyle, P., & Parkes, K. (1999). The effects of transition stress: A relocation study. *Journal of Organizational Behavior, 2,* 625-646.

Mudrack, P. E., Mason, E. S., & Stepanski, K. M. (1999). Equity sensitivity and business ethics. *Journal of Occupational and Organizational Psychology, 72,* 539-560.

Munton, A. G., & West, M. A. (1995). Innovations and personal change: patterns of adjustment to relocation. *Journal of Organizational Behavior, 16,* 363-375.

Munz, D. C., Huelsman, T. J., Konold, T. R., & McKinney, J. J. (1996). Are there methodological and substantive roles for affectivity in Job Diagnostic Survey relationships? *Journal of Applied Psychology, 81*(6), 795-805.

Nelson, D. L., & Sutton, C. (1990). Chronic work stress and coping: A longitudinal study and suggested new directions. *Academy of Management Journal, 33(4),* 859-870.

Netemeyer, R., Burton, S., & Johnston, M. (1995). A nested comparison of four models of the consequences of role perception variables. *Organizational Behavior and Human Decision Processes, 61*(1), 77-93.

Netemeyer, R. G., Boles, J. S., & McMurrian, R. (1996). Development and validation of Work-Family Conflict and Family-Work Conflict scales. *Journal of Applied Psychology, 81*(4), 400-410.

Netemeyer, R. G., Johnston, M. W., & Burton, S. (1990). Analysis of role conflict and role ambiguity in a structural equations framework. *Journal of Applied Psychology, 75*(2), 148-158.

Niehoff, B. P., & Moorman, R. H. (1993). Justice as a mediator of the relationship between methods of monitoring and organizational citizenship behavior. *Academy of Management Journal, 36*(3), 527-556.

Norman, P., Collins, S., Conner, M., Martin, R., & Rance, J. (1995). Attributions, cognitions, and coping styles: Teleworkers' reactions to work-related problems. *Journal of Applied Social Psychology, 25*(2), 117-128.

O'Driscoll, M. P., & Beehr, T. A. (1994). Supervisor behaviors, role stressors and uncertainty as predictors of personal outcomes for subordinates. *Journal of Organizational Behavior, 15*(2), 141-155.

Oldham, G. R., & Cummings, A. (1996). Employee creativity: Personal and contextual factors at work. *Academy of Management Journal, 39*(3), 607-634.

Oliver, N. (1990). Rewards, investments, alternatives and organizational commitment: Empirical evidence and theoretical development. *Journal of Occupational and Organizational Psychology, 63,* 19-31.

O'Neill, B. S., & Mone, M. A. (1998). Investigating equity sensitivity as a moderator of relations between self-efficacy and workplace attitudes. *Journal of Applied Psychology, 83*(5), 805-816.

O'Reilly, C. A., III, Chatman, J., & Caldwell, D. F. (1991). People and organizational culture: A profile comparison approach to assessing person-organization fit. *Academy of Management Journal, 34*(3), 487-516.

O'Reilly, C., III, & Chatman, J. (1986). Organizational commitment and psychological attachment: The effects of compliance, identification, and internalization on pro-social behavior. *Journal of Applied Psychology, 71,* 492-499.

Organ, D. W., & Near, J. P. (1985). Cognitive vs. affect measures of job satisfaction. *International Journal of Psychology, 20,* 241-254.

Organ, D. W., & Ryan, K. (1995). A meta-analytic review of attitudinal and dispositional predictors of organizational citizenship behavior. *Personnel Psychology, 48*(4), 775-795.

Ostroff, C. (1992). The relationship between satisfaction, attitudes, and performance: An organizational level analysis. *Journal of Applied Psychology, 77*(6), 963-974.

Parker, C. P., Baltes, B. B., & Christiansen, N. D. (1997). Support for affirmative action, justice perceptions, and work attitudes: A study of gender and racial-ethnic group differences. *Journal of Applied Psychology, 82*(3), 376-389.

Parker, D. F., & Decotiis, T. A. (1983). Organizational determinants of job stress. *Organizational Behavior and Human Performance, 32,* 160-177.

Parkes, K. R. (1990). Coping, negative affectivity and the work environment: Additive and interactive predictors of mental health. *Journal of Applied Psychology, 75*(4), 399-409.

Pearce, J. L., & Gregersen, H. B. (1991). Task interdependence and extra-role behavior A test of the mediating effects of felt responsibility. *Journal of Applied Psychology, 76*(6), 838-844.

Pearson, C. A. L. (1991). An assessment of extrinsic feedback on participation, role perceptions, motivation, and job satisfaction in a self-managed system for monitoring group achievement. *Human Relations, 44*(5), 517-537.

Pearson, C. A. L. (1992). Autonomous workgroups: An evaluation at an industrial site. *Human Relations, 45*(9), 905-937.

Pearson, C. A. L., & Chong, J. (1997). Contributions of job content and social information on organizational commitment and job satisfaction: An exploration in a Malaysian nursing context. *Journal of Occupational and Organizational Psychology, 70,* 357-374.

Peters, L. H., O'Connor, E. J., & Rudolf, C. J. (1980). The behavioral and affective consequences of performance-relevant situational variables. *Organizational Behavior and Human Performance, 25,* 79-96.

Peterson, M. F., Smith, P. B., Akande, A., Ayestaran, S., Bochner, S., Callan, V., Cho, N. G., Jesuino, J. C., D'Amorim, M., Francois, P., Hofmann, K., Koopman, P. L., Leung, K., Lim, T. K., Mortazavi, S., Munene, J., Radford, M., Ropo, A., Savage, G., Setiadi, B., Sinha, T. N. Sorenson, R., & Viedge, C. (1995). Role conflict, ambiguity, and overload: A 21-nation study. *Academy of Management Journal, 38*(2), 429-453.

Phelan, J., Bromet, E. J., Schwartz, J. E., Dew, M. A., & Curtis, E. C. (1993). The work environments of male and female professionals. *Work and Occupations, 20* (1), 68-90.

Pillai, R. I., Schriesheim, C. A., & Williams, E. S. (1999). Fairness perceptions and trust as mediators for transformational and transactional leadership: A two-sample study. *Journal of Management, 25*(6), 897-933.

Pines, A., & Aronson, E. (1988). *Career burnout: Causes and cures.* New York: Free Press.

Podsakoff, P. M., MacKenzie, S. B., Moorman, R. H., & Fetter, R. (1990). Transformational leader behaviors, and their effects on followers' trust in leader, satisfaction, and organizational citizenship behaviors. *Leadership Quarterly, 1(2),* 107-142.

Podsakoff, P. M., & Organ, D. W. 1986. Self-reports in organizational research: Problems and prospects. *Journal of Management, 12*(4), 531-544.

Pond, S. B., & Geyer, P. D. (1991). Differences in the relation between job satisfaction and perceived work alternatives among older and younger blue-collar workers. *Journal of Vocational Behavior, 39,* 251-262.

Porter, L. W., & Steers, R. M. (1973). Organizational, work and personal factors in employee turnover and absenteeism. *Psychological Bulletin, 80,* 151-176.

Price, J., & Mueller, C. (1986). *Handbook of organizational measurement.* Marshfield, MA: Pittman.

Quinn, R. P., & Shepard, L. G. (1974). *The 1972-1973 Quality of Employment Survey.* Ann Arbor: University of Michigan, Institute for Social Research.

Ralston, D. A., Gustafson, D. J., Elsass, P. M., Cheung, F., & Terpstra, R. H. (1992). Eastern values: A comparison of managers in the United States, Hong Kong, and the People's Republic of China. *Journal of Applied Psychology,* 77, 664-671.

Ralston, D. A., Holt, D. H., Terpstra, R. H., & Kai-cheng, Y. (1995). The impact of culture and ideology on managerial work values: A study of the United States, Russia, Japan, and China. *Academy of Management Best Papers Proceedings* 1995, 187-193.

Randall, M. L., Cropanzano, R., Bormann, C. A., & Birjulin, A. (1999). Organizational politics and organizational support as predictors of work attitudes, job performance and organizational citizenship behavior. *Journal of Organizational Behavior, 20,* 159-174.

Ravlin, E. C., & Meglino, B. M. (1987). Issues in work values measurement re-

search. *Corporate Social Performance and Policy, 9,* 153-183.

Reilly, N. P., & Orsak, C. L. (1991). A career stage analysis of career and organizational commitment in nursing. *Journal of Vocational Behavior, 39,* 311-330.

Remondet, J. H., & Hansson, R. O. (1991). Job-related threats to control among older employees. *Journal of Social Issues, 47,* 129-141.

Renn, R.W., & Vandenberg, R. J. (1995). The critical psychological states: An underrepresented component in job characteristics model research. *Journal of Management, 21*(2), 279-303.

Rentsch, J. R., & Steel, R. P. (1992). Construct and concurrent validation of the Andrews and Withey Job Satisfaction Questionnaire. *Educational and Psychological Measurement, 52,* 357-367.

Repeti, R. L., & Cosmas, K. A. (1991). The quality of the social environment at work and job satisfaction. *Journal of Applied Social Psychology, 21(10),* 840-854.

Rice, R. W., Gentile, D. A., & McFarlin, D. B. (1991). Facet importance and job satisfaction. *Journal of Applied Psychology, 76(1),* 31-39.

Riggs, M. L., & Knight, P. A. (1994). The impact of perceived group success-failure on motivational beliefs and attitudes: A causal model. *Journal of Applied Psychology, 79*(5), 755-766.

Riordan, C. M., & Vandenberg, R. J. (1994). A central question in cross-cultural research: Do employees of different cultures interpret work-related measures in an equivalent manner? *Journal of Management, 20*(3), 643-671.

Rizzo, J., House, R. J., & Lirtzman, S. I. (1970). Role conflict and role ambiguity in complex organizations. *Administrative Science Quarterly, 15,* 150-163.

Roberson, L. (1990). Prediction of job satisfaction from characteristics of personal work goals. *Journal of Organizational Behavior, 11,* 29-41.

Roberson, Q. M., Moye, N. A., & Locke, E. A. (1999). Identifying a missing link between participation and satisfaction: The mediating role of procedural justice perceptions. *Journal of Applied Psychology, 84*(4), 585-593.

Robie, C., Ryan, A. M., Schmieder, R. A., Parra, L. F., & Smith, P. C. (1998). The relation between job level and job satisfaction. *Group & Organization Management, 23*(4), 470-495.

Robinson, S. L., & O'Leary-Kelly, A. M. (1998). Monkey see, monkey do: The influence of work groups on the antisocial behavior of employees. *Academy of Management Journal, 41*, 658-672.

Rokeach, M. (1973). *The nature of human values.* New York: Free Press.

Roos, P. A., & Treiman, D. J. (1980). DOT scales for the 1970 census classification. In A. Miller, D. Treiman, P. Cain, & P. Roos (Eds.), *Work, job, and occupations: A critical review of the* Dictionary of Occupational Titles. Washington, DC: National Academy Press.

Rosen, C., Klein, K., & Young, K. (1986). *Employee ownership in America: The equity solution.* Lexington, MA: D. C. Heath.

Rothausen, T. J. (1994). Job satisfaction and the parent worker: The role of flexibility and rewards. *Journal of Vocational Behavior, 44*, 317-336.

Rothausen, T. J., Gonzalez, J. A., Clarke, N. E., & O'Dell, L. L. (1998). Family-friendly backlash—Fact or fiction? The case of organizations' on-site child care centers. *Personnel Psychology, 51*(3), 685-707.

Rowe, R., & Snizek, W. E. (1995). Gender differences in work values: Perpetuating the myth. *Work and Occupations, 22*(2), 215-233.

Rowley, D. J., Rosse, J. G., & Harvey, O. J. (1992). The effects of belief systems on the job-related satisfaction of managers and subordinates. *Journal of Applied Social Psychology, 22*(3), 212-231.

Roznowski, M. (1989). An examination of the measurement properties of the Job Descriptive Index with experimental items. *Journal of Applied Psychology, 74*, 805-814.

Roznowski, M., & Hulin, C. (1992). The scientific merit of valid measures of general constructs with special reference to job satisfaction and job withdrawal. In C. J. Cranny, P. C. Smith, & E. F. Stone (Eds.), *Job satisfaction: How people feel about their jobs and how it affects their performance* (pp. 124-159). Newbury Park, CA: Sage.

Rush, M. C., Schoel, W. A., & Barnard, S. M. (1985). Psychological resiliency in the public sector: "Hardiness" and pressure for change. *Journal of Vocational Behavior, 46*, 17-39.

Sagie, A. (1998). Employee absenteeism, organizational commitment and job satisfaction: Another look. *Journal of Vocational Behavior, 52*(2), 156-171.

Sanchez, J. I., & Brock, P. (1996). Outcomes of perceived discrimination among Hispanic employees: Is diversity management a luxury or a necessity? *Academy of Management Journal, 39*(3), 704-720.

Sanchez, J. I., Kraus, E., White, S., & Williams, M. (1999). Adopting high-involvement human resource practices. *Group & Organization Management, 24*(4), 461-478.

Sanders, M. M., Lengnick-Hall, M. L., Lengnick-Hall, C. A., & Steele-Clapp, L. (1998). Love and work: Career-family attitudes of new entrants into the labor force. *Journal of Organizational Behavior, 19*, 603-619.

Sapienza, H. J., & Korsgaard. M. A. (1996). Procedural justice in entrepreneur-investor relations. *Academy of Management Journal, 39*(3), 544-574.

Sargent, L. D., & Terry, D. (1998). The effects of work control and job demands on employee adjustment and work performance. *Journal of Occupational and Organizational Psychology, 71*, 219-237.

Sawyer, J. E. (1992). Goal and process clarity: Specification of multiple constructs of role ambiguity and a structural equation model of their antecedents and consequences. *Journal of Applied Psychology, 77*(2), 130-143.

Scarpello, V., & Jones, F. F. (1996). Why justice matters in compensation decision making. *Journal of Organizational Behavior, 17*, 285-299.

Scarpello, V., & Vandenberg, R. (1987). The Satisfaction With My Supervisor scale: Its utility for research and practical application. *Journal of Management, 34*, 451-470.

Scarpello, V., & Vandenberg, R. J. (1992). Generalizing the importance of occupational and career views to job satisfaction attitudes. *Journal of Organizational Behavior, 13,* 125-140.

Schaubroeck, J., Ganster, D. C., & Kemmerer, B. E. (1994). Job complexity, "Type A" behavior, and cardiovascular disorder. *Academy of Management Journal, 37*(2), 426-440.

Schaubroeck, J., Ganster, D. C., Sime, W. E., & Ditman, D. (1993). A field experiment testing supervisory role clarification. *Personnel Psychology, 46*(1), 1-26.

Schaubroeck, J., & Merritt, D. (1997). Divergent effects of job control on coping with work stressors: The key role of self-efficacy. *Academy of Management Journal, 40*(3), 738-754.

Schaufeli, W. B., & Van Dierendonck, D. (1993). The construct validity of two burnout measures. *Journal of Organizational Behavior, 14,* 631-647.

Scheck, C. L., Kinicki, A. J., & Davy, J. A. (1995). A longitudinal study of a multivariate model of the stress process using structural equations modeling. *Human Relations, 48*(12), 1481-1511.

Schminke, M., Ambrose, M. L., & Noel, T. W. (1997). The effect of ethical frameworks on perceptions of organizational justice. *Academy of Management Journal, 40*(5), 1190-1207.

Schriesheim, C., & Tsui, A. S. (1980). *Development and validation of a short satisfaction instrument for use in survey feedback interventions.* Paper presented at the Western Academy of Management meeting.

Schriesheim, C. A., & Hinkin, T. R. (1990). Influence tactics used by subordinates: A theoretical and empirical analysis and refinement of the Kipnis, Schmidt and Wilkinson subscales. *Journal of Applied Psychology, 75*(3), 246-257.

Schwartz, S. H. (1994). Are there universal aspects in the structure and contents of human values? *Journal of Social Issues, 50,* 19-45.

Seibert, S. (1999). The effectiveness of facilitated mentoring: A longitudinal quasi-experiment. *Journal of Vocational Behavior, 54,* 483-502.

Seibert, S. E., Crant, J. M., & Kraimer, M. L. (1999). Proactive personality and career success. *Journal of Applied Psychology, 84*(3), 416-427.

Shaw, J. D., Duffy, M. K., Jenkins, G. D., Jr., & Gupta, N. (1999). Positive and negative affect, signal sensitivity, and pay satisfaction. *Journal of Management, 25*(2), 189-206.

Sheridan, J. E. (1992). Organizational culture and employee retention. *Academy of Management Journal, 35*(5), 1036-1056.

Shirom, A., & Mayer, A. (1993). Stress and strain among union lay officials and rank-and-file members. *Journal of Organizational Behavior, 14,* 401-413.

Shirom, A., Westman, M., & Melamed, S. (1999). The effects of pay systems on blue-collar employees' emotional distress: The mediating effects of objective and subjective work monotony. *Human Relations, 52*(8), 1077-1097.

Shore, L. M., Newton, L. A., & Thornton, G. C., III. (1990). Job and organizational attitudes in relation to employee behavioral intentions. *Journal of Organizational Behavior, 11,* 57-67.

Siegall, M. (1992). Some effects of role conflict source on the experience of role conflict. *Journal of Applied Social Psychology, 22*(8), 628-638.

Siegall, M., & McDonald, T. (1995). Focus of attention and employee reactions to job change. *Journal of Applied Social Psychology, 25*(13), 1121-1141.

Sims, H. P., Szilagyi, A. D., & Keller, R. T. (1976). The measurement of job characteristics. *Academy of Management Journal, 19,* 195-212.

Singh, P. (1994). Perception and reactions to inequity as a function of social comparison referents and hierarchical levels. *Journal of Applied Social Psychology, 24*(6), 557-565.

Skarlicki, D. P, & Folger, R. (1997). Retaliation in the workplace: The roles of distributive, procedural, and interactional justice. *Journal of Applied Psychology, 82* (3), 434-443.

Skarlicki, D. P., Folger, R., & Tesluk, P. (1999). Personality as a moderator in the relationship between fairness and retaliation. *Academy of Management Journal, 42*(1), 100-108.

Skarlicki, D. P., & Latham, G. P. (1996). Increasing citizenship behavior within a labor union: A test of organizational justice theory. *Journal of Applied Psychology, 81*(2), 161-169.

Skarlicki, D. P., & Latham, G. P. (1997). Leadership training in organizational justice to increase citizenship behavior within a labor union: A replication. *Personnel Psychology, 50*(3), 617-633.

Small, S., & Riley, D. (1990). Towards a multidimensional assessment of work spillover into family life. *Journal of Marriage and the Family, 52,* 51-61.

Smart, R. M. (1998). Career stages in Australian professional women: A test of Super's model. *Journal of Vocational Behavior, 52*(3), 379-395.

Smith, C. A., Organ, D. W., & Near, J. P. (1983). Organizational citizenship behavior: Its nature and antecedents. *Journal of Applied Psychology, 68,* 653-663.

Smith, C. S., & Brannick, M. T. (1990). A role and expectancy model of participative decision-making: A replication and theoretical extension. *Journal of Organizational Behavior, 11*(2), 91-104.

Smith, C. S., Tisak, J., & Schmieder, R. A. (1993). The measurement properties of the role conflict and role ambiguity scales: A review and extension of the empirical research. *Journal of Organizational Behavior, 14*(1), 37-48.

Smith, P. C., Kendall, L. M., & Hulin, C. L. (1969). *The measurement of satisfaction in work and retirement: A strategy for the study of attitudes.* Chicago: Rand-McNally.

Smith, P. C., Kendall, L. M., & Hulin, C. L. (1985). *The Job Descriptive Index.* Bowling Green, OH: Bowling Green State University, Department of Psychology.

Smith, P. L., Smits, S. J., & Hoy, F. (1998). Employee work attitudes: The subtle influence of gender. *Human Relations, 51*(5), 649-666.

Snell, S. A., & Dean, J. W. (1994). Strategic compensation for integrated manufacturing: The moderating effects of jobs and organizational inertia. *Academy of Management Journal, 37*(5), 1109-1141.

Somers, M. J. (1995). Organizational commitment, turnover and absenteeism: An examination of direct and interaction effects. *Journal of Organizational Behavior, 16,* 49-58.

Somers, M. J., & Birnbaum, D. (1998). Work related commitment and job performance: It's the nature of the performance that counts. *Journal of Organizational Behavior, 19,* 621-634.

Somers, M. J., & Casal, J. C. (1994). Organizational commitment and whistle-blowing: A test of the reformer and the organization man hypotheses. *Group & Organization Management, 19*(3), 270-285.

Sommer, S. M., Bae, S. H., & Luthans, F. (1996). Organizational commitment across cultures: The impact of antecedents of Korean employees. *Human Relations, 49(7),* 977-989.

Spector, P. (1985). Measurement of human service staff satisfaction: Development of the Job Satisfaction Survey. *American Journal of Community Psychology, 13,* 693-713.

Spector, P. E. (1987). Method variance as an artifact in self-reported affect and perceptions at work: Myth or significant problem? *Journal of Applied Psychology, 72(3),* 438-443.

Spector, P. E. (1992). *Summated rating scale construction.* Newbury Park, CA: Sage.

Spector, P. E. (1994). Using self-report questionnaires in OB research: A comment on the use of a controversial method. *Journal of Organizational Behavior, 15,* 385-392.

Spector, P. (1997). *Job satisfaction.* Thousand Oaks, CA: Sage.

Spector, P. E., & Jex, S. M. (1991). Relations of job characteristics from multiple data sources with employee affect, absence, turnover intentions, and health. *Journal of Applied Psychology, 76,* 46-53.

Spector, P., Jex, S., & Chen, P. (1995), Relations of incumbent affect-related personality traits with incumbent and objective measures of characteristics of jobs. *Journal of Organizational Behavior, 16,* 59-65.

Spector, P. E., & O'Connell, B. J. (1994). The contribution of personality traits, negative affectivity, locus of control and Type A to the subsequent reports of job stressors and job strains. *Journal of Occupational and Organizational Psychology, 64,* 1-11.

Spector, P. E., Van Katwyk, P. T., Brannick, M. T., & Chen, P. Y. (1997). When two factors don't reflect two constructs: How item characteristics can produce artifactual factors. *Journal of Management, 23* (5), 659-677.

Spreitzer, G. M. (1995). Psychological empowerment in the workplace: Dimensions, measurement, and validation. *Academy of Management Journal, 38(5),* 1442-1465.

Spreitzer, G. M. (1996). Social structural characteristics of psychological empowerment. *Academy of Management Journal, 39(2),* 483-505.

Spreitzer, G. M., Kizilos, M. A., & Nason, S. W. (1997). A dimensional analysis of the relationship between psychological empowerment and effectiveness, satisfaction, and strain. *Journal of Management, 23(5),* 679-704.

Steel, R. P., & Rentsch, J. R. (1995). Influence of accumulation strategies on the long-range prediction of absenteeism. *Academy of Management Journal, 38(6),* 1616-1634.

Steel, R. P., & Rentsch, J. R. (1997). The dispositional model of job attitudes revisited: Findings of a 10-year study. *Journal of Applied Psychology, 82(6),* 873-879.

Stephens, G. K., & Sommer, S. M. (1996). The measurement of work to family conflict. *Educational and Psychological Measurement, 56(3),* 475-486.

Sutton, C. D., & Harrison, A. W. (1993), Validity assessment of compliance, identification, and internalization as dimensions of organizational commitment, *Educational and Psychological Measurement, 53,* 217-223.

Sweeney, P. D., & McFarlin, D. B. (1993). Workers' evaluations of the "ends" and the "means": An examination of four models of distributive and procedural justice. *Organizational Behavior and Human Decision Processes, 55(1),* 23-40.

Sweeney, P. D., & McFarlin, D. B. (1997). Process and outcome: Gender differences in the assessment of justice. *Journal of Organizational Behavior, 18(1),* 83-98.

Taber, T. D., & Alliger, G. M. (1995). A task-level assessment of job satisfaction. *Journal of Organizational Behavior, 16,* 101-121.

Taber, T. D., & Taylor, E. (1990). A review and evaluation of the psychometric properties of the Job Diagnostic Survey. *Personnel Psychology, 43*, 467-500.

Taylor, J. C., & Bowers, D. G. (1974). *The survey of organizations: Towards a machine scored, standardized questionnaire.* Ann Arbor: University of Michigan, Institute for Social Research.

Taylor, M. S., Tracy, K. B., Renard, M. K., Harrison, J. K., & Carroll, S. J. (1995). Due process in performance appraisal: A quasi-experiment in procedural justice. *Administrative Science Quarterly, 40*(3), 495-523.

Thomas, L. T., & Ganster, D. C. (1995). Impact of family-supportive work variables on work-family conflict and strain: A control perspective. *Journal of Applied Psychology, 80*(1), 6-15.

Thompson, H. B., & Werner, J. M. (1997). The impact of role conflict/facilitation on core and discretionary behaviors: Testing a mediated model. *Journal of Management, 23*(4), 583-602.

Tsui, A. S., Egan, T. D., & O'Reilly, C. A., III. (1992). Being different: Relational demography and organizational attachment. *Administrative Science Quarterly, 37*(4), 549-580.

Van DeVliert, E., & Van Yperen, N. W. (1996). Why cross-national differences in role overload? Don't overlook ambient temperature! *Academy of Management Journal, 39*(4), 986-1005.

Van Dyne, L., Graham, J. W., & Dienesch, R. M. (1994). Organizational citizenship behavior: Construct redefinition, measurement, and validation. *Academy of Management Journal, 37*, 765-802.

Van Dyne, L., & LePine, J. A. (1998). Helping and voice extra-role behaviors: Evidence of construct and predictive validity. *Academy of Management Journal, 41*(1), 108-119.

Vancouver, J. B., & Schmitt, N. W. (1991). An exploratory examination of person-organization fit: Organizational goal congruence. *Personnel Psychology, 44*, 333-352.

Vandenberg, R. J., & Lance, C. E. (1992). Examining the causal order of job satisfaction and organizational commitment. *Journal of Management, 18*(1), 153-167.

Vandenberg, R. J., & Scarpello, V. (1994). A longitudinal assessment of the determinant relationship between employee commitments to the occupation and the organization. *Journal of Organizational Behavior, 15*, 535-547.

Vandenberghe, C. (1999). Organizational culture, person-culture fit, and turnover: A replication in the health care industry. *Journal of Organizational Behavior, 20*, 175-184.

VanYerpen, N. W., Van Den Berg, A. E., & Willering, M. C. (1999). Towards a better understanding of the link between participation in decision-making and organizational citizenship behavior: a multilevel analysis. *Journal of Occupational and Organizational Psychology, 72*, 377-397.

Viswesvaran, C., Sanchez, J. I., & Fisher, J. (1999). The role of social support in the process of work stress: A meta-analysis. *Journal of Vocational Behavior, 54*, 314-334.

Wahn, J. C. (1998). Sex differences in the continuance component of organizational commitment. *Group & Organization Management, 23*(3), 256-267.

Wall, T. D., Jackson, P. R., Mullarkey, S., & Parker, S. K. (1996). The demands-control model of job strain: A more specific test. *Journal of Occupational and Organizational Psychology, 69*, 153-166.

Wallace, J. E. (1997). It's about time: A study of hours worked and work spillover among law firm lawyers. *Journal of Vocational Behavior, 50*, 227-248.

Wallace, J. E. (1999). Work-to-nonwork conflict among married male and female lawyers. *Journal of Organizational Behavior, 20*, 797-816.

Wanberg, C. (1995). A longitudinal study of the effects of unemployment and quality of reemployment. *Journal of Vocational Behavior, 46*, 40-54.

Warr, P. B., Cook, J. D., & Wall, T. D. (1979). Scales for the measurement of work attitudes and psychological well-being. *Journal of Occupational and Organizational Psychology, 58,* 229-242.

Watson, D., & Slack, A. K. (1993). General factors of affective temperament and their relation to job satisfaction over time. *Organizational Behavior and Human Decision Processes, 54,* 181-202.

Wayne, S. J., Liden, R. C., Graf, I. K., & Ferris, G. R. (1997). The role of upward influence tactics in human resource decisions. *Personnel Psychology, 50,* 979-1006.

Wayne, S. J., Shore, L. M., & Liden, R. C. (1997). Perceived organizational support and leader-member exchange: A social exchange perspective. *Academy of Management Journal, 40*(1), 82-111.

Weiss, D., Dawis, R., England, G., & Lofquist, L. (1967). *Manual for the Minnesota Satisfaction Questionnaire (Minnesota Studies on Vocational Rehabilitation, Vol. 22).* Minneapolis: University of Minnesota, Industrial Relations Center.

Welbourne, T. M. (1998). Untangling procedural and distributive justice: Their relative effects on gain-sharing satisfaction. *Group & Organization Management, 23* (4), 477-493.

Welbourne, T. M., Balkin, D. B., & Gomez-Mejia, L. R. (1995). Gainsharing and mutual monitoring: A combined agency-organizational justice interpretation. *Academy of Management Journal, 38*(3), 881-899.

Welbourne, T. M., & Cable, D. M (1995). Group incentives and pay satisfaction: Understanding the relationship through an identity theory perspective. *Human Relations, 48*(6), 711-731.

West, M. A. (1987). A measure of role innovation at work. *British Journal of Social Psychology, 26,* 83-85.

Westman, M. (1992). Moderating effect of decision latitude on stress-strain relationship: Does organizational level matter?

Journal of Organizational Behavior, 13 (7), 713-722.

Westman, M., & Eden, D. (1997). Effects of a respite from work on burnout: Vacation relief and fade-out. *Journal of Applied Psychology, 82*(4), 516-527.

Wiersma, U. J., & Van den Berg, P. (1991). Work-home role conflict, family climate, and domestic responsibilities among men and women in dual-earner families. *Journal of Applied Social Psychology, 21*(15), 1207-1217.

Williams, J. R., & Levy, P. E. (1992). The effects of perceived system knowledge on the agreement between self-ratings and supervisor ratings. *Personnel Psychology, 45,* 835-847.

Williams, K., & Alliger, G. M. (1994). Role stressors, mood spillover, and perceptions of work-family conflict in employed parents. *Academy of Management Journal, 37*(4), 837-869.

Williams, L. J., & Anderson, S. E. (1991). Job satisfaction and organizational commitment as predictors of organizational citizenship and in-role behaviors. *Journal of Management, 17*(3), 601-617.

Williams, L. J., Gavin, M. B., & Williams, M. L. (1996). Measurement and non-measurement processes with negative affectivity and employee attitudes. *Journal of Applied Psychology, 81*(1), 88-101.

Williams, M. L., Podsakoff, P. M., & Huber, V. (1992). Effects of group-level and individual-level variation in leader behaviors on subordinate attitudes and performance. *Journal of Occupational and Organizational Psychology, 65*(2), 115-130.

Winefield, A. H., Winefield, H. R., Tiggemann, M., & Goldney, R. D. (1991). A longitudinal study of the psychological effects of unemployment and unsatisfactory employment on young adults. *Journal of Applied Psychology, 76*(3), 424-431.

Witt, L. A., & Nye, L. G. (1992). Gender and the relationship between perceived fairness of pay or promotion and job satisfaction, *Journal of Applied Psychology, 77*(6), 910-917.

Wong, C., & Campion, M. A. (1991). Development and test of a task level model of motivational job design. *Journal of Applied Psychology, 76*(6), 825-837.

Wong, C. S., Hui, C., & Law, K. S. (1998). A longitudinal study of the job perception-job satisfaction relationship: A test of the three alternative specifications. *Journal of Occupational and Organizational Psychology, 71*(2), 127-146.

Wright, B. M., & Cordery, J. L. (1999). Production uncertainty as a contextual moderator of employee reactions to job design. *Journal of Applied Psychology, 84*(3), 456-463.

Wright, T. A., & Bonett, D. G. (1992). The effect of turnover on work satisfaction and mental health: Support for a situational perspective. *Journal of Organizational Behavior, 13*, 603-615.

Xie, J. L. (1996). Karasek's model in the People's Republic of China: Effects of job demands, control, and individual differences. *Academy of Management Journal, 39*(6), 1594-1619.

Xie, J. L., & Johns, G. (1995). Job scope and stress: Can job scope be too high? *Academy of Management Journal, 38*(5), 1288-1310.

Zeffane, R. (1994). Patterns of organizational commitment and perceived management style: A comparison of public and private sector employees. *Human Relations, 47*(8), 977-1010.

Zeitz, G. (1990). Age and work satisfaction in a government agency: A situational perspective. *Human Relations, 43*(5), 419-438.

Zellars, K. A., Perrewé, P. L., & Hochwarter, W. A. (1999). Mitigating burnout among high-NA employees in health care: What can organizations do? *Journal of Applied Social Psychology 29*(11), 225-235.

Zohar, D. (1995). The justice perspective of job stress, *Journal of Organizational Behavior, 16*(5), 487-495.

Zohar, D. (1997). Predicting burnout with a hassle-based measure of role demands. *Journal of Organizational Behavior, 18*(2), 101-115.

Name Index

Subject Index

315

About the Author

Dail L. Fields (Ph.D., Georgia Tech, 1994) is Associate Professor at the Regent University School of Business. His research interests include measurement of employee perspectives on work, cross-cultural management, human resource management strategies, and leadership and values in organizations. He has published research studies in the *Academy of Management Journal, Journal of Management, Journal of Organizational Behavior, Educational and Psychological Measurement*, and the *International Journal of Human Resource Management*. He is a member of the Academy of Management and the Academy of International Business. Prior to beginning an academic career in 1994, he was a management executive with MCI Communications Corp. and a management consultant with Touche Ross & company